October 31st 1998

To Mum

with love

Rich

# SOME YOU WIN

# SOME YOU WIN

## *A Life in Racing*

## *Julian Wilson*

CollinsWillow
*An Imprint of* HarperCollins*Publishers*

*To Alison and Thomas . . .*
*and the horses that made it happen.*

First published in 1998
by CollinsWillow
an imprint of HarperCollins*Publishers*
London



1 3 5 7 9 8 6 4 2



A CIP catalogue record for this book is available from the British Library

ISBN 0 00 218825 2

Typeset by Palimpsest Book Production Limited,
Polmont, Stirlingshire
Printed and bound in Great Britain by
Caledonian International Book Manufacturing Ltd, Glasgow

All photographs supplied by Julian Wilson with the exception of the following: **Alpha/Sport & General** picture no. 13; **BBC** 11; **Gerry Cranham's Colour Library** 22, 29; **Srdja Djukanovic** 17; **Express Newspaper** 25; **Les Hurley Photography** 32; **Mirror Syndication International** 10; **Desmond O'Neill Features** 4; **PA News** 20, 23; **Bernard Parkin** 12, 24, 33; **Popperfoto** 26, 38; **Lesley I Sampson** 16; **George Selwyn** 14, 21, 27, 28

# Contents

# *Prologue*

It was 2.45 am and the band were thinking about Auld Lang Syne and getting paid. I picked up my twelfth – or was it thirteenth? – glass of champagne. Then came a familiar voice in my ear: 'Are you going to take me home?' asked Suzanne.

We were celebrating the 'coming-out' of a girl called Honor Saul at a typical debutante's dance at the Hyde Park Hotel. The 'season' was coming towards its end and the talk was of holidays, skiing – and Gina Mostyn's 'cockers-p' on Thursday.

I turned to Suzanne. Taking her home was an enjoyable, if exhausting pursuit, ending, as it did, with the rays of autumn sunshine peeping through the fading curtains of my Chelsea flat. But I said: 'Suzanne, I'd love to, but I've got to be up really bright and early tomorrow. I'm going to an interview for a job. It's quite important.' 'I thought you'd got a sort-of job?' Suzanne queried. 'Yes, but this is a proper job. I haven't had one for nearly three years. I think I'd better be there.' With the words 'Well, I think you're jolly mean and I don't like you any more', Suzanne flounced away in search of another suitable chauffeur.

With mixed feelings, I thanked my hostess and went home alone. The following morning I arrived at 5 Portland Place, W1, bang on the dot of 10 am.

The interview proved unchallenging. I was greeted by a charming kindred spirit in Harry Middleton, an Old Etonian and legacy of the BBC's past. Harry puffed furiously on a cigarette and conveyed the image of a man already dreaming of his first Bloody Mary or pink gin of the day. He asked me a handful of innocuous questions: Who was Lord Rosebery's jockey? Where did Vic Smyth train? . . . and other similar long-hops. Whereupon we chatted amiably and probably realized there and then that we would be friends for life.

After several similar interviews by various BBC personnel, the 800 applicants for the job advertised two months earlier in the *Sporting Life* were narrowed down to six. Those on the shortlist were invited to attend a day at Newbury races to undertake a race commentary, a paddock commentary and a 'piece to camera' – the latter being a one-minute monologue, facing the camera and previewing the afternoon's racing. So five other optimistic contenders for the position of BBC Television Racing Correspondent gathered with me at Paddington Station.

There are several descriptive variations of the ensuing events, and notably of the rail journey to Newbury!

We were a mixed bunch. Three of the team were professional journalists: David Phillips, who became racing editor of the *Daily Mirror*; Jack Millan, 'Robin Goodfellow' of the *Daily Mail*; and Tim Richards of the *Sporting Chronicle* and latterly of the *Racing Post*.

There was also a young man called Gavin Pritchard-Gordon, who had some freelance work experience with the *Brighton Evening Argus*, and an unfamiliar individual recently arrived from Barbados, called Michael Stoute.

A BBC administrator issued us with third-class day-return tickets to Newbury. Now, group travel has never held particular appeal to me – during a journey I like to read, think and sleep in comfort. So I looked at my ticket and at the amiable administrator. 'Would you mind terribly if I upgraded my ticket?' I asked, 'I normally travel first class.' Tim Richards, who had been a friend during our newspaper days in Manchester, looked at me open-mouthed.

What the privacy of a first-class compartment enabled me to achieve was rehearsal of my 'piece-to-camera' without embarrassment, and a thorough perusal of the newspapers and of the day's form; and a sleep!

We arrived at Newbury mid-morning. It was a crisp, bright, November day, with a good-class National Hunt racing programme on the eve of the Hennessy Gold Cup.

The audition was managed by the BBC's senior racing producer, Dennis Monger, a kindly, immensely likeable man, who had flown spitfires with astonishing courage during the war and who had been one of the pioneers of BBC's outside broadcasts in the ensuing 20 years. I came to regard Dennis, his assistant Pam Guyler, and the senior stage manager, Ronnie Pantlin, as an irreplaceable institution. I missed them all terribly when they left the Corporation.

On this occasion we were briefed, allocated our respective races for the three disciplines, in rotation – and taken to Dennis's favourite bar for a drink. I have often thought in retrospect that the decision that faced the BBC 'examiners' was not 'Which of the six was best?' but rather 'Shall we turn them all down and start all over again?'

Poor Michael Stoute, in a climate roughly 40 degrees colder than his native country, was confronted by a scene that he found totally baffling. He had never visited a National Hunt meeting in his life! His disappointment over failing to win the job may have been compensated by subsequent events. He has been champion trainer on the Flat five times, is a multimillionaire, and won over £5 million for his patrons worldwide in 1997. In June 1998, he received a knighthood.

Of the others, Gavin – who later became my racehorse trainer – was hesitant; while David Phillips with his south London accent and Jack Millan with a deep Scots brogue were hindered by their voice tone. These, remember, were still the days of Richard Dimbleby. Twenty years later and the regional accents would have been a considerable plus for those candidates.

As for Tim, in the midst of his 'piece to camera' he dried up. We died for him. He just stood there with his mouth opening and shutting, with no words emerging. If ever a contest was won by default, it was at Newbury that day!

On Friday 17 December I was invited to meet the head of outside broadcasts, Peter Dimmock, and his head of sport, Brian Cowgill. I had got the job, and it was a position that I held on to for 32 years – over 80 per cent of my working life.

Tim Richards was the first on the phone to congratulate me on my appointment. 'Mind you,' he added, 'we all knew that you'd get the job when you travelled first class. What a rotten trick.'

## ONE

# 'The Best Days of Your Life'

My father died on 5 October 1981. At his Memorial Service held at the Church of St Bride in Fleet Street, I read the following passage from the book of Ecclesiastes:

> *To every thing there is a season and a time to every purpose under the heaven: a time to be born and a time to die . . .*

It was a very moving service, conducted within the square mile where he had worked for over 40 years, stage-managed by his long-time employers the Mirror Group – and notably his great friend Lord Cudlipp – and attended by the many hundreds of colleagues and friends for whom he was an irreplaceable, larger-than-life, Fleet Street legend.

In the hour or so after the service I came to understand how estranged I had become from my father, his friends, his values and his life. Peter Jardine Bonhote Wilson had belonged to these other people, so this was not a family affair. We were all there, of course – myself, my wife and ex-wife, my brother, my stepmother, her family and one or two more distant relations – but we were onlookers, bit players in a Fleet Street event. My father's heart and soul had lived in the newspaper industry and they were his people. His wife, Sally, was a peripheral part of this scene and was warmly loved by his friends. But seldom had I felt more alone, and remote from the father whom it now seemed I had never really known.

> *. . . a time of war, and a time of peace . . .*

My parents were married in 1936. It was a marriage that

appeared perfect in concept, but was nevertheless violently opposed by my mother's family. I was born on 21 June 1940, almost exactly nine months after the declaration of the Second World War. My parents at that time were living in Kensington and my father was already a force in Fleet Street. He had joined *The Times* in the early thirties, but his provocative ways were incompatible with that esteemed newspaper's balanced reporting, and by 1935 he had moved to the *Daily Mirror*. In 1938 he made two-inch headlines himself when he resigned from the *Sunday Pictorial* because the editor refused to publish his opinion that a well-known cricketer was 'scum'. He was subsequently reinstated, but already the seeds were sown of the famous epithet 'The Man They Can't Gag' – although in this case they had tried very hard.

Even at Harrow he had been confrontational. His school house, Elmfield, was known to be the most 'snobbish' on the Hill – so much so, my father claimed, that even the Archbishop of Canterbury was unable to claim a place in the Old Boy's XI. At an early stage he espoused the politics of the Left, and was considered argumentative and a non-conformist.

My father had covered the 1936 Olympic Games and been outraged by the conduct of Herr Hitler towards the black athlete Jesse Owens. The incident when Hitler turned his back on the multiple gold medal winner enflamed his life-long hatred of, and outspoken opposition to, the doctrine of *apartheid*. Now he was only too anxious and willing to confront the Nazi leader. Although Cecil King, the *Sunday Pictorial* chairman, offered to apply for exemption, my father joined up with the Dorsetshire Regiment.

Going back a generation, my two grandfathers – Freddy Wilson and Eric (E. W.) Mann – were both outstanding cricketers. They played together in the Harrow School XI and for Cambridge University: Eric Mann captained Harrow, while each in turn captained the Cambridge side. But after university the two friends went in very different directions.

Freddy Wilson, who was also an outstanding rackets and real tennis player, became a journalist and was eventually appointed rackets and cricket correspondent of *The Times*, earning the princely salary of £600 a year. He was hugely popular and much loved and, according to E. W. Swanton, never made an enemy in his entire life. Jim Swanton received a letter from Freddy's widow thanking him for some kind remarks broadcast about Freddy at the Eton & Harrow Match in 1939: she referred to 'the dearest of sons . . . and no-one could have a sweeter daughter-in-law than I have'. Sadly for her and my father, Freddy Wilson died in 1932. He, too, was commemorated at St Bride's Church, which was packed beyond capacity. The closing hymn was 'Fight the Good Fight' and the collective chorus of the hundreds whom he had befriended and helped could be heard beyond Aldwych.

Freddy's legendary generosity had cost him dear. He died leaving an estate worth just £1371, so no resources existed to enable my father to study at university. My father left Harrow and went almost straight into journalism. He had inherited his father's talent for writing – and more as well.

My other grandfather, Eric Mann, had travelled in a different direction. After playing cricket for Kent in 1905 and captaining an MCC side to Philadelphia in 1907, he went into the family coal business and married into society: his wife was 'Kitzie' Cameron, daughter of Sir Euan Cameron, founder of the Royal Hong Kong and Shanghai Bank. His many interests outside business included stamp collecting, and he became President of the Royal Philatelic Society.

The extended family (my mother had two sisters and two brothers) lived during the 1920s and 30s at Kitemore House, near Faringdon in Berkshire – a vast, monolithic building latterly acquired by a Far East businessman and restored to its former glory at a cost of millions. This was an idyllic home in which to grow up. Built in 1867 and set in 44 acres of parkland and paddocks, there were stables for the children's ponies and woodland for the boys to explore. It was a regular meeting place for the Old Berkshire Hunt and a wonderful house for parties.

My mother also enjoyed the London season. She was presented

at Court and, through hunting, made many friends in the world of racing. Indeed, in 1930 her dance card for the Royal Military College Ball contained several well-known racing names, including the late Fulke Walwyn who was to win the Grand National both as an amateur jockey and as a trainer. Whether my mother viewed Fulke as a potential husband I do not know, but the following year – on Derby Day – she consulted Gypsy Rose Lee on the Downs at Epsom. The old soothsayer looked deeply into her crystal ball and pronounced that she saw the letter 'W' . . . yes, my mother was going to marry someone whose name began with that letter. My mother had a fit, because the only 'W' she knew well was Colonel Dick Warden, one-time Master of the Old Berks, whom no-one had regarded as a candidate for marriage!

It was against this background that my father met and courted my mother. From the start he was not a popular house guest, being viewed as unconventional, argumentative with his fellow guests, and not especially fond of fox-hunting. He was also late for breakfast. Nonetheless, the more hostility he invoked in my maternal grandparents, the more devoted to him my mother became. At the time they were married there was no question that they were madly in love.

In the spring of 1940 London was in a state of evacuation: Hitler's bombers were threatening to launch night raids and the major cities were under threat. Since Eric Mann had an interest in the Belmont Hotel in Sidmouth, Devon, my mother was moved to the West Country to await my birth. Sidmouth is a charming seaside resort that has changed extraordinarily little in the past 50 years, and the hotel is pleasant and well-sited, overlooking a cricket ground. Here I was born at around midnight on 21 June, and I am told that within ten minutes one of the other residents was wheeled out into the lift (the hotel was occupied substantially by elderly or retired people!). My father did not travel to Devon – he spent the night of my birth in a nightclub in Mayfair.

Meanwhile, my grandparents had bought a house near Sidbury, called Littlefields, where the Mann family were to settle for the war years. My grandfather played cricket in Sidmouth regularly in the 1900s, and late in his career took eight wickets for 17 runs against the Devon Regiment. Fifty years later I played on the same ground with my school friend, the Harrow captain Anthony Cable, during the school holidays. The ground is the same today as I remember it being then.

I have fleeting memories of Littlefields . . . the sounds of the bombers passing overhead . . . a large lawn that I was anxious to explore away from the confinement of my pram . . . peaches growing in the sun on the wall of the orchard . . . and a day school down the hill in Sidbury. Then in 1943 my brother Rodney was born and my father was billeted in the barracks at Colchester. We moved to that town for the summer months.

Perhaps I was a frequent embarrassment to my father throughout his life, but the first recorded occasion was at these quarters in Colchester. My father's Colonel was paying a visit and enjoying a quiet drink in the drawing room. At the age of three, I was barely able to see over the back of the sofa. On spying a round, whitish, shiny object – the top, it transpired, of the Colonel's balding head – I grabbed hold of a large spoon and gave a resounding tap to what I perceived to be a hard-boiled egg. The Colonel reacted as if a bomb had landed, and the miscreant – for a reason he could not understand – was sent to bed.

My father spent the latter part of the war in Italy, and my mother returned to Devon with Rodney and myself.

At last the ghastly war in Europe was over. It was 1946, but a whole generation of young people, on the threshold of adulthood, had lost six years of their lives. For many it would never be the same again. Ravaged by the emotional and physical savagery of war – crippling wounds, torture, the trauma of prison camps and the loss of fellow soldiers – the road to rehabilitation was to be far from easy. Many returned as heroes but had no jobs awaiting them, nor the emotional strength to carry on where they had left off six years earlier. No-one was unaffected, and even the families who were reunited without personal loss had to rebuild their relationships.

I never did get around to asking my own father exactly what happened in the months after the war. There was a hardened reluctance on the part of my generation – and generations before – to discuss affairs of a personal nature. This was, I suppose, a 'code of conduct' imposed at public school: Don't ask personal questions. Don't show emotion. If something improper, scandalous or unwholesome occurs, keep your counsel, and turn a blind eye. So, in particular, I never did ask my father or mother what went wrong with their marriage. For that matter there was very little of a personal nature that we did discuss.

It was not long before my father was re-established in Fleet Street when he rejoined the *Sunday Pictorial*. We bought a house in Bedford Gardens, Kensington, very close to where my parents had lived before the war. I remember little of my father's presence there, partly because he was a late riser and I was packed off to day-school in the adjacent Sheffield Terrace before he was sighted. My bedroom was adjacent to that of my parents, and I can recall a series of noisy and animated arguments in the night. Their marriage lasted barely 18 months after the war. There had been no family life as such, and I cannot remember a single occasion when my father, mother and their two sons were all together.

The war had thus created two more orphans, but my mother ensured that we had a wonderful life, with walks in Kensington Gardens, entertainments and ice-creams.

My father had moved to Mayfair to share a flat with the show-business writer Dick Richards, and so almost inevitably he came up with more spectacular 'treats'. By the age of nine his eldest son was committed to football, and soon after to racing. My father took me to watch Luton, Chelsea and, joy of joys, Leyton Orient – dare I confess, the very first team to win my support. What on earth the club's directors, notably Harry Zussman, made of Peter Wilson's presence at Leyton Orient versus Northampton Town in Division Three (South) can only be imagined, but Wilson junior had a magical day and met Leslie Welch the Memory Man! There were also trips to the circus at Harringay and to a pantomime starring Norman Wisdom. One of these expeditions ended at Harry Meadows' Churchill's Club, my presence in which must have stretched legality to the limit!

My mother bought a smaller London house in Phillimore Terrace, off Kensington High Street. My grandparents had moved back from Devon and bought a house called Woodrising, near Rye in Sussex. By now I was attending preparatory school at Summerfields, St Leonards, and the holidays were spent between London and Rye. There was always plenty to do in London, but I preferred the country life, with tree houses, bicycle rides, secret places and cricket on the lawn.

My father's widowed mother lived in a top-floor flat in Airlie Gardens, Kensington. She was a wonderful enthusiast for expeditions to the park, to Whiteley's Store and to the cinema. As my enthusiasm for horse racing developed and the need for racing results to be obtained became urgent, we would always return via Kensington High Street underground station to acquire the most up-to-date edition of the *Evening News*, the *Standard* or *The Star*. The 'stop press' would be feasted on and delight or disappointment manifested.

This daily obsession originated from one day in 1949. My grandfather would rattle through *The Times* crossword at breakfast, but eventually he would lose interest and make the newspaper available to others. One morning my aunt Sylvia – my mother's younger sister – pushed the paper to me, opened at the racing page. 'Julian, see if you can pick some winners,' she challenged. I had not the remotest idea how to go about it, but it occurred to me that form figures of 330 must be better than 112. How wrong can you be! In the event, on that first day, Lady Pappageno with the 330 form finished unplaced and I had learned my first lesson in racing. Every morning for the next ten years I made a list of selections for every race meeting in a private notebook.

Summerfields was a privately owned, traditional 'prep' school, designed to prepare boys for the Common Entrance examination to a public school. It was what was then known as an 'Eton school' because the majority of pupils were being prepared for entry to Eton. This enabled me to enjoy the best of both worlds: as a future Harrovian I made many friends destined to become Etonians, whom otherwise I would never have met. One such friend was Lord Charles Spencer-Churchill, brother of the Eleventh Duke of Marlborough. Churchill, as we called him, was a noisy and vibrant individual, already a skilled raconteur, with the ability to capture an audience and dominate a discussion. He held his own through dint of his personality, although he was not a gifted games-player. The star athletes were inevitably the élite of the school: to win your school 'colours' was everything, and to be in a school team was socially obligatory.

At Summerfields my best friend became a boy called Jimmy Armstrong, whose parents owned a stud and several racehorses in Australia. Jimmy was equally obsessed with racing, so every day we staked our daily ration of five boiled sweets on the outcome of our equine selections. Soon, my mother and aunt were persuaded to take me to a point-to-point at Charing, and then to racing at Wye. It was hypnotic. Every day, hours were spent studying the form, reading every word that was written on racing, listening to the radio commentaries of Raymond Glendenning, and never missing – during the holidays – the racing results on the radio in the evening. At school we had access to a daily newspaper, while the Matron would allow Jimmy and myself a quick peek at her evening paper.

But there were other games to play at school: cricket, football and rugby, and later squash, tennis, golf, billiards and athletics. It was heaven for me. For almost a week before it was time to return to school, I was counting the days. The work was not challenging and the hours spent on the playing fields, in friendly competition, were the ultimate pleasure.

My brother Rodney (now Steve Wilson, author and journalist) was a pleasant companion during the holidays, but neither cricket nor football was high on his daily agenda. As we grew older, occasionally a sixpenny bribe would entice him out on to the lawn. Otherwise, at Woodrising, it was my grandfather (then in his late sixties!) or my aunt who provided the obligatory bowling or batting.

My grandfather was tall and distinguished-looking, with a grey moustache and the air of a patriarch. I was able to admire his cricketing achievement through dusty and disintegrating copies of *Wisden*. When he died in 1954 I was distraught: he had coached me, encouraged me, and once turned a blind eye to what could have been seen as a severely punishable offence. His study window extended about two feet from the outside wall to maximize the light on to his desk. One day whilst playing cricket on the lawn with my next-door neighbour I struck an extra cover drive which arrowed upwards, hit the outside wall of the house, crashed through the lateral window into the study and back out into the garden through the central window. There was broken glass everywhere! Grandfather walked calmly into the garden and said: 'I saw that. I've told you before, for goodness sake keep your left elbow straight.' When he died he left me a personal letter from W. G. Grace, whose admiration he had earned with a particular innings.

This grandfather's experience with 'WG' was, however, happier than that of my other grandfather. The great cricketer was notorious for his gamesmanship and was never happy if a player was getting the better of him. One day in a match between Cambridge University and London County, as Freddy Wilson was scoring freely, Grace was becoming more and more exasperated. A wicket fell and he said to grandfather: 'Look at the ducks, Freddy.' 'What's the matter with them?' enquired the other. 'You keep on watching them and you'll see something funny in a minute,' said Grace. Grandfather watched them flying around, looking full face into the sun. The following ball my grandfather missed a full toss and was stumped down the leg side!

It was in 1950 that my father took me on our first holiday together, to the Cornish seaside resort of St Mawes. I was looking forward to it immensely, but the day before we were due to leave London I developed a pain in my left groin. My mother noticed my limp but I made nothing of it. Father and I took the train to Paddington and arrived at our destination on a sunny summer evening. There we checked into a pub called the 'Ship and Castle' – but for me it could well have been called 'The Titanic'. My limp worsened and after the first day I was compelled to stay in bed. It transpired that an infection had worked its way up from a toe and the poison had caused a swelling of a gland. There was considerable parental concern as my pain became more severe, and father confessed subsequently that he feared my leg would need to be amputated. At the time he reacted in the only way that he knew: he made some delightful friends in Alan and Mary Slater from Yorkshire and another charming couple from Leicestershire, who proved to be the durable drinking companions he needed!

After a week in bed at the Ship and Castle, young Julian was returned to his mother with a pair of crutches and a sallow complexion. The Slaters, meanwhile, are convinced to this day that I was spending my time 'messing about in boats' with the local fishermen!

Happily the poisoned leg had cleared up before the start of the new term at Summerfields. I was fit and healthy, with only one other discomfort – a painful ingrowing toenail. I had two operations on the toe, the first during the spring term of 1950. I can remember vividly the miserable journey to Hastings Hospital after a football match – in which, ironically, I had scored a hat-trick – and wondering for how long sporting activities would be prohibited. The second, more serious, operation which removed half of the toe was in the summer of that year, when my convalescence was eased by sitting in bed, listening to the BBC radio commentary on the famous Test series between England and the West Indies, whose unforgettable heroes included the three 'W's' – Walcott, Worrell and Weekes – and 'those two little friends of mine', Ramadhin and Valentine.

I had started my schooling at Summerfields in the autumn of 1949. A tribe of small boys gathered at London's Victoria Station for the train journey to Hastings. We were an assorted assembly in varying states of enthusiasm and distress. There were the show-offs, the braggadocios, the bullies, the whimperers and the 'total inadequates'. We scrambled with our luggage into old-fashioned, reserved, 3rd Class carriages. The 'new boys' were apprehensive, some terrified; the older boys were assured and patronizing. One small boy, unforgettably, spent the journey in the overhead net luggage rack. On arrival at school I was allocated a five-bedded dormitory, with a 'dorm captain' to teach us new boys 'the ropes' – such as no talking after lights out, and washroom procedure.

Summerfields was a large, rambling, but comforting building, with a broad front stairway leading from the hallway to the first floor – for the exclusive use of the staff – and a narrow back stairway for the boys. On the right of the main hall were the majority of classrooms, all overlooking the terrace and gardens, rolling downhill towards the sea. Straight ahead was a long wooden corridor (the marbles playing ground) leading to the library-cum-assembly hall, where prayers would be 'held' every morning. Up a narrow staircase from the library was the long dining room, where breakfast, lunch and high tea were served to the fifty-odd pupils. At the back of the school buildings there were sports changing rooms and a vast gymnasium. Behind this, the playing fields were sited about 100 yards up a lane and a staircase.

As in all similar establishments, the meat was overcooked, the cabbage invariably contained a population of caterpillars, and the puddings would have weighed down a battleship. Mrs Savage, the school cook, was a formidable but benign autocrat, with heavily dyed red hair. An early indication of my ability to 'sweet-talk' and to employ my inherited 'gift-of-the-gab' was my special relationship with this lady. I would arrive in the kitchen several minutes before the other boys had come downstairs, to ask for – and invariably acquire – a pre-breakfast bowl of steaming-hot porridge. By the time it arrived at the boys' table it was usually cool and lumpy!

We played soccer in the autumn, rugby in the spring and cricket during the summer. There was a Sports Day (athletics) during the summer term, invariably followed by the Hay picnic. This was an annual celebration of the cutting of the hay in one of the meadows below the playing fields, an event that I never looked forward to or enjoyed. I was soon to understand why. All my life I have suffered from chronic hay fever, which manifests itself towards the end of May and continues until Glorious Goodwood week – the last week of July.

Hay fever has been one of the great scourges of my life. From the early 1950s I have submitted to every form of treatment or 'cure' known to man, with minimal success. For almost 15 years I visited the 'foremost specialist' in Harley Street and subjected myself each spring to a course of 'specific injections' over a three-month period. No good. The worthy doctor eventually admitted that I was his longest-running patient and there was nothing more he could do for me.

I have taken antihistamines that have sent me to sleep, nasal sprays that made me sneeze even more violently, enough injections to bring a rhinoceros to its knees, and even goat's milk – all to no good. The only substance that has provided any degree of relief is Depo-Medrone which was recommended to me by Nigel Dempster in 1974, to whom I am indebted. Injections of this have enabled me to get through Royal Ascot for many years without recourse to antihistamine pills, and I still rely on it. It used to be said that sufferers 'grow out' of hay fever, usually in their thirties. At 58 I am still a sufferer.

Because of this afliction I was mercifully 'excused' the Hay picnic in my final year at Summerfields. I was also an absentee from another memorable school outing.

The Queen, in her Coronation year, was coming to Hastings on an official visit, so the entire school was given a half-day holiday to welcome her at the County Ground. I asked permission to stay at the school because I had decided to be an anti-monarchist. Permission was granted. Already the legacy of my father's rebellious instinct was permeating through! Looking back, I view this episode with a mixture of amusement and embarrassment. It is certainly ironic: after describing, for 30 years, the procession at Royal Ascot for the benefit of BBC television viewers, my feelings for the Royal Family could rightly be described as rock-solid. Sadly, this is far from a universal sentiment at the Corporation.

If the masters at Summerfields were concerned at my contrariness they did not show as much. Probably, wisely, they viewed it as a childish whim. Nonetheless, if there was mischief about, I was normally in the thick of it. A favourite adventure was to slip out of the back door of the gymnasium after supper, run across the playing fields, drop over the school wall, and buy as many sweets as we could afford in the local shop. We were never caught at this, but other mischief did not always escape detection. I was caned on several occasions. Group canings were the least agreeable because no-one wanted to be first, but the longer it was necessary to wait, the more disturbing it became. I recall one little group of miscreants waiting outside the Headmaster's study for the first victim to emerge, to be asked: 'Was it hard?'

Boxing was a popular school sport. To what degree it was obligatory I cannot recall, but the annual boxing championships were well subscribed. To contest the middleweight title, in my penultimate year, I had to fight three times during the afternoon.

The first bout was against a boy called Stephen Spurrier, now a successful wine merchant. He was far from enthusiastic, and in the changing room beforehand whispered: 'Don't hit me and I'll let you win.' Consequently the first two rounds resembled an indifferently choreographed slow foxtrot. The judges looked unimpressed, so in the third and final round I landed a conspicuous slap on the side of my opponent's jaw. His eyes misted and he had the look of a wounded animal. After the fight he complained bitterly, but I retorted: 'Well, I had to do something!' My next bout was against a boy called Muers-Raby, which I scrambled through to reach the final against Nicholas Spurrier, the older brother of my first-round opponent.

Spurrier major, at least a year older than me, was uncompromising. 'I saw what you did to my brother. He says you double-crossed him. I'm going to make you pay,' he snarled. There is little doubt that Nick Spurrier was the superior boxer and he was certainly stronger and fresher than me. At the end of the second round, forced back into a corner, I put my gloves to my face in defence. Spurrier stood back to wind up a huge haymaker for a spectacular knockout. Peering cautiously through my gloves, inquisitive as to the reason for the cessation of pain, I saw a monster blow leave its launching pad on its slow and laborious journey. I stepped aside and Spurrier all but fell out of the ring. Amazingly I survived the third round, whereupon the judges, unamused by Spurrier's buffoonery, decided to award the bout to me. I have often contemplated the disposition of a schoolmaster when confronted with the knowledge that he is obliged to sit through an afternoon such as that!

During my last year at Summerfields, another boy and I rose to the surface of a rather shallow pool of athletes. The other boy's name was William Wilks. We were deadly rivals and had separate groups of friends. Wilson and Wilks! In the eyes of the school he was the personification of everything worthy and good. He was a school monitor and captain of cricket, whilst I was vice-captain of cricket and football. He was school champion at tennis, table tennis and squash, whilst I won the golf and billiards competitions. He was a thoroughly 'good egg', whilst I was becoming argumentative and expressing a desire to be 'different'. In the end it was a case of 'good' triumphing over 'evil': Wilks won our private battle hands down, and for good measure went on to win a scholarship to Eton.

It was the summer of 1953. We listened on the radio to Sir Victor Sassoon's Pinza winning the Derby for Gordon Richards, beating the Queen's Aureole. It seemed that the sun was always shining.

There was just the tiniest cloud in the sky – the Common Entrance examination and graduation to public school. I had read Horace Vachell's famous romantic eulogy of Harrow, *The Hill*, and heard the stories of my grandfather's days at the school. But what truly lay in store? There was that indefinable fear of the unknown.

I was sad to say goodbye to Summerfields for the final time. Perhaps instinct was telling me that life would never be quite as easy again.

## TWO

# *The Hill*

Harrow School, founded by John Lyon in 1584, is a large, sprawling, multi-purpose, up-market academy, covering much of a windy hilltop village in north-west Middlesex. It is probably the best school in the world: every Harrovian knows that the only reason people speak of the Eton & Harrow Match, rather than the other way round, is that 'E' comes before 'H' in the alphabet.

It comprises 11 residential houses, a large, windy concrete yard in front of an historic building, a church, a library, a gymnasium, a sports centre, an athletics track, a huge swimming pool (known as 'Ducker'), and acres and acres of magnificent playing fields. Quite simply it is an epicentre of education and of fun. Lord Byron and Sir Winston Churchill are included amongst many distinguished Old Harrovians.

The school is internationally famous and, nowadays, internationally patronized. But if the Harrow of today sounds like a happy-go-lucky holiday camp, it was not always so.

In the nineteenth century there was more than one Headmaster who believed that the best aid to a boy's education was the cane, and the flogging block in the old Fourth Form room remains a testimony to that philosophy. The system had occasional justification, but sadly failed to take into account the elements of dyslexia and sheer inability to learn. Nonetheless, the severity of school discipline – abetted by the habitual arctic conditions in draughty, unheated houses on top of that icy hill – served its students well in other respects. An Old Harrovian, like many ex-public school boys, was almost immune to pain and discomfort. Whether shooting in driving rain, fishing in the gusty north of Scotland, hunting all day on an uncomfortable saddle, or indeed facing unspeakable conditions in war, the Old Harrovian was conditioned to cope. It was a tough regime and not everyone saw it through.

I arrived at Harrow-on-the-Hill in September 1953. As I travelled with my mother on the Metropolitan railway from Baker Street station, the words of the famous school song echoed through my mind:

*Five hundred faces and all so strange,*
*Life in front of me, home behind . . .*

Yet I knew that I came to the Hill with a great advantage as a third-generation Harrovian. As well as my grandfathers, my uncle Teddy (Mann) – killed in Libya in 1942 – had played in the cricket XI, and my great-uncle Thomas (Wilson) had played at Lord's in the three years between 1909 and 1911. He, too, was killed in hostilities – at Ypres in July 1917. My father, predictably, had forsworn cricket, but he had represented the school at squash and was a finalist in the Surrey Junior Covered Court Tennis Championships in 1931.

We newcomers were welcomed with tea and friendship, and I was delivered into the hands of a 'second-termer' whose duty it was to acquaint me with the house and its customs. My house was West Acre, whose Housemaster, a likeable, middle-aged bachelor named Philip Boas, had been a popular young master while my father was in the school. I was allocated a bed in Room 40, at the very top of the house. This was a disadvantage: it was the room furthest away from the majority of House Monitors.

If a Monitor needed an errand to be run, or a package delivered, or any other task fulfilled too tiresome for his 'special' fag, he would yell at the top of his voice: 'B-o-o-y-y, b-o-o-y-y, b-o-o-y-y'. The last fag to arrive at a 'boy call' was given this tedious duty to perform. All this was explained by my mentor with a combination of gloom and glee. He added that the penalty for avoiding a 'boy call' was a beating. 'So,' I enquired, 'one of us three in here is almost certain to get most of the boy calls?' 'Yes,' said the boy, 'but the other fellow hasn't arrived yet. I'd take that desk near the door if I was you.' The remaining desk was in the far corner of the study, so I would have three yards start on the other new boy at every call!

This was one of a hundred or so customs and rituals, along with names, initials, abbreviations, houses, masters (or 'beaks'), senior boys, institutions, and rules that had to be learned by heart by every new boy in the first two weeks. Failure to attain an acceptable level of knowledge would entail chastisement. Worse still, the new boy's mentor would also be beaten.

> *Who is the Head of Elmfield? . . . What are the privs (privileges) of Phil (the Philatelic Society)? . . . What are the colours of the Headmaster's House? . . .and so on.*

And so it went on, an endless litany of parochial knowledge, to be absorbed, on pain of . . . pain!

The 'special' fags were a privileged élite, chosen personally by the House Monitors, on the grounds of either good looks or general efficiency. Their duties were to make fires, clean shoes, press trousers, make beds, and occasionally to cook meals. They were, however, exempt from day-to-day fagging.

There was much to assimilate in those first few days – the locations of classrooms, the acquisition of books, and achieving an element of comfort in one's dormitory and study. It soon became clear, for example, that I needed a lamp for my desk. Having acquired one, with difficulty, the task of making it work had to be faced. All my life I had been indulged by my mother in domestic matters while my grandparents enjoyed the privilege of living-in staff. I had no more idea how to wire an electric light than to split an atom. So I did what seemed the obvious thing: I connected the wires from the ceiling to the wires of my new lamp, taped the two together and turned on the light switch. There was the most almighty flash and every light in the immediate vicinity went out. I was shaking with shock. Somehow a senior boy assessed the damage, repaired the fuses and restored electricity to the house.

I was expecting serious trouble and severe punishment for my stupidity. Whether it was because of my evident shock, or the sympathy of the senior boy, I got away with it scot-free. I have always avoided electrical appliances ever since.

Two days a week (and three if you were involved in matches) we would play rugby. On the first day of term the new boys were put under the microscope in 'house practice'. The training was severe. The nucleus was a training routine known as 'Stevers', after a rugby master called Stevenson. You would walk 25 yards, run 50 yards, and sprint the final 25 yards. Every session started and ended with ten Stevers. On my first day the House Captain was determined to make us work, the 25-yard sprint being accompanied by a bastinado of blows from his Corps cane. There was no slacking that day. We even ran most of the half mile uphill back to the house.

Nevertheless I came to love those playing fields, perforated by a thousand sets of rugby studs. On less intense days we would idle back from an exhausting game, in the autumn twilight, with the lights of North London twinkling across the fields and the gentle hum of the distant traffic wafting up towards the Hill.

Those who played longest, or returned the slowest, faced an unwelcome penalty. The house baths, or 'toshes', numbered just six on the top floor, to accommodate upwards of 50 mud-soaked rugby players. Latecomers bathed in a darker version of Brown Windsor soup, without the fragrance and with a thick layer of scum! Showers, there were none.

I had passed into Remove 1(a), a level below the standard of scholarship. My form-mates included Anthony Cable, who was to become captain of cricket and a lifetime friend, William Fox (later to become James Fox, the actor), and Peter Ohlson, whose father Sir Eric had owned the 1945 Derby winner Dante.

Few of our scholastic tasks were unduly challenging, except that learning poetry was extremely difficult for me. I discovered that reciting last thing at night enabled me to remember a few verses for a while in the morning. This technique became helpful to me later in life when it was important to learn owners' colours for racing commentaries.

Homework, between 'bill' (roll call) and prayers, was the most boring and arduous part of the day, then after prayers it was bed at 9.30 pm for junior boys. The sleeping facilities did not represent the height of comfort. We had hinged bunk-beds which, when not in use during the day, were strapped together and tilted upwards into their framework. This of course represented a heaven-sent instrument of torture for sadistic older boys who, sensing the possibility of claustrophobia in a junior boy, would lift up the bed and its occupant, confining the victim to an airless, upside-down prison.

In truth I recall little bullying during my time at the school, although weaker individuals may have suffered in silence. The behaviour was a far cry from my grandfather's day. A letter written by him to his parents from his Eastbourne preparatory school, Warren Hill, began pathetically:

> *Dear Mother and Father*
> *I am all right and not quite so much bullied . . . I do not find the work too much for me, but the bullying makes me quite unfit for it . . .*

I can only speculate why my grandfather should have been bullied, but suspect that he may have been spoiled by his mother, who sent him baskets of fruit. Parental interference was always frowned upon at school: we saw our parents once or twice every term but regular visits were viewed as over-indulgence.

We survived mostly on a weekly allowance of two shillings, dispensed by the Housemaster after lunch on Fridays. Invariably boys with unwise or *nouveaux riches* parents came back to school with bulging wallets. In this respect my uncomfortable relationship with my father cost me dearly. On the few occasions we met he would invariably ask: 'Are you all right for money?' Either through pride or embarrassment my reply was always 'Oh yes, fine' – a response similar to that given to my mother. It was, of course, quite untrue, so it became all the more necessary as the years passed by to supplement my modest allowance through successful betting.

Those with money would invariably take tea on half-holidays at the Hill teashop, or at an establishment called Anne's Pantry where egg and chips, sausage and tomato were on offer – a veritable feast. The rest of us satisfied ourselves with bread and jam and cake in the house. Only once did I envy the 'Anne's Pantry' élite, when my rival for a place in the Harrow Football XI in my last year was able to invite the School Captain regularly to tea.

While I made a handful of good friends in West Acre, sadly none of those friendships has survived the passage of the years. My best companions were all in other houses, and some of those are still my friends today. Notwithstanding this it was always important to establish a working friendship with at least one West Acre contemporary, because at the end of each term, until seniority earned you a single study, it was necessary to find a kindred spirit with whom to share a study the following term. Anyone unable to do so would be burdened with harbouring a 'new boy', or a social pariah. The choice, of course, was hugely significant: you would spend over 12 hours a day with your companion, in a confined space, smelly socks and all. In some respects it was a good training for marriage.

The juxtaposition of two healthy young men, of pubescent sexuality, almost inevitably encouraged homosexuality, even if it was largely experimental. I had only second-hand experience of this. I was sharing a study with an individual who was attractive in every way, and who represented my new 'William Wilks' – we were friends and rivals. Long after 'lights-out' the door of our study (on the quiet, private side of the house) opened and a senior boy came in. 'Now then young –,' he demanded, 'would you like to come down for a party?' The inference was obvious and, naively, I called out to the older boy: 'Don't be a fool, –.' He took no notice. My room-mate was away for about an hour and we never discussed the matter again.

The following day the senior boy saw the contempt in my eyes. For the remainder of his time in the school there was a mutual distaste between us. Unhappily, as he attained an important status, I suffered from his antagonism.

In the immediate period after arrival at Harrow, it was exceptionally difficult to avoid calling the House Monitors 'sir' – as one called the Masters. Through the eyes of a 13-year-old the Monitors were large, strapping individuals, built like gods and with considerable authority, as well as the power to discipline. In my first term I was especially in awe of the captain of rugby, a large, robust boy called Cecil-Williams with a deep booming voice. He turned out to be a benign despot. At the end of my first term, during which I played in the winning 'Cock Torpid' XV (the inter-house Under-16 Rugby tournament), Cecil-Williams came crashing into Room 40 after House Supper with a huge bottle of kirsch, from which all of the team were invited to burn their throats. That was my first experience of spirits and to this day kirsch remains one of my favourite liqueurs.

There was so much sporting activity available at Harrow. On the days when Harrow Football or rugby were not played, there was the choice of a 'Short Ducker' (a three-mile run around the perimeter of the Hill, ending with a steep uphill climb), squash, rackets, boxing, fencing or fives. In the first two years most of my non-football afternoons were spent in the boxing gymnasium. I truly felt that my boxing was progressing until a setback occurred. There was a short, stocky youth in West Acre called Simpson, son of Ernest Simpson, the erstwhile husband of the late Duchess of Windsor. He was a pugnacious individual who had boxed successfully for the school. I had finished training for the day when Simpson challenged me to three rounds of sparring. I had no particular desire to spar with him, especially as he seemed in a strange frame of mind, and I told him so – but he insisted. It got a little out of hand. Seconds were called to monitor what had become a full-blown contest, and the outcome was that Simpson landed a telling blow and broke my nose. The legacy of that blow is still evident today.

It was around this time that the new intake of boys were given a general medical examination by one of the school doctors, in the gymnasium. We were weighed, measured, checked for blood pressure, heart-beat, lung capacity and the rest. I have always had the misfortune to have a concave chest, as well as the respiratory problems brought on by my hay fever. The doctor checked me over, made some notes and shook his head. I moved on and heard him make a comment to the next in line. After the 'medical' was over I asked the boy what the doctor had said. 'Oh,' he exclaimed, 'he just said that you'd be lucky to live beyond the age of 20!'

My first year at Harrow passed enjoyably and without major trauma. I played in the House Torpid team in all three sports and played in the games from which the Junior Colts were selected, in rugby and cricket. In the case of Harrow Football, there were no school games other than the Sixth Form game since, other than Old Boys' XIs, there were no other opposing teams, so competition was entirely inter-house.

Harrow Football was played with a large, heavy ball the size of a medicine ball as used in the gymnasium, and was a hybrid cross between soccer and rugby. It was created in the early part of the twentieth century on the grounds that the clay-based playing fields of Harrow were unsuited to soccer, being always waterlogged in the spring. So, for most of the century, no soccer was played at Harrow. This was a personal disadvantage as the sport was certainly my favourite at the time – so much so that I was inclined to play Harrow Football as if I were playing soccer. This was frowned upon and consequently I was regarded as too 'lightweight' to be a serious player.

When the summer arrived I was placed, on the basis of my record at Summerfields, in the cricketing Junior Colts (under-15), but failed to make the XI. I was a medium-fast, left-arm, round-the-wicket bowler capable of swinging the ball in and cutting it back, but there was an awkwardness about my delivery. A left-arm bowler's tendency is to run away to the right on delivery. This leaves you liable to run on to the wicket – disallowed! – and to lunge in front of the umpire, which irritates him and invariably leads to a refusal of even the most straightforward lbw decision.

At the time, young cricketers were simply not encouraged to bowl *over* the wicket – on the right side of the umpire for a left-arm bowler. That would have been so much easier for me and, in my view, would have allowed me to be considerably more effective. Later in life I continued to bowl at medium pace until the age of 40, when I switched to leg spinners. Ironically, I have taken far more wickets in recent years – over 250 since 1990 – than I ever did bowling at medium pace.

At Summerfields I had opened the batting for the school, but now I was dropping rapidly down the order. Indeed, apart from in 'house games' I was not scoring many runs. Then, during one holiday that we shared together, my father noticed that I was squinting and screwing up my eyes. He insisted on an eye test, which revealed that I had a significant astigmatism in my left eye, impairing my sight. Now I knew why I was 'picking up' a cricket ball so late: as a right-handed batsman it is the left eye that does the significant work. A less vain individual would have batted in glasses, but I always possessed an obsessive dread of joining the 'four-eyed' brigade!

At the end of my second year at Harrow I sat my O-level examinations and, miraculously, managed to pass the lot – although geography was a photo-finish. This was a significant period in the scholastic cycle for another reason because by now a boy would have a coveted 'single' study, was exempt from fagging and had a degree of self-esteem. But there was a negative period until the authority and privileges arrived that came with being a 'three-yearer'.

I had finally completed my period of sharing a study in the company of a pleasant-enough boy with whom I had nothing special in common except that we seemed to be socially compatible. We had the same room, on the 'private' side, that I had occupied previously. One day as I was reading quietly at my desk there arose a gurgling sound behind me. My companion was hanging by a belt from a hook on the back of the door with a chair a few feet away. His face was damson-red. Blood vessels were bursting from his forehead and cheeks and his eyes bulged from their sockets. At first I froze but then rushed to him and lifted him upwards – luckily he was neither tall nor heavy – and eased him to the floor. He had urinated and defecated into his grey trousers. After loosening the belt I rushed downstairs to locate the House Matron, and of what immediately happened next there is no recall. I suppose I was in shock.

The following day my friend returned from the school sanatorium and life reverted slowly to near-normal. Bloodshot eyes and protruding vessels were the only manifest signs of his trauma. I never did ask him why he did it, but I mused: Was it an accident? Was there unhappiness at home? Or was he under the threat of a beating? The following term, when we were bathing one day after rugby, I found him lying in a muddy bath, front-down, with his backside above the scum of the water. I thought for a moment that he must have sat on a red-hot barbecue because his seat was crossed with five or six vivid purple lines. Then the penny dropped. Once again I did not ask why he had been beaten. Sometimes it was just for having an 'attitude'.

The most savage beating endured by one of my contemporaries was that inflicted on a boy called James Lotery. His executioner, the Head of House, was a School Rackets player, with a wrist like flexible steel. Lotery, who himself was pretty tough, was obliged to acquire the services of first his neighbours and, latterly, the House Matron to attend his wounds. He had suffered the misfortune of being beaten in his pyjamas, which were rendered unwearable.

Beatings would take place in the Head of House's study, in the presence of other House Monitors, about one hour after evening prayers. They would be preceded by a single 'boy call' for the Head of House's 'special', whose task it was to inform the victim that his presence was required. Of all the fearsome sounds that I have encountered in my life, none created such a clammy feeling of sheer terror as that awesome late-night 'boy call'.

Yet most of us lived our lives dangerously. A popular entertainment during the summer term was 'bombing the oiks'. This constituted throwing carefully prepared water-bombs out of a top-floor window, at local boys walking by in the street below. This particular diversion was brought to a rather dramatic end when one of the victims, with no little justification, responded by throwing a thunderflash through a study window. The effect was fairly spectacular.

West Acre was not ideally situated for the mainstream of school activity. It was, for instance, the furthest house from the school chapel, where attendance was obligatory at 9 am every morning. At nine on the dot the gates would be closed, forcibly, by the school custodians and anyone excluded would be duly punished. On the other hand the house was well-sited for mischief. It had a perfect back exit for after-dark expeditions to the public house/off-licence; it was handily placed for Newlands Wood, the favoured location for illicit smoking; and it was closest to the school sanatorium for those who wished to take their chance of a heterosexual relationship with a nurse.

I indulged in all of these activities in the fullness of time, to the extent of taking a nurse called Jane Camden-Field to the Eton & Harrow Match in my last year. Unhappily, despite much scheming and day-dreaming on my part, our relationship was never consummated at Harrow, although it was several years later in a flat in North Kensington. She was dark and petite, with an excellent figure and I shall always remember her.

Life really began at Harrow in the fourth year, when 'three-yearer' privileges created so much more freedom. The privileges involved comfort possessions (a wireless and gramophone), deregulation and authority. The next step was to become a House Monitor with a status akin to membership of an omnipotent oligarchy. A simple 'boy call' ensured that every task was fulfilled and every comfort created. A highlight of the weekly despotic ritual was the 'Fines Breakfast' on Sunday mornings. The monitors would be served a breakfast of bacon, eggs, sausage, tomato, fried potatoes and kidneys, by their selected 'specials'. These banquets were financed by fines levied on miscreant boys. At the time it seemed an admirable system.

One of the privileges of older boys was the facility to visit friends in other houses. This was the basis of my most enjoyable times at Harrow. A friend called Philip d'Abo and I launched a card school that occupied hours of leisure time during the winter months. Philip, now the father of actress Lucy d'Abo, later became a professional croupier and more recently a Steward at Dubai's Nad Al Sheba racecourse. We would play poker, brag and vingt-et-un. The sums involved were not substantial, but occasionally a poker pot would reach several pounds. Philip, an excellent cricketer, had a cheerful, almost impenetrable smile, which was a formidable weapon. Neither of us will forget the day he bluffed me out of a monster pot with a pair of two's!

I was also established before long as one of the school's leading bookmakers. We bet on house matches, school matches, marathons and occasionally outside events. In my last year I made an especially good book on the Harrow Football house matches. I laid several houses to win, but refused to lay West Acre. The latter won the final 2-1. Unfortunately, the following term, while I was anticipating settlement by my clients of between £20 and £30, I was summoned on a Sunday afternoon by the Head of School, Michael Connell.

'I understand,' said Connell, 'that there is a great deal of betting going on in the school and that you and Sidebottom are the leading miscreants. It's got to stop.' I tried to explain – 'Well, I know that Sidebottom has been a bit indiscreet. It wasn't a smart move to shout "On the Eton 'n' Arrer . . . even money Eton" in the Hill. I gather it caused a riot. But surely you know that my business is much more discreet?' That was not enough – 'Discreet or not,' replied Connell, 'it has got to stop. All bets are cancelled as of now.' I insisted – 'Yes, but there are several boys in your house who owe me a few quid. They've got to pay up.' But no – 'You heard what I said. All bets are cancelled. That's it. You may go.'

And my clients never did pay me. Sir Michael Connell is now

a High Court Judge, a Master of Foxhounds and a member of the Jockey Club. I have often thought about taking him before Tattersalls' Committee!

In contrast, my mother was sympathetic towards my love of racing and betting. In the summer of 1953 she sold the house in Kensington and moved down to Berkshire, just a few miles from where she had grown up. She took Rodney and myself with her. We bought a cottage in Little Coxwell, near Faringdon. A near-neighbour was one of mother's oldest friends, Betty Berners, daughter of the trainer Bert Gordon, and whom mother had introduced to her husband Geoffrey Berners. Mother was back among old friends in the heart of the Old Berkshire Hunt. For my part, this was the start of an involvement that was going to last for 40 years – with Swindon Town Football Club. Early that autumn my mother drove me to the County Ground for the first time, with instructions to catch a bus home after the match. When I had not returned by 8 pm she must have been mildly worried, but the fact is that every bus home was packed to capacity, so I ended up walking the entire 10 miles. Thereafter I made the journey there and back on the A420, on my bicycle. It is laughable to contemplate such a journey nowadays.

During the weekdays I would spend hours with my racing books and diaries, analysing form, compiling lists of horses to follow and working out systems. (There was a system involving the Tote Double which invariably showed profit.) In many ways I was a 'loner', content with my own company. In particular this manifested itself in a dread of the annual ordeal of the Old Berks Pony Club Dance. I had never learned to dance properly – when there was dancing instruction at Summerfields I played billiards instead – and spent most of the autumn plotting a way to evade it. In 1956 I went to exceptional lengths.

As a student of modern languages at school, I was due to take my A-levels the following summer. It was suggested that I would benefit from staying with a family in France ('en famille') to improve my colloquial French. Thus it came about that I stayed for two or three weeks with a pleasant family near Nancy. Ironically, during the first weekend they dragged me to a dance, to be partnered by a swarthy, Gabriella Sabatini lookalike! But thereafter they respected my introspective ways and left me to read French books and magazines, mostly about horseracing. I spoke not a word of English during the entire trip and in the end was dreaming in French.

On my last night in France I had a vivid dream that a horse called Bremontier had won the Grand National. I had no knowledge of any such horse in England so put the dream out of mind. Four months later, on the day of the Whitbread Gold Cup at Sandown, I saw to my amazement that a horse called Bremontier, bred in France, was entered and was a 'probable runner' (there were no overnight declarations in those days). I travelled to Sandown only to find that Bremontier was a non-runner. It was only in the evening that I learnt that Bremontier had run in the *Scottish* Grand National at Bogside earlier that afternoon – and won at 10/1. He was ridden by the jockey who had won on him in France, A. Rossio.

It must have been nightmarish for my mother to coerce me to the Pony Club Dance. The ordeal was softened one year when my great Etonian friend Jimmy Armstrong came to stay. Otherwise, it was a war of attrition: 'I want to wear this tie.' . . . 'It's not suitable.' . . . 'But it's my lucky tie' . . . and so on.

We would dine beforehand with the mother of an old friend of my mother's, Lady Vi Page. Lady Page had two pleasant granddaughters with whom I was required to dance. The scenario was similar to the start of a horserace, with the stalls handlers heaving, shoving, blindfolding, threatening and finally imploring the reluctant competitor. I could get through the reels, but the waltzes and slow foxtrots were too much. My friends and I were a shameful disgrace.

In the summer of 1956 I had a hugely sobering (and philosophical) experience. A friend and I would go on long bicycle rides as an early conditioning for rugby training – and the dreaded 'Stevers' – on return to school. One day we stopped by the main railway line from Swindon to London, near Challow. The line was high on an embankment, so we left our bikes on the side of the road and climbed up the embankment. We heard, from away to the east, the distant rumble of the express train from Paddington to the West Country, perhaps a mile away.

'Let's play chicken,' ventured my friend. 'What do you mean?' 'Well, I'll put my foot on the rail this side and you put yours on the rail that side and the last to jump wins.' I do not remember who won the game, but the express thundered by with a clatter of endless carriages, as I stood exhilarated on the east-bound line. Then, almost before that train had passed I was aware of a sharp, shrieking whistle to my right and was aghast to see the London-bound train no more than 50 yards away from us. Instinctively I dived head-first through the air, feeling the rush of the violently displaced air against my legs as I hurtled over the embankment. I rolled down the grassy edge and slithered to a halt. In the distance the sound of the express grew ever fainter and the calm of the beautiful Berkshire countryside was slowly restored. 'Tim, where are you? Tim, for Christ's sake!' (Tim had been a nickname for many years.) My friend was convinced that my carcass was already halfway to London, but I put him out of his misery – 'I'm down here. Great game!' We were shaken but neither of us wanted to show it. I did not tell my mother what had happened, but thought about it for months and years.

What did it mean? Was that really – just a split second – the margin between life and death? Why did it happen? If I had died . . . what a waste: a life thrown away, for nothing. But I would have been unaware, untouched by the tragedy. Only my mother and brother and others would have borne the pain. So many questions and so few answers. If anything the episode drew me a shade closer to God.

In the summer of 1957 it was time to sit my A-levels. I had specialized in French and German – sound advice from my father – and with the benefit of my trip to Nancy sailed through my French. I failed my German exam, which was a mixed blessing: with a further year to spend in the school, but with no wish to go to university, I did not have to move on to scholarship level in the coming year. Instead I could gently go over the A-level syllabus again. A year of free-wheeling – what bliss! I had already decided my destiny in my early years at Harrow. I harboured the idea of becoming a schoolmaster, for which the motivation was simple: I adored school life – never wanted to leave – and envisaged becoming a sports master so as to be able to continue to play games every day. I had not got as far as working out academic responsibilities, this was simply a free passage to a Peter Pan lifestyle. What could be better?

Mercifully, by the age of 16 I had grown out of this fantasy and was determined that my career would be in the world of horseracing. My father and grandfather had been journalists, so what could be more obvious? I would be a racing journalist.

I think that it was widely accepted that my future lay in this direction. In my last year, studying some mandatory 'optional extra', I was rewarded with an end-of-term report from the benign master in charge, Roger Ellis, which read as follows:

> *Wilson has sat quietly at the back of the form throughout the term, evidently pursuing his own agenda. I can only hope that his deliberations have been of profit!*

With a true spirit of adventure my mother allowed me to use her credit betting account with a firm called 'Derridge' and sent on any winnings through the post. Conveniently there was an old-fashioned, red telephone box outside West Acre, and one school master described me to another as 'that boy who is always hanging about outside the telephone box'.

There were several contemporaries with racing connections. As well as Peter Ohlson, there was Peter Robertson, whose father had horses trained by the late Ryan Jarvis, and Sandy Taylor, whose father was Chairman of Newcastle Racecourse. Sandy and his friend Patrick Hume suffered a desperate blow when their betting account was intercepted by their Housemaster and they were 'gated' for the Lord's Exeat – the weekend of the Eton & Harrow Match. At the time it was difficult to think of a more severe punishment. Of course we had setbacks. Peter Ohlson took a long time to forgive me for persuading him to back a horse called Brother Birdbrook, which (as he correctly anticipated) was 'having a run'.

We were greatly assisted by information from Jeremy Rugge-Price, whose stepfather, Tom Blackwell, was a leading owner and member of the Jockey Club. We therefore had a useful network.

An individual on the fringe of our group was a large, untidy boy called McCririck. This individual was not pleasing to the eye, being scruffily dressed, looking thoroughly unwashed, and invariably sporting a damaged straw boater. He had, though, one notable talent: he was an able table tennis player, with the help of the latest of Chinese foam-covered bats. He was a good opponent and enjoyed a bet on the outcome. Eventually he became the school's 'third bookmaker'. In our last year he invited me to watch Royal Ascot on television in the Headmaster's House senior boys' room.

Judith Chalmers' fashion commentary, as she walked among the racegoers in the Ascot paddock area, was memorable. Ever-present behind her, holding a large umbrella or parasol, was a substantial, rather flushed looking gentleman. I was to meet the same man in person exactly seven years later. He was Ronnie Pantlin, BBC TV's senior stage manager. It took a while for recognition to set in, but suddenly the familiar face fell into place. Of course – the man behind Judith!

And so my last year at school drifted pleasantly by. I was a House Monitor and life, as they say, was easy. In the spring term, James Lotery, who had left the school but kept in touch, took me surreptitiously to watch Swindon at Brentford one Saturday. Swindon won 2-1. Not surprisingly, I was undetected.

West Acre won the Harrow Football House Matches and looked certain to win the Rugby Cock House Match. However, for me the week leading up to this climax of the term was traumatic. I was again afflicted with the poisoned leg that had ruined the holiday with my father in St Mawes. I spent several days in the sanatorium in a race against time to be fit to play. Released on the eve of the match, I trained hard in the afternoon and slept fitfully, dreaming of a glorious win against our arch-rivals Rendalls, Michael Connell's house. But there was to be no match: the playing fields froze solid overnight, so the match was abandoned and the trophy shared.

The summer was an idle paradise of playing cricket for the Outcasts XI and lazing in my room listening to the music of Eartha Kitt. The Outcasts was a team of older boys, of Second or Third Eleven standard, who were leaving that summer and resigned to not playing at Lord's. We had entertaining fixtures, mostly away from Harrow, at grounds like the Rothschild Estate near Tring and the Hendon Police College. Alcohol was allowed on the journey home.

It was a bitter disappointment to me, and no doubt to my father, that I failed to play in the Eton & Harrow Match at Lord's. It was probably the biggest disappointment of my life. But thanks to my friend, Anthony Cable, and the reputation of my card school, I was selected just once as twelfth man for the Harrow XI. At least I had sniffed lightly at the scent of success.

There was one great day at Harrow yet to be lived. Every morning I would read the astrology column in the now-defunct *News Chronicle*. On one Saturday the star sign of Gemini was promised:

> *This is a day on which everything that you attempt will succeed!*

My bet was doubled – to £10 – on a horse called Radiancy, running at Wolverhampton that afternoon. The horse duly obliged at 100/30. I bowled with unusual accuracy for the Outcasts – five wickets and my Outcasts cap was my reward. It was such a perfect day.

Now the day that we pretended to welcome, but some of us secretly dreaded, was drawing closer. It was the custom, on leaving the school, to present the Housemaster with a small token of appreciation. I had a friend, in Bradby's House, called Julian Barrow, whom I had seen painting in oils and watercolours from time to time and whose work, to the untrained eye, looked exceptional. I commissioned him to paint West Acre as my leaving present to Philip Boas. I think I paid Julian, who is now a world-renowned landscape and portrait painter, 30 shillings for that effort. The West Acre painting has subsequently been reproduced in prints and enamels and is familiar to almost all West Acre Old Boys.

Mine may not have been an outstanding scholastic career, but at least it ended on a worthy note!

# THREE

# *No Mean City*

We were a strangely subdued group during the walk down to Harrow-on-the-Hill station for the last time. There were echoes of a hundred 'goodbyes' following distribution of our 'Leavers' – personal signed photographs for our friends and younger boys who had earned admiration. Now, bravely defiant of our headaches – the legacy of the previous night's excesses – we were London-bound:

*Life in front of us,*
*School behind . . .*

Four of us reassembled at Alexandra Park for the evening race meeting, after which we headed for the West End and checked into the Regent Palace Hotel, near the Strand. We had dinner and roamed the West End and Soho. At some point the idea developed that we should pick up a prostitute and take her back, surreptitiously, to our hotel. This we did. Choosing the 'batting order' produced a scenario reminiscent of punishment at prep school: would it be better to go in first or last? In the end I went in nervously at number three, but proved to be unsuitably prepared for this keenly anticipated landmark and quite inadequate.

We slept, somehow, all four of us in the single room and in the morning went our separate ways. We were Men! Well, that was the theory.

I walked down the Strand to Charing Cross station to catch a train to Chichester, for the races at Goodwood. Glorious

Goodwood! I had first been taken there in 1952 by my mother and grandmother Wilson. We picnicked on Trundle Hill and enjoyed the amazing visual panorama of the Sussex Downs. It is an image that has always remained romantic in my memory.

Now I was staying with a school-friend, Nick Mayer, whose family had a holiday home on the Sussex coast. I would run down the beach with Nick's sister Peta in the morning, go racing in the afternoon and lie in bed lusting after the gorgeous Peta at night. We remained great friends for seven or eight years, but sadly it was a relationship that was never consummated. That was a wonderful week at Goodwood. The sun seemed to shine incessantly. We had lunch with parents of friends – including Sir Eric Ohlson – in the Chalets and, as one invariably did at Goodwood, won money.

The previous year Jimmy Armstrong and I had taken the train to York for the Ebor meeting. It had rained for most of the day, and almost every favourite had been beaten. Lester Piggott had several fancied rides and none won. In the last race he rode a filly called Street Singer for our next-door neighbour in Berkshire, Major Jack Paine. According to Jack, Lester was so distraught by the events of the day that he appeared to be on another planet. He either did not hear, or took no notice of, what he was asked to do and did the opposite! Street Singer was unplaced. This was an interesting lesson for me: it takes a jockey of exceptional character to bounce back in the last race after a nightmare afternoon.

I spent that summer going to the races at Newbury, Salisbury, Bath and on the Devon circuit, with my friend Anthony Cable. August and the Bank Holiday passed away and now the next ordeal was to be faced.

Financial and emotional support may have been in short supply from my father, but to his credit he helped to provide a perfect springboard for my journalistic career. He had arranged, with the help of the *Daily Mirror* sports editor, Jack Hutchinson, for me to be employed as a sub-editor on the *Noon Record*, the companion newspaper of the *Daily Record* in Glasgow and part of the Mirror Group.

The *Noon* was, in theory, the noon edition of the *Daily Record*. In reality it was a hugely popular sporting tabloid – filled with horseracing, greyhounds and football – which sold more copies in the three counties around Glasgow than did the *Sporting Life* and *Sporting Chronicle* collectively in the whole of England. These extraordinary sales were not unconnected with the fact that, at the time, there were 600 illegal, but flourishing, betting shops in Glasgow. The Betting and Gaming Act of 1961, permitting off-course betting, had yet to be drafted and Glasgow was the epicentre of off-course cash betting. Any punter in England who did not possess a credit account was obliged to send cash in an envelope to Glasgow, postmarked prior to the 'off' of the race or races in question. A firm called McLachlan was the brand leader in this market. My grandmother's domestic help would bet with McLachlan every day without fail!

So, in early September I packed my cases, said goodbye to Berkshire and the dogs, and embarked with my mother on the great journey by road to north of the border. The following day we both went racing at Lanark. That was a weird afternoon. I fancied the first five winners without having a bet, simply recording my selections in my notebook. The biggest 'certainty' of the day was in the last race – a useful animal that had travelled over on the ferry from Ireland. However, in the betting it drifted from 2/5 to even money. I could not believe that my selections would 'go through the card' so I decided against having a bet. The Irish horse 'bolted' in and I returned to Glasgow utterly bemused.

I was no stranger to Scotland. Since the age of nine we had spent part of our summer holiday fishing for brown trout in Invernesshire from a village called Whitebridge. That was a tradition that I maintained, on and off, until 1983. But Glasgow was different. It was raw, urban, dirty, beset with slums and, in some areas, still bearing the scars of the war. It was brought to life memorably by the book *No Mean City* which captured the spirit and despair of the great city.

At the *Noon* I was to be paid a basic wage of £3 10s 0d a week, plus a further £6 a week subsistence allowance for accommodation and food. By keeping a diary of every penny spent (in addition to my betting book) I tried to live within my means.

My accommodation had been arranged in Dowanhill Street, a long road linking Patrick Cross with Anniesland in the north-west of the city. This was close to the university, to Kelvinhall where the big boxing promotions took place, and to the Great Western Road leading out of Glasgow towards Stirling and Loch Lomond. It was also about two miles from Partick Thistle Football Club. I had a bed-sitting room with bathroom on the first floor, and that was it. For this I paid the whole of my weekly wage for bed, breakfast and an evening meal. In my case the latter was at 4.15 pm so that I could catch the tram at Partick Cross and be in the office in Hope Street, opposite Central Station, at 5.00 pm sharp.

I reported for duty on Monday afternoon, and any apprehension was quickly swept away. The editor, an Airdrie fanatic called Bill Harley, and the deputy editor Gordon Stephen, an ardent 'blue-nose' (Rangers supporter), were both kindness itself. I was coached and encouraged by my fellow racing sub-editor, Roy Brown, while the football writer, Dixon Blackstock, was equally helpful. Another good friend was Ian Paul, who worked on the *Daily Record* racing desk, and is now one of the top sports writers in Scotland.

On the racing side the routine was pretty straightforward. First we would sub-edit the race cards as they came in from the Press Association, add the 'late' jockeys and alterations, adjust the PA betting forecasts, and send the copy upstairs to be set in hot metal. This we followed up with the results from the previous day. Next was the PA preview copy which constituted, on a normal day, the front-page lead published under the fictional by-line of 'Meridian'. Finally came the reports of the previous day's racing, either from the PA or from the *Daily Mirror* course correspondent.

The sub-editors' job was to package the copy in a readable format, think of suitable headlines, and advise the editor of any major stories that might be brewing and that could break during the course of the evening. It was Bill Harley's job to prepare a page plan that gave proper prominence on the front and back pages to the major features and news stories, and to present the racecards on the inside pages in a way that was attractive and readable both to the punters and to the betting shops.

The 'cherry on the cake' was the duty of choosing the Three Best and One A Day – the *Noon*'s special selections which had a great following in Glasgow and which had hitherto been the responsibility of Roy Brown. On a day when Roy was off work I was invited to make these selections and they all won. Thereafter, every evening the tension rose after our meal-break as to who would be allocated the privileged duty. It was the last editorial judgement of the day, and Roy and I would sit, seemingly nonchalantly checking proofs, but with just half an eye on the editor. Eventually, as the tension became almost unbearable, Bill would look up, clear his throat, and say: 'Roy, do the Three Best and One A Day.' The reply would be 'Thank you, Bill', while I carried on with my work as if I had not heard!

Our working evening was carefully structured. At about 8.15 pm, when all the copy except for evening results had been 'subbed' and sent upstairs, we would file down to a pub called 'The Garrick' for a couple of pints. There followed an expedition to the canteen for the evening meal, although in my case, having already had my 'tea' at the bed-sit, this was not a great deal. At about 9.30 pm we would return to the office, deal with the late racing, greyhounds and football copy – and await Bill's key judgement!

Between 10.00 and 11.00 pm we would go up to the printer's 'stone' to re-read the proofs, make late adjustments, and put the paper to bed at around midnight. God protect any young enthusiast who laid a hand on the galleys: union power was still dominant and lines of demarcation carefully observed.

At midnight came 'decision time' for me. Should I catch the last tram back to Partick Cross, or should I join Gordon Stephen and the gang for drinks in the Press Club? Most often it was the latter, so I would catch the 2.15 am tram, scramble into bed at around

3.00 am, get up for my breakfast at 9.00 am, and return to bed until mid-day.

Lunchtimes were spent in the local pub, with frequent breaks to duck in and out of the Hyndland betting shop. This was hardly a lifestyle to prepare a man for the Olympic Games! It was as well, perhaps, that I was dependent on public transport, having on two occasions failed my driving test.

The first test was taken in Swindon, in the summer of 1958. I arrived for my test at 12.00 noon to be told that I was due at 2.00. After enjoying a couple of pints of Arkell's '3 B's' beer for lunch, I was failed on the grounds of 'over-confidence'! My second test was in Glasgow, where I failed because I had not the faintest idea where I was going.

Bill Harley's deputy, Gordon, was of the old school – hard-drinking, hard-talking. He wrote a popular weekly column on football betting, and besides Rangers FC his interests were in 'a wee hauf' (a small whisky) and an enormous-breasted copy-typist named Rita. Whether Gordon ever made it with Rita we never discovered, but his courtship was an on-going topic of considerable interest.

The social and cultural highlight of Gordon's year was the 'Old Firm' match on New Year's Day between Rangers and Celtic. This was an event of frightening emotional intensity, looked forward to for weeks ahead. Glasgow was divided – and is to this day – between the 'Blues' of Rangers, located at Ibrox Park in Govan in the west side of the city, and the 'Greens' of Celtic, situated at Parkhead, between Bridgeton and Carntyne in the East End. The atmosphere at an Old Firm game is impossible to conceive without being at the ground. The decibel level is awesome. It is a traditional and personal religious rite, to which no-one impartial is relevant, or required. For most of this century, until Mo Johnston found his way to Ibrox, no Roman Catholic wore the blue shirt of Rangers. It is a rivalry that impinges on everyday life.

As I was still maintaining my 'want-to-be-different' mentality, I supported Partick Thistle!

The principal difficulty created by a desk journalist's working hours is that of creating a social life. My day off, in common with all daily newspaper journalists, was Saturday. I came to Glasgow with just one name in my address book, that of Jimmy Stevenson, the *Daily Mirror*'s highly respected Scottish football correspondent, and an old friend of my father. Jimmy lived in Pollockshields, in the south-west of the city, with his wife Betty and daughter Maureen.

The family were quite the kindest and most hospitable people I had ever met. They fed me and made truly welcome. I would be entertained for lunch on Monday in a house where humour and love radiated and where dozens of friends from the world of football, both north and south of the border, were regularly given the warmest of welcomes. Maureen, with auburn hair and a model-girl figure, combined with the same radiant personality of her parents, had recently been crowned Glasgow University Charities Queen. She was stunningly nice and always beautifully dressed, but she was engaged to be married. I could only admire from afar.

As I was pondering the question of how on earth I was going to make any friends outside the office, to my rescue came a colleague called Rodger Baillie. He recommended the Saturday night dance at Whitecraigs, a tennis club on the outskirts of Glasgow. It was there that I met my first serious girlfriend – her name was Mairi Fleming and her father was a general practitioner in Paisley.

Mairi and I made love for the first time in the Station Hotel after an evening meeting at Ayr races. We were both virgins. I won't claim that the roof fell in, but a whistle blew on Platform 3!

It was thus that I came to know Paisley quite well – I even went to see St Mirren play football one Saturday. The Flemings were also kind and welcoming and not for one moment did I feel an iota of loneliness in Glasgow.

Nonetheless, I was thrilled when my friend Frank Crocker announced that he was coming to stay for the weekend. Frank and I have been 'best friends' for over 40 years. We met at school, played cards together, went racing together, and – most important

– went to Swindon Town FC together. Frank has always lived in Gloucestershire and I have stayed with him and his family for the Cheltenham races almost every year since the mid-50s. Originally a farmer, he now has a successful business renting and erecting marquees. It was traumatic for his family and friends when his marriage broke up in 1988 and his wife, Chickie, later married his next-door neighbour, Lord (John) Oaksey. But Frank bore it bravely and remains a matchless host.

When he visited me in Glasgow, in the spring of 1959, Frank was on leave from the Army. He had narrowly fallen liable to two years of National Service and was engaged in 'winter warfare' (i.e. skiing). I arranged accommodation in the adjacent room in my lodgings, bought tickets for a show at the Alhambra Theatre, and asked Mairi to bring her best friend Aileen to make up a foursome. The evening was a rip-roaring success. We dined after the theatre and Frank drove us all back to Dowanhill Street. Mairi and I went to bed, while Frank and Aileen were clearly hitting it off.

After about half an hour I heard a knock on my door. It was Frank. 'I say, you haven't got a spare French Letter?' he pleaded. 'No,' I said, 'but you can borrow this one I've just used.' Frank wisely declined the offer, but it is an episode he has never forgotten.

Aileen was an extremely attractive girl and, as my passion for Mairi faded, I must confess to having had designs on her. When the day came to suggest to Mairi that we should not see each other any more, she was ready for me. 'All right,' she said, 'I understand – but just promise me one thing.' 'What's that?' I demanded, to which she replied: 'Promise you won't take out Aileen.' I had no choice and was seething with frustration.

Now I was starting to get some work outside my sub-editing duties. On Saturday afternoons I was paid ten shillings for 100-word reports on local rugby matches, often at West of Scotland RFC. Jimmy Stevenson commissioned me to file a report for the *Daily Mirror* on the Scotland versus Wales rugby international at

Murrayfield. While I thought my work was ordinary, he claimed to be impressed by my description of a Welsh try:

> *10,000 tammies spiralled skywards as the Welsh three-quarter crossed the line . . .*

I was also sent by the *Noon Record* to report on the game between Partick Thistle and Clyde from Firhill. This was a big one! For some reason it was my one and only football report: quite clearly, Dixon Blackstock felt threatened.

More important, I was authorized by Bill Harley to rewrite the PA copy for the 'Meridian' column, and to make my own selections. This was a major breakthrough, as was the invitation to take over the 'Noel Day' racing column in the *Sunday Mail*, the group's Scottish Sunday newspaper. I continued with that column until 1965, when I joined the BBC. My demise as Noel Day may or may not have been in some way connected with a letter to the editor from a 'friend' (his name was Mark Saleby), dated 5 December 1965:

> *Dear Sir*
> *If Noel Day spent less time in the Turkish Baths with Christopher Collins* [the champion amateur jockey] *and more on the racecourse, less time looking through the bottom of a glass, and more looking through his 10 × 30's, he might occasionally tip us a winner.*
> *Yours faithfully*
> *John (Losing) Streak*

It was a letter entirely without justification. But Saleby – of whom more later – was a rotter through and through.

I was also sent out one day to report on National Hunt racing from Ayr, but did not make the most of the opportunity, being overawed by the local leviathans in the press box and having no-one to show me the ropes. Three races were won by Stan Hayhurst and two by Mick Batchelor – I managed to get a 'quote' from Mick Batchelor, but my report was not impressive.

The essence of the Noel Day column was to preview the following week's racing. To achieve this I needed information about running arrangements – remember, there were no early declarations in those days, merely an early entry and a forfeit stage on the Thursday prior to the race – so a great deal of telephoning around the stables was required. The Scottish and northern trainers were generally very helpful, but I well remember a call to a legendary Newmarket trainer: 'Good evening, sir, this is Noel Day of the *Sunday Mail*, Glasgow. Could you please tell me if you run -- at Newmarket next week?' 'Why do you want to know?' 'So that I can write about him in my column.' 'Well, that's my business and the owner's business and no business of yours at all. Good night.' He was not alone in his attitude, making for difficult days for journalists other than those in the golden circle.

There is not the slightest doubt that I was greatly advantaged by my father's status at the *Daily Mirror*, which he had rejoined from the *Daily Express* in 1954. But there were times when the soubriquet of 'Peter Wilson's son' was an irritation.

One such was when the American boxing circus came to town. Angelo Dundee, who won boxing immortality in steering the raw Cassius Clay to the heavyweight championship, was staying with a large entourage at the Central Station Hotel, opposite the *Record* building. He invited me across the road for a drink and Bill Harley acceded. Dundee was holding court in a vast suite, with bottles of scotch, vodka and beer on every table.

'Come in, have a drink, have some salami,' he called out. 'Hey, guys, this is Peter's son.' I was presented in turn to seven or eight characters straight out of Damon Runyon, being billed to every one as 'Peter's son'. None would have known my own name at the end of the evening. It was that night that I determined that one day Peter Wilson would be 'Julian Wilson's father'.

After my fling with Mairi, I was gaining confidence with the opposite sex. One of my new friends was a young girl still at school, who even then bore a remarkable resemblance to Penny Irvine, the 1960s model – I have often wondered if that was who she became. Although young she was extremely self-possessed and would visit my bedsit during her lunchbreak. But, despite a great deal of fumbling, I never persuaded her to miss afternoon school.

It was towards the autumn of 1959 that I became closer to Maureen Stevenson. Although for some time she had been 'an item' with her fiancé, an older boy called Ernie, I sensed that there was a small doubt in her mind. At last she was persuaded to dine with me. I was thrilled: just to spend an evening with the stunningly beautiful Maureen was a fantasy-come-true. As we became closer, I begged her relentlessly to sever her ties with Ernie and cast in her lot with me.

It was a war of attrition, my cause being helped by the fact that our fathers enjoyed a special friendship. Jimmy would poke gentle fun at Ernie, whom he called 'Snow heid' – his hair was unusually fair, almost white. But Ernie was mature and I was two or three years younger than Maureen. It was an obsession that came to preoccupy me for most of the time and I was determined to win her. I was falling in love, and the first time that Maureen allowed me to kiss her I was assuredly in love.

But for a while Maureen was still seeing Ernie. When that happened I would spend Saturday night in a pub at Hillhead and imbibe as much 'heavy' as I could afford to absorb. In truth, three pints was my limit: one evening I returned home through gardens and over garden walls, merely on an intake of three pints of 'heavy'. It was lethal stuff.

By Christmas 1959 it seemed that I was winning the battle of the love stakes, especially when Maureen accepted my invitation to a Hogmanay party at Bearsden. Regrettably this night that promised so much turned into one of the worst of my life. I drank an inordinate amount of whisky and by 3.00 am was disgracefully drunk. Maureen, understandably, asked to be taken home. We searched unavailingly for a taxi and I begged her to stay at the party we had just left. She refused and I slapped her face. I had never previously struck a woman and I have never done so since. Now, even to think of that grotesque night fills me with a sense of nausea.

Worse still, I left Maureen alone on the roadway and returned to the party. The next 48 hours were the most miserable beyond description. In the morning, filled with shame and remorse, I went round to the Stevenson's house to beg forgiveness. Jimmy was civil beyond the requirements of courtesy, but the atmosphere was chilling. Maureen would not see me; indeed, her mother added, she never wished to see me again. It was in the ensuing days that I learnt the true meaning of the 'pain of love'. I was beside myself with misery.

I travelled down to London to stay a night with my father, who now lived in Twickenham. I was pitiful and self-pitying: my world had come to an end, I just couldn't imagine life without Maureen, I was totally besotted. I wept and thought about suicide.

Heaven knows how I clawed my way back into her affections. Perhaps I was helped by the benign understanding of Jimmy and Betty. Maureen was bombarded with flowers and *billets doux* of repentance. In the end, within ten days, I had won a period of probation, and by the end of the month appeared to have gained Maureen's total forgiveness.

Certainly, by the end of March I was a welcome guest in the Stevenson's house to watch the first televised Grand National. It was an awesome televisual experience, with amazing camera production and the BBC's outstanding commentary. If anyone had suggested that within ten years I would be part of that famous commentary team – and indeed for the following 23 years – I would have laughed them out of court.

The previous year I had taken the special race train from Glasgow to Aintree to see my first Grand National in the flesh. Until then it had always fallen during term time and had been listened to avidly on the radio. Mirabel Topham, the owner of the racecourse, held out against television coverage for many years until Peter Dimmock

– who married her goddaughter Polly Elwes – sweet-talked her into signing a contract which relaxed her grip on the race's copyright.

That National was an enthralling race. I watched from the top of the grandstand as Tim Brookshaw, legs flapping, drove the courageous Wyndburgh in pursuit of Michael Scudamore on Oxo up that long and gruelling run-in. What we did not know was that Brookshaw's stirrup leather had broken at Bechers second time round, which meant that he had ridden the remainder of the race without stirrups. It was almost too amazing a feat to contemplate. Brookshaw, from farming stock, was a colossus of a man, but in 1963 suffered a crashing fall over hurdles that left him paralysed for the rest of his life. Even in his immobilization he refused to give up riding and designed a pulley system to hoist himself on to his mount without assistance.

A more memorable train journey from Glasgow – for all the wrong reasons – was an expedition to the now defunct Hurst Park Races near Hampton Court, for the Victoria Cup. There was a cheap return fare to London because it was the weekend of England versus Scotland at Wembley. So it came about that I joined over a thousand football supporters on the 'special' leaving Central Station at 10 pm on the Friday evening. It was soon evident that sleep would not be an option: the group in my compartment were intent on drinking the train dry, in competition with practically every other passenger. By 3 am they had almost drunk themselves to sleep, until one of their number managed to cut off the end of his finger in the sliding door of the compartment. There was blood everywhere, accompanied by a wide range of expletives of quite unusual originality. Not even the anaesthetic of the whisky could help the wretched man, who alternately groaned and mouthed obscenities for the remainder of the journey. The return trip was more subdued: Scotland had been beaten, most of the passengers had played themselves out, and a great many had missed the train!

Jimmy Stevenson continued to provide wonderful treats. Thanks to his provision of a coveted ticket, I was on the terraces at Hampden Park for the greatest football match I have ever seen, the epic between Eintracht Frankfurt and Real Madrid, which ended 7-3 in favour of the Spaniards, led by the legendary Ferenc Puskas.

My career was ticking over nicely, but I was swimming around in a relatively small pool. It was time to move on. I cannot remember when I first asked Maureen to marry me, but by the time I left Glasgow we were betrothed. My twentieth birthday was still two weeks away, but I could not imagine a life without loving Maureen.

If only, when we are young, we could zoom out, as with a television camera, from our close-up image of life and see the broader stage and the wider spectrum. How much pain and sadness would be avoided.

# FOUR

# *Newmarket: A Hard School*

My father and Jack Hutchinson had arranged for me to be based at Newmarket as a local correspondent. The prime purpose of this move was to enable me to become acquainted with the big names in racing – the top trainers and the top jockeys. I would also file copy when required, although the *Daily Mirror* already had a local 'stringer' in Bob Rodrigo. This was to be another important step up the ladder for me and it was a wonderful opportunity.

I called into London for a day before I started the new job. My father had moved from central London out to Twickenham and remarried in the mid-fifties. His new wife – my stepmother – was Sallyann Thompson, the American-born widow of Cecil ('Tommy') Thompson, a distinguished war correspondent who had run the New York office of the *Daily Express* after the war and was a close friend of Lord Beaverbrook. His father, in turn, was Edward Raymond Thompson, a former editor of the *Evening Standard*, who was sent to jail for contempt of court between the wars. Thompson had interviewed a notorious murderer while he was on the run and was imprisoned in a *cause célèbre* for refusing to reveal his sources.

My father met Sally while she was working for the *Daily Express* in 1952. The previous year her husband had died aged 46 from a heart attack and Sally was struggling to bring up two young children. By all accounts she did not respond to my father's initial romantic overtures, and an early approach brought the response: 'That's enough of that, Buster!' But they became a devoted couple, and Sally's support as housekeeper, chauffeur, confidante, mediator and (ultimately) nurse was the backbone of my father's happiness and continuing professional success.

Their registry office wedding, with Sally unavailable to stage-manage, was typically chaotic. It was my mother who arrived with my father's suit from the cleaners, while the best man, Dick Richards, was nowhere to be seen and arrived late. But Sally, despite the regular scourge of debilitating migraines, ensured that 'Tottering Towers' (47 Cole Park Road) ran smoothly and was always a welcome haven to my father's itinerant Fleet Street friends and colleagues.

The most regular and companionable of these were Gerard Walter, former sportswriter of the *News Chronicle* whom father helped to obtain a position on the *Mirror*, and Geoffrey Green, outstanding and lyrical football correspondent of *The Times*. Father always gave a huge party on New Year's Eve, with oysters and champagne, and Gerry Walter's major task of the year was to open at least 50 dozen oysters – an activity that left his hands unserviceable for several days afterwards. Geoffrey Green, too, was a wonderful companion and raconteur, and a simultaneous visit from Geoffrey and myself would ensure that father's bar, in the corner of his living room, would be in service until 6.00 am Sally would retire to bed at 3.00 am while father had usually had enough by 4.30!

I often wondered how my father maintained such remarkable grasp of facts and an ability to conjure magical language from a turmoil of ring-side chaos. He took little or no exercise in his latter years and was quite liable to have a glass in hand for up to 12 hours at a time. The secret may have lain in the fact that he soaked in a hot bath, reflecting, every morning for upwards of three quarters of an hour. On a Sunday from around mid-day he would write his copy for the Monday morning, phone it over at around 2.00 pm and be ready for lunch (after a Sherry Cobbler or two) at 3.00 pm. His guests, meanwhile, would have been entertained by Gerry Walter from mid-day onwards. It was a system that worked and, thanks to Sally, confrontations at lunch amongst our disparate group were normally nipped in the bud!

These disagreements, if allowed to run loose, could involve politics, personalities, foxhunting, hare-coursing, South Africa, the integrity of boxing and the integrity of horseracing. On every single issue my father and I had different views. Gerry Walter would be liable to take my side. Sally would interject with 'Now then, you two', and relative calm would be restored.

When I arrived in London from Glasgow that early June weekend, my father was horrified. 'Good God', he exclaimed, 'you sound like a poor man's Harry Lauder!' It was true that my accent had taken on a Glasgow inflection: it had been difficult to avoid it since all my colleagues at work spoke broad Scots and the Stevenson's likewise. I just slipped into the vernacular.

The *Mirror* had booked me a room at the Rutland Arms Hotel in Newmarket until I found my feet and some accommodation. I arrived in the Rutland on the Sunday evening before the Derby. 'Noel Day' had tipped St Paddy. It was a happy swansong: Lester Piggott's mount was to win at 7/1.

I had never previously visited Newmarket, and now was not a good time to arrive as an unfamiliar press man. The previous year there had been a contentious stable lad's strike, with the local trainers blaming the press for fanning the flames of discontent. The Fourth Estate, outside of the trusted few within the golden circle, were looked upon with suspicion and, in some cases, contempt.To arrive in Newmarket wearing the badge of the *Daily Mirror* was not a passport to the inner sanctum of the élite.

By now I had passed my driving test and was the owner of a Mini Minor. As for accommodation, I decided that the bar of the Rutland Arms was as good a meeting place as any and I made it known that I was on the lookout for a bedsit. Almost immediately I met a jumping jockey called Pat Mahoney who became a good friend – he was later to win the Topham Trophy at Liverpool on Georgetown. Pat was about to move out of his digs on the Old Station Road, where he was occupying a room on the first floor of the off-licence, and so I moved in the following day. My landlord here was a middle-aged bachelor who lived with his elderly mother. As in Glasgow, I was served breakfast and an evening meal. The landlord was friendly, but I was never entirely comfortable in his presence.

Most mornings I would be up early to watch horses exercising and, every Wednesday and Saturday, galloping. The touts – the professional gallop watchers – were an assorted bunch, but for the main part were extremely helpful. Their job was to report on the gallops for the *Sporting Life* and *Sporting Chronicle*, and feed information to those newspapers' resident correspondents, Warren Hill (Richard Galpin) and Old Rowley (Richard Onslow).

The touts' ability to identify horses was remarkable. We would be positioned on the far side of the main road adjacent to the Limekilns – we were not allowed to place one foot on the gallops which were owned by the Jockey Club – and were obliged to identify horses galloping up to 200 yards away. Nowadays there are 2800 horses in training in Newmarket, with 80 trainers, so the task is unthinkable, but in the early sixties there were fewer than half this number of horses on view.

George Robinson was widely regarded as the top man. George's trick was to keep a notebook with the markings of every older horse in each leading stable. He would compile his list in the spring, while the horses were on the Walking Grounds, checking the identity of each with a friendly stable lad. Soon the horses – at least in the big stables – became familiar and, as the season progressed, he would add two-year-olds to his list. Gradually, he built up a complete portfolio. What was most challenging was when different gallops took place simultaneously on parallel work grounds!

Eventually I too learnt to recognize the key horses in the town. For example, while St Paddy was being trained for the King George VI and Queen Elizabeth Stakes as a four-year-old, I witnessed a quite stunning gallop on the Limekilns. St Paddy was working with two good-class older handicappers called Sunny Way and Off Key. (The latter was to win the Vaux Gold Tankard, one of the top handicaps in the racing calendar, and the former had just beaten Predominate in a conditions race at Sandown.) St Paddy won that particular exercise gallop by 15 lengths, unextended, simply annihilating those two very good horses. I have rarely, if ever, seen a more impressive performance. Nowadays such a gallop is rare because trainers are less anxious to extend horses on the training grounds and like to keep them 'undercooked'.

I enjoyed the company of some most entertaining drinking companions in the Rutland Arms, amongst them the top jockey Willie Snaith and his wife Sylvia, and Jean Hayes, the wife of jockey Michael Hayes, who was later killed in a high-speed car crash near Newmarket.

Time was also spent with a few stable lads who drank at the Rutland, notably an ex-jockey called Ken Thompson who worked for Jack Clayton's stable. This lad took his meals and comforts from a wonderful woman called Muriel Pritchard who had earned the distinction of becoming the first female travelling head lad to Harry Thomson Jones. Ken hoped to encourage me to become one of his 'punters' (someone who places bets on a lad's advice), but I did not have the resources – or the belief in Ken! – to bet at that level. However, one Friday night at around closing time at the Red Lodge, just outside Newmarket, he said: 'There's a good thing at Newton Abbot tomorrow you know – Thomson Jones' in the third'. 'Well let's go down and back it', I said. So we jumped into my car and drove down, a journey of almost 300 miles. When we reached Denham at about half past midnight, I discovered that my car choke was still full out! At 6.00 pm we had a short sleep on the Exeter bypass: we had no luggage or toiletries, just the clothes we were wearing.

The first race at Newton Abbot, a market town between Teignmouth and Torquay in Devon, was at 2.15 pm. We arrived at the races soon after mid-day and counted our money – Ken had been paid that Friday morning. We decided to put the entire bank, less return petrol money, on Ling Hills who was an even money shot. I fiddled around the ring, taking every best price that was offered, and he shortened to 7/4 on. The horse's pilot, Johnny Gilbert, jumped off in front and made every yard of the running, allowing us to collect a thick wad of West Country money. Consequently we checked into the Imperial Hotel at Torquay, had an expensive dinner and a long sleep, and drove back to Newmarket on Sunday evening. When the motorways were built in the following decade, these journeys became a shade easier!

It was Ken who invited me to a party outside Newmarket during the July Meeting of 1960. The participants were a mixed bunch – stable lads, servicemen from nearby Mildenhall, and assorted women of no clearly definable origin. I spotted Ken talking to a couple of lads in conspiratorial tones. 'What was that about?' I asked later. 'There's going to be a job done tonight', he replied. 'They're going to 'do' a horse that's running tomorrow'. The horse was Sing Sing, one of only two runners in the following day's July Cup. In the end the race was a walkover: the dopers overdosed Sing Sing and he was withdrawn, comatosed, on the morning of the race. Tin Whistle collected the prize by default.

When I left Glasgow I was convinced that I would love and be faithful to Maureen for the rest of my life. Now, just four weeks later, I found myself taking home a married woman whom I had never previously met. By an extraordinary coincidence she turned out to be the wife of a stable man, who was one of the gang responsible for a spate of dopings in the early sixties – possibly including Sing Sing.

It was through the Rutland Arms that I made some other friends who had a thoroughly beneficial influence on my life. While I was in Glasgow I had taken virtually no exercise at all. Now, as I was drinking Worthington E with the Newmarket 'All Blacks' RFC, two of them – Tony Bailey and David Taylor – asked if I would like a game. I ended up playing a full season for the club, and according to the *Newmarket Journal* rarely played a bad game. (I was writing the reports!)

My finest hour was on 29 September 1960 when Newmarket beat Norwich Union 'A' by 13-3. I managed to score all three tries and converted two of them. As we were walking off the park I was already composing my introduction: 'A game dominated by the All Blacks' wing forward, Wilson . . .' At that moment I felt a tap on the shoulder. 'I'm sure you would rather that I wrote the report this week, old man,' said our Captain. Wilson was mentioned briefly in the final paragraph, after a eulogy about a fine team performance!

I was back on form against Ely (19-3) the following Saturday, and Wilson was noted as scoring a penalty goal, a conversion and a try and conversion, and was described as 'ever present'. I must have written that one!

The rugby players, to whom I introduced a dangerous and exciting card game called 'Newmarket Shoot' after matches, were good companions, but I was not breaking into the inner circle. The *jeunesse dorée* of Newmarket were a group headed by Gay Leader (now Gay Slater) the daughter of trainer Harvey Leader; Julie Murless the daughter of Noel Murless; and Hugh McCalmont, a rather louche amateur rider. There were also the Cecil twins, Henry and David, who were younger. These people were simply not interested in sharing my company, nor can I blame them!

McCalmont once played an expensive practical joke on a young, rather decadent assistant trainer and amateur rider called Simon Blow. Simon, now the author of some excellent books on hunting, was assistant to the crusty disciplinarian trainer Sam Armstrong, who was shortly to become Lestor Piggott's father-in-law. McCalmont decided to arrange a large drinks party at the Bedford Lodge Hotel in the name of Simon Blow. All of the local glitterati were invited, from Cecil Boyd-Rochfort to the more modest training practitioners like 'Fiddler' Goodwill and Percy Allden. Blow, needless to say, was not informed, but on the night in question was rung up by McCalmont and advised that there was a party at the Bedford Lodge. Would he like to come? Poor Simon had a baffling evening as countless strangers came up to him to thank him for a splendid party! He was less than enchanted when a bill was presented for over £100.

Feeling that I was on the wrong side of the tracks in the Old

Station Road, in the spring of 1961 I heard of accommodation available in the Bury Road, close to some of the leading stables. The house in question, Lyndhurst, belonged to a delightful couple called Michael and Lavender Horne, and the vacancy occurred because Tim Forster, who had been assistant trainer to Geoffrey Brooke at Clarehaven Stables and was later to train three Grand National winners, had moved on.

It was a happy house. Simon Blow was another lodger, much of whose time was spent driving Sam Armstrong's vast academy of apprentice jockeys around the country. Also lodging there was a young man called Leslie Harrison, who was then working as private handicapper for the Armstrong stable and has gone on to become one of the leading figures in the thoroughbred breeding industry, notably managing Lord Howard de Walden's Plantation Stud.

Lyndhurst was a short distance away from Carlburg Stables where Fergie Sutherland trained. Fergie's wife, Judy, was a close friend of Lavender Horne and I was obliged to play squash once a week with Fergie. He had lost a leg during the Korean War, but that did not stop him riding to hounds – or playing squash, one of the severest athletic disciplines to which I have ever been subjected. Since Fergie's movement was somewhat laborious, it was obligatory to hit the ball roughly in his direction. Fergie, meanwhile, hit the ball as hard as he could, as far away from me as possible. They were always exhausting games, invariably followed by a journey home in Fergie's Mercedes with the heater on full blast! 'We had a good sweat today', was Fergie's usual summing-up, but I was often too exhausted to speak.

One of Lavender's very best friends was a long-time resident of Newmarket, Bunty Richardson, who – in addition to bringing up four children – took in boarders at the family's capacious house, Bury Hill, overlooking the Severals. Bunty saw many celebrated and notorious racing personalities pass through her house, including the Irish trainer and dealer Adrian Maxwell, the NH jockey Danny Mellen (now dead), the leading bloodstock agent Tote Cherry Downes, and the Duke of Roxburgh's stepson, Jeremy Church.

Bunty was terrific fun and dispensed gin and tonics with a pleasing liberality. Her son Jeremy became a leading local solicitor (notably representing Lester Piggott on various high-profile occasions), while her daughter, Patsy-Anne remained a pen-pal when she went to work for the legendary trainer Paddy Sleator in Ireland. Jeremy and I play cricket to this day – it was he who was seen completing a fumbling catch off my bowling on BBC-TV's 'Grandstand' in the autumn of 1997!

And so now I was finding myself in the mainstream. In the spring of 1961 I was invited to go round Noel Murless's and Cecil Boyd-Rochfort's stables, along with the correspondents Galpin and Onslow. This was a fascinating and instructive exercise, if obstructed by Galpin who insisted on viewing every horse as if he were a potential purchaser. In the end Murless became rather tired of it. Galpin, who became the bloodstock agent responsible for buying foundation mares for the hugely successful Meon Valley Stud (One In A Million etc.) was training at Harraton Stables, Exning, at the time. But because he was a journalist, the licence had to be held by his father, a distinguished former army officer. Unhappily, a rather small animal from the stable was found to have raced at an unlicensed track – Hawthorn Hill – and Brigadier Galpin faced the social stigma of being warned off.

It was this spring that Noel Murless had in his stable a horse called Pinturishcio which he regarded as the best he had ever trained. Pinturishcio was unraced as a two-year-old, but even before he ran as a three-year-old he was substantially backed to win the Derby. One evening in the Rutland Arms I met an associate of Murless who confided that he had placed a substantial commission on Sir Victor Sassoon's colt. The details of his gallops – although Murless rarely extended horses – were hair-raising indeed. Pinturischio won his first race, the Wood Ditton Stakes, very comfortably, but was only fourth in the 2000 Guineas where the distance was regarded as insufficient.

Three weeks before the Derby, Pinturischio was off-colour and missed several days' work. On the Saturday before the Derby I watched him gallop and reported to the *Mirror* that he looked back to himself, but the following day he was declared a non-runner. It transpired later that he had been doped not once, but twice. It was thought that the first dose would rule him out of the Derby, but after the Saturday gallop the dopers made certain and 'did' him again. A firm of bookmakers, who had taken most of my friend's commission and other substantial wagers, simply could not afford for him to win. The horse never raced again.

The three weeks leading up to that Derby were a journalistic nightmare. The *Mirror* was clamouring for news but Murless remained silent and a visit to the stable was fruitless. I even invited the amusing and statuesque Julie Murless out to dinner – although news of Pinturischio was not the only intended topic of conversation on the agenda – but she refused. The full story of Pinturischio was never revealed, but the following year several of the gang involved were arrested after a doping-that-went-wrong at Bob Read's stables in Lambourn.

Maureen Stevenson and I had seen little of each other in the past ten months, but our letters and telephone calls had kept us close. Now it is difficult, with the passage of time, to recall the exact sequence of events in the months between April and July 1961, and the full roller-coaster of our emotions. In the spring I remained obsessed with the determination to marry Maureen. She had completed a successful modelling show in March, and on 7 April, on the eve of her birthday, we became secretly engaged. The engagement was announced officially at my twenty-first birthday party, at Skindles Hotel, Maidenhead, two months later. We were blissfully happy and planned excitedly for the future. We stayed the night with my father and Maureen's family in Twickenham, and both of my parents gave their whole-hearted support, whatever their possible misgivings. The Stevensons, likewise, were overjoyed.

How the picture changed so dramatically in the following weeks remains a mystery, obscured by the traumas of the forthcoming months.

I had met a delightful girl called Therèse Theodas the previous week at Royal Ascot. She was racing with a wealthy Ayrshire owner, Ian Murray, with whom I had become friendly whilst based in Glasgow. Ian was a friend of Therèse's father, who owned a hairdressing business in Ayr, and had collected the exceptionally attractive student cook from the nearby culinary college-cum-finishing-school, Winkfield Place, in the morning.

After racing I invited Therèse to dinner in Windsor and took her back later to Winkfield Place. I slipped over the wall and 'skinny-dipped' in the college pool. It was a hugely enjoyable evening and 'Terry' was terrific fun. The following month, with Maureen back in Glasgow, I took Terry to the Eton & Harrow Match at Lord's. Looking back, just two weeks into an engagement it seems an extraordinary act. I cannot start to rationalize or justify the invitation, although the relationship between Terry and myself was perfectly innocent.

I was also spending some weekends at the home of an old schoolfriend in Simon Smith, who lived with his parents at Howe Green in Hertfordshire. His sister Harriet, in the year before her debutante season, was growing into a classic English rose.

In a matter of weeks there had within me been a metamorphosis from the ecstasy and aspirations of my birthday party, to the belief that I had made a terrible mistake and that the commitment to marriage was impetuous and ill-conceived. After all, I had no clearly defined career, no property and no capital. I had been driven by an obsession. Suddenly I had an entirely new vision of life.

Hence the decision I made, one weekend in Newmarket, I knew to be correct. Nonetheless, the way in which it was implemented, insensitively and with ill-chosen words, over the telephone, was unacceptable and unforgivable. Maureen, who had given me so much and had given up so much for me, was brutally betrayed. I have never subliminated the shame that I feel when I reflect on those events and the pain I caused to those I had loved.

At the time, selfishly, I submerged myself in the lotus life of Newmarket.

I was swimming in gin, but I was in for a shock. The worst few months of my life lay ahead.

## FIVE

# *Manchester Madness*

Within three weeks of the end of my engagement to Maureen, I received an entirely unexpected telephone call from the *Daily Mirror*. The call instructed me to leave Newmarket immediately and to start work as a reporter-cum-sub-editor in Manchester on Monday 28 August.

This was an unpleasant shock, especially as I had expected to stay in Newmarket for at least another six months. I was enjoying the lifestyle, making new friends, and looking forward to playing another season of rugby. I shall never know what triggered the conspiracy to move me on, although there is no doubt that my father was involved. I suspect it was activated by rumours of my having an affair with a married woman.

In Manchester there were no lodgings arranged and I had no contacts whatever in the city. It was unknown territory. I packed my cases and, having said a sad farewell to the Hornes, the Richardsons and my friends at the Rutland Arms, set off north at lunchtime on the Friday following the Ebor meeting at York and checked into a central Manchester hotel. My little mini was jam-packed with suitcases and other paraphernalia, the assorted acquisitions of the first 21 years of my life. I parked my car in the hotel car park, which was a mistake.

The following morning virtually all that remained was the car. It is hard to explain the feeling of sheer devastation that follows the realization that you have lost everything. In my cases had been my entire wardrobe, my books (including my form books), my cuttings and my sporting scrap book. My typewriter, radio and gramophone had gone, as well as a new overcoat and my raceglasses. Every significant possession, except for an overnight bag and the clothes that I stood in, had gone for ever. A world-weary policeman advised me that the thieves would have removed the valuables and tipped the remaining contents of my case into the River Irwell, which was very comforting.

The full gamut of emotions: I was stunned, shattered, angry, empty and above all impotent. I checked into a cheap hotel – the Antrim – in the south of the city, climbed back into my car, and drove south to be with Harriet and Simon Smith for the weekend. For the second time in nine months I felt suicidal. I could see no glimmer of consolation, no possible good that could emerge from this ghastly evil. I was quite simply devastated.

My mother was wonderfully supportive in the aftermath of this drama. She offered immediately to drive up to Manchester to stay with me and to help me through the days of rehabilitation. I did not know that at the same time she was facing her own personal crisis.

She had visited her doctor in London in July – she had a pied-à-terre in Turk's Row, near Lower Sloane Street – following some abdominal discomfort. Her doctor was concerned by the results of some tests he had made and immediately wrote to mother stating that he must see her before he went on holiday on 5 August. However, mother had moved back to Great Coxwell where she had been living since 1957, and the letter had not been forwarded. She did not receive it until 28 August. By the Monday after my robbery she had suffered four successive days of stomach pains and diarrhoea, and when she finally got to see her doctor the following week, on 5 September, it became clear that she was suffering from cancer of the ovaries. She would be dead within two months.

It was typical of my mother that her concern for my predicament far outweighed concern for her own health. While she should have been resting she was chasing around Faringdon trying to untangle the complications of our respective insurance policies. (Inevitably, I was substantially under-insured.)

For my part, I had no idea of the extent of my mother's illness. My brother and grandmother Wilson were with her at home, but any suspicions my mother had of her predicament she made certain to conceal from me. Then when she wrote to me on 4 October she confessed that she had been taken very ill again. She was admitted to St Thomas' Hospital on Friday 13 October. When I visited her in hospital on 26 October it was tragically obvious that there was no way back: she was unable to digest any food and was pitifully weak.

When mother died I was numb. I did not weep. I knew that she would have expected me to be strong, to look after my brother, and to keep a cool and unemotional head while the funeral arrangements were made and the cascade of letters from friends flooded in and had to be answered. If I had ever underestimated my mother's qualities of sweetness and kindness, they were now brought home to me in letter after letter.

Now she was dead, struck down – like her parents – by the scourge of cancer. Thirty years later her two sisters, Diana and Sylvia, were to succumb to the same disease.

We held the funeral at Great Coxwell on Saturday 11 November – ironically the day of Manchester's biggest race of the year, the November Handicap. For once the result was not a priority.

Following mother's death I was determined to throw myself into my work. I had started on the 'desk' in Manchester and was to move into a comfortable apartment in a house called Langroyd in Fielden Park, West Didsbury, in the southern suburbs of the City. It is now a public house called the Woodstock Tavern. The jumping season was well under way and there were some high-class steeplechasers trained in the north.

Harriet Smith, to whom I had become very close and who had come to stay for a weekend at Great Coxwell before the acceleration of my mother's illness, had been sent to a finishing school in Megeve. I missed her considerably and wrote to her regularly. In December, before the snow had submerged the French Alps, I flew out to spend a weekend with Harriet. We had a tender, innocent relationship and I was sad to say goodbye to her.

I had very few friends in the north. Harriet's brother, Simon, had moved to Huddersfield, where his uncle had an accountancy business and where Simon was preparing to enter the legal profession. I stayed a few weekends in his uncle's house, when Simon and I would go to the pub on a Saturday night, 'pick up' a party, and take our chances. On Sunday morning I would return the worse for wear to Manchester – except on one occasion when, following a row with Simon, I drove back over the Pennines in the middle of the night!

Another old schoolfriend based in the north was Peter Szechenyi, a descendant of an aristocratic Hungarian family, who was at the army camp at Catterick. Peter kept a couple of racehorses at the nearby stables of the young trainer Bill Haigh. One weekend I booked into the Old Bridge Hotel in Catterick with a view to riding out one of Peter's horses on the Saturday morning. Unfortunately we spent all of Friday evening in the bar at the 'Bridge', by the end of which I had decided that the well-endowed barmaid, who lived on the premises, was one of the most beautiful women that I had ever seen. Having finally been persuaded to go to my room, I undressed, climbed out on to the slate roof of the hotel, sidled along the wall and knocked persistently on the barmaid's window. I have often wondered in retrospect about the possible outcome of that scenario, the most likely of which were arrest, or a serious fall into the road below. In the event the mission was a harmless failure.

In the morning, feeling like death, I was a pitiful passenger at full throttle up Bill Haigh's gallop. Luckily the gallop ended with a steep incline, otherwise I should have missed breakfast. Bill was not amused and I was not invited again.

Peter and I both took out, at different times, Bill's wife-to-be, Vanessa Marsh, the daughter of the Classic-winning trainer, Marcus Marsh, and sister of Robert Armstrong's wife-to-be, Liz. At other times I would go riding with a journalist colleague, Tim Thompson, in Cheshire. Tim, who became a successful racecourse manager, would arrange mounts for us at the Livery stables of Alec Bennett and we would stage private races on the nearby gallops.

For no acceptable reason I was becoming an extremely heavy drinker. Perhaps alcohol was a type of fuel to sustain energy and good humour, or maybe it was an opiate to overcome the loneliness of an empty life.

Whatever the reason, inevitably my lack of self-discipline created a crisis. I had driven two newspaper colleagues, Tim Richards and Noel Winstanley of the *Daily Mail*, back from Catterick races via Huddersfield. We regrouped in Manchester at around 11 pm and decided to drive out to a party in Cheshire. We bought a bottle of gin as our entrance ticket and set off on the A56 out of Manchester. Just beyond Old Trafford we came to a set of traffic lights at crossroads. I drove across an amber light, while a driver coming at 90 degrees from the right had the same idea. We crashed violently. Poor Noel, in the passenger seat, was thrown headlong through the windscreen and landed yards away. Whenever I see his bald patch nowadays, I feel guilt! The steering wheel took my full impact and snapped. Tim Richards, in the back seat, had damaged legs.

Tim's first reaction was to dispose of our bottle of gin by hiding it surreptitiously in an adjacent graveyard. In the morning when we searched for the bottle it had gone: a case of 'spirits departed'? My car was a write-off and Noel was taken to hospital. We never did make it to the party.

The crash had a very sobering effect on me. I lay awake long that night, thinking what might have been. If there was a lesson to learn from that episode – and there was – I failed to learn it.

Meanwhile I was enjoying my work on the newspaper. Two or three days a week I sat on the racing desk with the editorial staff, Alf and Ernie, but for the rest of the week covered race meetings and visited stables. On the 'inside' days we finished work around 8.30 pm and crossed the road from Withy Grove for a pint or three at a pub called the Lower Ship, on Shude Hill. Thereafter we would enjoy a curry and return home at a reasonable hour – although occasionally I was obliged to drive home Dickie Onslow of the

*Sporting Chronicle*, who lived in Higher Disley, in Cheshire. If Dickie was late he needed moral support to face his wife Barbara!

Occasionally, however, on the way home I would drop in at the bar of a hotel in the Wilmslow Road. There one evening I ran into Gerald Williams (a journalist and subsequently a broadcaster) who, like my father, spent the summer on the tennis circuit. Gerry was in Didsbury for a tennis-connected event and he introduced me to someone with whom he had been having a couple of drinks. For the purposes of this story I shall call him 'Charlie'. Charlie wanted to go to a club, one where female company was available, so I took him to a twilight club in the centre of Manchester. We had a few drinks and Charlie picked up a prostitute. I did the same – she was a pleasant young girl, a nurse, 'moonlighting' for some extra money. Charlie's hooker was a hard-liner whom I'll call 'Ruth'.

'What happens now?' I asked. 'We go home.' 'Where?' I demanded. 'Well, we can't go to my hotel', said Charlie, 'we'll have to go to your place.' So I drove the four of us back to Langroyd. It was now about 2.30 am and the next four hours were among the worst in my life.

As far as I was concerned the sooner the 'business' was done the better. Ruth had other ideas. She spied the display of bottles on my cocktail tray and determined to drink her way through the lot. She was manic. Charlie realized he had been caught by a monster and the nightmare became a stale-mate. Eventually Charlie did a most despicable thing: making the excuse of going for some cigarettes, he disappeared for good with the nurse. I have never knowingly seen him again.

Ruth, transparently a paranoid schizophrenic, was beside herself when realization dawned. 'Where's my punter?' she demanded. 'I don't know. He's gone home, and I want you to go home', I replied. 'I'm not going until you pay me,' she insisted. When I said that I was not going to pay her the ghastly stale-mate continued. Eventually, as the light was flooding through the windows, Ruth consented to leave if she was paid. She could also take with her the remaining bottle of sherry, and I would drive her home.

It was a dreadful journey. As we set off, Ruth, in the passenger seat, smashed me full in the mouth with the sherry bottle, leaving fragments of front teeth all over my mouth. Two teeth were knocked clean out. My mouth was bruised and swollen. For an hour I sought the help of police and public to rid me of this creature. No-one was interested, and she refused point-blank to get out of my car. Eventually, at almost 7 am, Ruth 'remembered' where she lived in Moss Side and I was rid of her at last.

I booked an early appointment with my dentist, a charming man called Wigoder, whose son Basil Wigoder was to become an eminent QC and, in 1974, a life peer. Over the following few days he did a wonderful restructuring job on my mouth and finally installed a bridge which has only been replaced once in 35 years. If I had harboured the remotest idea of appearing on television at the time I would have been distraught. As it was, Dr Wigoder's work achieved a re-assembly that has gone generally unnoticed, although for many years I was disinclined to smile and show my artificial incisors.

It had been quite a year. I was still 21, but inside 12 months I had lost my mother, my property and now my front teeth.

But my career was flourishing. As well as reporting for the *Daily Mirror* I was 'moonlighting' for the *Daily Telegraph*. I would file my race report for the former, then sit down and write a differently phrased story for the broadsheet. It was good experience and pressure reporting.

Jack Hutchinson, the *Mirror*'s London sports editor, asked me to initiate a horserace, to be called the 'Andy Capp Handicap' after the tabloid's popular cartoon character. Sponsorship in racing was still relatively new – less than five years old – and newspapers were yet to be involved. I chose the go-ahead Major Lesley Petch, who had transformed the north-east seaside 'gaff' track at Redcar into a major racecourse, as the man to stage this revolutionary concept. We decided on a valuable handicap for three-year-olds over a mile and a quarter, to be run at Redcar on the Saturday of Royal Ascot week, so exploiting the one major omission of Ascot's programme.

I was proud to see the race grow in stature as the years rolled by – long after I left the *Daily Mirror* – until it was transferred to York's Ebor meeting.

I enjoyed reporting a pre-season tour of the leading north-country stables, notably those of 'Buster' Fenningworth and the bluff and burly Sam Hall. Sam was a delightful man. He was assisted at the time by his niece, Sally – now a successful trainer – whom the following spring I invited to dinner, near Middleham, after evening stables. Sally was charming and companionable, but unimpressed by my advances – it was another case of 'That's enough of that, Buster!'

But the story that earned a rave review from my sports editor, Peter Thomas, centred around a selling race at Pontefract. A trainer called Ted Gifford, whose stables were at Skipton in Yorkshire, ran two horses. One, Eastern Tor, had been in the stable for some time and appeared fully exposed; he was ridden by the stable apprentice Brian Henry and started at 13/2. The other, Melozzo, had been bought out of a selling race - in which Eastern Tor had finished second – two weeks earlier and was ridden by Lester Piggott. He was the one carrying the stable's money and he started at 7/4.

The race was extraordinary. In the uphill straight Piggott's mount battled his way into contention, whilst Brian Henry was cantering in the lead on Eastern Tor. Piggott rode a finish that Melozzo would have remembered for a few days to come. It was a kitchen sink job. Brian Henry, meanwhile, sat as if totally immobilized, without moving a muscle. The two horses passed the post locked together. If Brian Henry had merely sneezed Eastern Tor would have won outright. All hell broke loose. The punters – or more likely the bookmakers – remonstrated. There were catcalls and derision. Eventually the judge called a dead heat and the stewards awarded Brian Henry a lengthy suspension.

It was a dream story to write. Later that evening I dropped into the Press Club in Manchester, where Peter Thomas welcomed me with open arms: 'Great story!' he shrieked. 'Terrific stuff. It's led the back page. Give me something like that every day and we'll really give racing a major show!' I didn't like to tell him that I would not expect to write another comparable story for at least a decade!

I was seeing a lot of a girl called Virginia Hutchinson. Her father was managing director at Ripon racecourse and a leading shareholder. Virginia was an attractive, if provocative, girl who rode out for a local trainer called Herbert Clarkson. I did a pre-season photo-story with her and a horse called The Quare Fellow, which she rode and was being trained for the Lincoln Handicap. The family lived in a delightful country house with beautiful gardens (it is now a hotel) in a village called Markington, between Harrogate and Ripon. Ginnie was 'doing' a London season and I drove her to several parties.

The tempo of life was now relentless. One Thursday morning in July I drove from Manchester to Catterick to report on the day's racing. (It was the day that Willie Carson rode the first of his almost 4000 winners.) From Catterick I then drove Ginnie Hutchinson to the coming-out dance of a girl called Catherine Berry in Buckinghamshire. At 4.00 pm I snatched an hour's sleep, drove back to Manchester, worked on the desk and set off to Lavinia Beasley's dance that evening. (Lavinia's father, Rufus, had been a hugely successful jockey and trainer.) On the Saturday I took Ginnie to York races.

My poor old mini was taking a terrible hammering, but before long I was to exchange it for a sleeker conveyance. Mother's house in Great Coxwell having been sold meant there was cash in the bank, so I toyed with the idea of acquiring a Facel Vega, which was the height of fashion, but ended up buying a Volvo P1800 – known as a 'Saint' car because Simon Templar drove one in the popular television series.

I sold Chapel House for £3300 to our erstwhile neighbour in Little Coxwell, Major Jack Paine, the former stud manager to Lord Derby. It is a pitiful reflection on contemporary prize money in British horseracing that the value of the Royal Hunt Cup at Royal Ascot that year was a comparable £3863; nowadays, Chapel House would fetch upwards of £150,000 while the value of the Hunt Cup is less than one third of that figure.

In all, I was invited to a dozen debutante dances in 1962. Harriet shared a dance with her next-door neighbour, Susan Wigan. Harriet's family had discouraged her from continuing to see me, on the grounds that doing so would have rendered her 'season' rather pointless. Understandably, they had loftier aspirations for their daughter. Harriet's mother buttonholed me one day and asked, perfectly seriously, 'Julian, when are you going to get a *proper* job?' In the end, Harriet married a worthy fellow called John Dutton, who worked for an American oil company, and fitted comfortably within the parameters of Mrs Smith's ambitions.

I met another Virginia – slightly older – during the summer. She was Virginia Richards. I had been invited to the Jesus College May Ball in Cambridge and took as a partner a girl that I hardly knew. Partners were at a premium! It was unthinkable for a debutante to go, unchaperoned, to a May Ball; besides, it was in the middle of Royal Ascot, the axis of the social season.

It was a fantastic evening. The band was a young group called the Rolling Stones, whose lead singer was a long-haired, thick-lipped student at the London School of Economics. We rocked and we rolled until the dawn crept in along the banks of the Cam. Ginnie Richards, who was vibrant and inexhaustible, was in a neighbouring party and we clicked straight away. Since my partner and I had run out of words hours earlier, I took her to Cambridge station and put her on the 6.00 pm train to London. Ginnie begged leave of her partner and I drove her over to Newmarket – still in evening dress – to watch the dawn gallops on the Limekilns.

It was a glorious, lazy morning, on the Wednesday of Royal Ascot. I had parked my car next to that of the top northern jockey, Geoff Littlewood, who was riding work. 'Any chances today, Geoff?' I asked. 'I think I might win the Bessborough on Better Honey,' he replied. 'I think the trip will suit him and he'll be a nice price!' he added with a wink.

We drove back to Cambridge, had breakfast and rejoined

Ginnie's party. Having changed clothes and regrouped at 11 am, we took an early lunch and moved on to the Pitt Club to watch Royal Ascot on television. By mid-afternoon the champagne and the anticipation of a decent bet on Better Honey were keeping the adrenaline flowing, but towards 4 pm – by which time I had been awake for 33 hours – a feeling of torpor overwhelmed me in the comfortable chair. I nodded off, and awoke to the tones of Peter O'Sullevan calling home Better Honey at 10/1! I was shattered, but had the consolation of driving Ginnie back to London. We kept in touch, but it was Ginnie Hutchinson I took to Lord's for the Eton & Harrow Match.

Ginnie Richards had a flat in London, but spent the summer holidays with her parents in Devon. At the end of July she went abroad – we had lunch together at Heathrow – and then returned for a holiday in Cornwall. She was proving elusive, but her niceness and effervescent character made the chase worthwhile. Finally, towards the beginning of October, Ginnie rang from London to tell me that she was coming to stay the following weekend with me in Manchester, and I arranged accommodation for her. I was overwhelmed with excitement. A few days later I was filled with horror, and all because of an indiscretion in Paris.

On 23 September my aunt Sylvia and I had embarked on a long weekend to that city. We stayed in a hotel near the Place de la Madeleine and planned some serious eating. After a long and esoteric lunch, flushed with cognac, I spent a pleasant mid-afternoon in the company of a prostitute. I thought no more of it, until two or three days before Ginnie's arrival in Manchester I was beset with what I was convinced were the symptoms of venereal disease. Horror! Unfortunately there was no time to arrange a test and obtain the results before Ginnie's arrival.

Thus it transpired that Ginnie's visit was quite the most frustrating weekend of my life. What must have gone through her mind as we lay together and I tried to explain: 'Ginnie . . . I can't . . .'? We had waited for this moment for almost four months. Now I was rejecting her and, worst of all, I could not tell her the truth! Ginnie and I never did consummate our relationship, but we remained great friends. Luckily my 'symptoms' were a false alarm.

I was playing a fair bit of cricket, both for the *Daily Mirror* eleven and for the Northern Press team. The former had fixtures against teams like the *Daily Telegraph*, *The Herald* and the local taxi drivers. On one occasion I had an unusual preparation for a match in outer Manchester at the end of August.

I had spent the previous weekend, after racing at Ripon, at the home of a wealthy Yorkshire divorcee called Ruth Whittingham, who lived at Bramham Hall near Boston Spa. Another member of the house party was Michael Cox, a young man whom I had never met previously. He had an address in Montpelier Square, Knightsbridge, and was what was once described as an adventurer. He had considerable charm and lived, very successfully for a while, on his wits.

Michael was impressed by my judgement and asked me where I was racing next. I told him that I would probably go on Monday to Warwick, where there would be two possible winners to back. 'Great,' said Michael, 'I'll stay the night with you in Manchester and drive you to Warwick. Then we'll make some money.' In the event, I told Michael to back three winners from three selections. He was betting with Laurie Wallis and won £1750 – the equivalent of well over £20,000 nowadays.

The plan was that a colleague would drive me home, but Michael insisted that I travel with him to London. We dined, at ridiculous expense, drinking exceptional claret, at the Café Royal, and Michael insisted that in the morning I should order a suit, at his expense, from his Savile Row tailor.

The following day I caught the first train to Manchester, nursing a monster hangover, and arrived at the cricket ground for an 11 am start. I batted with unusual confidence and timing, until having scored 19 runs I was overcome by complete exhaustion and was run out by a wide margin. Back in the pavilion I slept for two hours!

Michael was on the phone that evening – I had tipped him another winner that day – to ask where I was next going racing.

'I'll be at Hurst Park at the weekend,' I replied. (I was standing in for 'Newsboy', the *Mirror*'s senior correspondent Bob Butchers, while he was on holiday.) Michael arrived, but his luck had left him: by the end of the two-day meeting he had lost £4000. We kept in touch periodically, but eventually Michael's lifestyle caught up with him and creditors were not satisfied. The measures that he took to improve his circumstances did not find favour within the law and inevitably he spent a period as a guest of Her Majesty. His friendship with Ruthy Whittingham was thus one that she preferred to forget!

I was making some good friends in Cheshire, notably two girls called Caroline Doniger and Diana Carnegie, who shared a coming-out dance in September. Caroline was lively, amusing and sparky and we enjoyed a friendship that was very closely monitored by her family! She eventually married Nick Cowan the manager of Ronnie Wood amongst others. Cowan, with the Old Harrovian Anthony Speelman, won the biggest-ever exotic bet payout in the history of American racing – over $2 million. Caroline and I are still very good friends.

Another 1962 debutante was Anne Baring, who has remained a lifetime friend. Her parents, Desmond and Mollie Baring, owned horses with the late George Todd and spent a deal of time with John and Jean Hislop, the owner-breeders of the great Brigadier Gerard. Before Anne's dance I dined with Francis and Anna Byrne at Hurlingham. Francis was racing correspondent of *The Times* and their daughter, Jane, was to marry Anne's brother, Nigel Baring. It was marriages like this that were the justification of the London season: matches made on the dancefloor and consummated only on the wedding night.

Life in and around Cheshire was fun – there were Hunt Balls and cricket club dances – but more and more I was attracted to London. It had become fashionable to go ice-skating on Monday evenings at Queen's ice-rink in Bayswater. One would meet one's friends, have supper and make plans for the week.

At this time I was having a relationship with an attractive

dark-haired twin called Antonia Trechman. Her family lived in Haslemere and several weekends were spent enjoying their warm hospitality. Antonia was charming, but self-disciplined, and I always felt that marriage was high on her agenda. She proved me right by marrying the following October, and she and her husband moved to Portugal. Antonia was soon the mother of three children. Antonia's twin sister Fanny was of a different colour. A lively, bubbly blonde with an infectious laugh, she lived life to the full and we had lots of fun after I had broken up with Antonia.

In the spring of 1963 I again threw myself into my work. My pre-season tour included the stables of Avril Vasey, Sam Hall and Rufus Beasley, who was especially hospitable. Rufus loved to play poker and was regularly relieved of £20 a night by a young man about Malton called Pat Rohan. It was Rohan – a brilliant trainer of sprinters – with whom Michael Stoute began in racing as an assistant trainer.

I dined at the Rising Sun in Cheltenham with the legendary Dan Moore and his brilliant and stylish jockey Willie Robinson. That was a privilege in terms of journalism and of friendship.

However, I was finding it increasingly hard to reconcile my life as a working journalist for the *Daily Mirror* – encompassing the office's political agenda and the occasional industrial disputes in which I was involved as a member of the NUJ – and my fantasy life as a deb's-delight wannabee. So, towards the end of March, to the fury of my father and the bemusal of my colleagues, I announced that I was leaving the newspaper 'to take a break'. On 26 March I gave a final party for my colleagues and friends at 'The Ship' and cleared my desk.

I watched, from the County Stand, Pat Buckley's thrilling Grand National win on 66/1 shot Ayala, from John Oaksey on Carrickbeg; spent the weekend with Di Carnegie in Cheshire; and on Sunday drove south to begin my new life.

# SIX

# *Dancing Days*

I spent the first day of the rest of my life as I meant to continue – at a party. An old school friend, Aubyn de Margery, lived with his father in the historic – if crumbling – Lympne Castle, near Folkestone in Kent.

Aubyn had arranged a house party for Folkestone races on the Monday. I travelled from London by train and was collected for lunch at the castle before racing. Aubyn's companion was an attractive girl with stunning eyes and high cheekbones. Her name was Penny Walker. After racing, as the evening progressed, I determined to get to know Penny much better. It took me almost six weeks to persuade her to dine with me in London, and then we became an intermittent 'item' until August.

Penny invited me to stay with her parents for Glorious Goodwood. Her father was stud and racing manager to Percy Wright, a leading owner at the time. Her grandfather was one of Noel Murless's leading owners, Colonel Hornung, who entertained us to lunch during the meeting in his private chalet. It was a magical week, but the Walkers – as Harriet Smith's mother had done earlier – made it clear that they had greater expectations of their daughter than a liaison with an out-of-work racing journalist. Penny eventually married Anthony Oppenheimer of the de Beers diamond family and a leading racehorse owner and breeder, whom she irreverently called 'Rocks'. 'Rocks' came up with the goods, and I was just happy to have been a small station on the exotic route of her life.

I was sharing a house in South Kensington with three schoolfriends and an Old Etonian called Robert Bonham-Christie. Robert's family owned Brownsea Island, in the Solent, where we spent a memorable water skiing weekend.

It is not clear, looking back, whether I had a game plan for the year, but activities can be summarized as follows: 26 dances, 28 cocktail parties, 21 games of cricket. My earned income was limited. I was still writing the 'Noel Day' column in the *Sunday Mail*, and I had 'sold' the *Daily Mirror* a mystery-man bet under the pseudonym of 'The Man In The Trilby'. Otherwise I was living on what I won betting on horses or playing cards.

Other than Penny Walker, I had four special girlfriends in 1963: Susan Anderson, whose father Sir Donald Anderson was chairman of the P&O shipping line, Buddy Green, whose father owned racehorses, Aubyn Angus, whose stepfather John Miller owned a stud near Newbury, and a girl called Nancy Meade.

Sue Anderson was an intelligent, responsible and thoroughly self-disciplined girl. She married an earl, whom I imagine she regulated with a rod of iron. When she asked me to dinner before her dance her instructions were: '8.00 for 8.30 (punctually!) . . . and *please* have your hair cut (and washed!)'. I probably complied. Sue was fairly special then and she is now a Justice of the Peace. I hope never to appear before her!

Buddy Green was a stunning-looking girl, with model looks and figure. I met her through Christopher Collins, who owned a steeplechaser in partnership with her father. I took her racing at Sandown on Whit Monday, just two days after we had met. Four days later I invited her to 'Boats' at Cambridge, an all-day party starting with drinks with a group called The Natives and ending with a dance in the evening.

Buddy turned heads wherever she went. During the evening, exhausted by champagne cocktails and the heat of a long day, I decided to take a discreet forty-winks. I asked three of what I believed were my friends – Richard Worthington, Simon de Zoete and Jake Morley (now the part-owner of Gold Cup winner Celeric) – to 'look after' Buddy while I was asleep. Worthington, tall and good-looking, made a totally dishonourable attempt to spirit

Buddy away. Happily, she behaved impeccably. When I awoke, we danced and finally returned to our arranged accommodation. I dived into our shared bathroom first, washed and brushed my teeth and lay back on my bed, anticipating a night of unparalleled pleasure. I awoke six hours later: 'I didn't like to wake you,' said sweet Buddy, 'you looked so content.' It was a classic case of Paradise Lost.

The following week I took Sue Anderson to the Jesus College May Ball. This year it was held in the week before Royal Ascot and was an altogether more orderly evening.

Aubyn Angus came into my life in the autumn. I stayed with the family for the Newbury Race Ball and John Miller showed me his mares. Aubyn and I clicked straight away. We were both out for fun and understood each other perfectly, so it was a perfect relationship with no strings attached.

The girl who had most influence on my life that year was Nancy Meade. I met Nancy at the Eton & Harrow Match. I had gone to Lord's with a girl called Clarissa Kershaw, but it was Nancy I took out to dinner that night and squeezed into my diary whenever possible in the next months. She was outrageous, uninhibited and outspoken. When we made love she made her requirements explicitly clear: she showed me the 'manual' and the right buttons to press! Any pleasure that I have managed subsequently to transmit to a member of the opposite sex is largely attributable to Nancy. She disappeared out of my life almost as rapidly as she appeared and I have not heard of her or from her for over 30 years. But I will always be grateful.

It was the week after the Eton & Harrow Match that Clarissa Kershaw had her dance in Hampshire. I stayed with a delightful family called Dereham, who lived at Old Basing, near Basingstoke. I came across Jenny Dereham regularly in later years. She became a senior publishing assistant at Michael Joseph, the publisher of Dick Francis's novels.

My behaviour at Clarissa's dance sank to a new depth of unacceptability. Sue Anderson would have been appalled; even now I am deeply ashamed. For a simple wager a friend and I lined up 13 glasses of champagne on the bar. The plan was simple: we were to start at different ends, down six glasses of champagne each, while the man who reached the central thirteenth glass first won the bet. I won, but shortly afterwards fell flat on my back in the centre of the dance floor. Then, on arriving back at Old Basing House, I inexplicably turned on the tap in my room, collapsed on the bed and passed out. The following morning I was found fully dressed, the tap still running.

A wild Irish girl at that party was Diana Hallowes, whose family lived at Fethard in County Tipperary, the local village of the now world-famous Coolmore Stud. Her father, Colonel Jos Hallowes, was a bloodstock breeder and Master of Foxhounds. Di has followed in his footsteps.

If I have ever been more damaged by alcohol than during that weekend at Old Basing, it was probably by a concoction called an 'Attitude Adjuster' in McCarthy's pub in Fethard, following a trip to Coolmore!

Two weeks later, for Juliet Harrison's dance, I stayed with a fascinating man in Colonel Bill (later Sir William) Dugdale. Both he and Juliet's father, Bill Harrison, had horses in training with Rufus Beasley. Dugdale, a steward, told me stories about the integrity of certain jockeys that changed my image of them for ever. Some years later I did a television programme with Sir William about the finances of racing.

The morning after Juliet's dance I drove from Derbyshire to play cricket for my housemate Tim Duke, one of my co-residents in South Kensington, at his family home in Surrey. I bowled unusually well, took three wickets for 10 runs and was taken off! It was probably as well: after my three overs I was quite exhausted.

I played most of my cricket for three clubs that year: Essendon, the local club to Harriet Smith's family; Rye CC in Sussex; and the Blue Angel, a travelling team whose roots were the fashionable Blue Angel nightclub in Mayfair, where David Frost and Lance Percival cut their teeth.

The 'Angels' were an entertaining bunch of itinerants, probably comparable to the Captain Scott Invitation XI described so hilariously in Marcus Berkmann's classic cricket liturgy, *Rain Men*. Our fixtures included matches against Littlehampton, Fleet and Tatty Bogie, where or whatever that was. The squad included Bob Gibbons, the solicitor who was largely responsible for introducing the Maktoum family – notably Sheikh Hamdan – to British racing, and who won the 1998 Lincoln Handicap with his mare Hunters of Brora. We took our cricket seriously enough to have pre-season nets at Alf Gover's cricket school in South London, but it was extremely rare for us to win a match.

Nevertheless, a memorable game was against Littlehampton in June 1963. I had been kept awake through the previous night by a sexual predator of quite inexhaustible rapacity, to the extent that I had barely an hour's rest. In consequence I slept in the back of the car throughout the entire journey to Littlehampton. My bowling was appalling, but amazingly I scored 19 runs before fatigue overcame me. I slept exceptionally well on the Saturday night.

By and large, until August, I played most weekends for Essendon. After Goodwood, from the start of August, I spent the following six weeks playing for Rye. London becomes a social vacuum in August: it is holiday time, whether that be sunning in the South of France, fishing in the north of Scotland, or shooting grouse on the Glorious Twelfth. I decided to stay for several weeks with my Aunt Sylvia in Sussex.

Sylvie, who was closer to being a sister than an aunt, had established a small high-class restaurant called 'The Playing Card' in Rye. Her business partner and long-time friend was the delightful and long-suffering Adrienne Gurr – long-suffering, that is to say, from the Wilson and Mann families! Sylvie and Adrienne had worked together at Bletchley Park, the wireless and telegraph headquarters of the SIS during the war. That was vital and enervating work in the height of wartime and their activities were covered by the Official Secrets Act for 50 years. We never did discuss their precise role.

I went to Rye with three main purposes – to play cricket, to write a novel, and to wean myself from drinking gin and tonic.

At cricket I enjoyed varying degrees of success. I played nine games for Rye, who were one of the better club sides in Sussex, and could call upon two Sussex 2nd XI players. I was in the side against Westminster Bank, The Dragons, North Kent, Peasmarsh, Folkestone, the Sussex Martlets, and Hastings Priory. The most memorable game was against Folkestone on the County Ground. In one respect it was an eerie experience, to play on a near-deserted, first-class ground, but it felt special. We won the match and our dinner at an Indian restaurant stays in the mind.

I found it surprisingly easy to eliminate gin from my staple diet. This was probably helped by something that I read in a book about fitness and rugby. So, after cricket, our group – the Matthews brothers, Robert Hacking, Richard Merricks and others – would down several pints of beer and gradually I eliminated spirits from my life . . . for a while.

Michael Matthews was one of our Sussex 2nd XI players, but I was closer to his brother Peter. Thus I was stunned beyond belief when Peter was arrested and convicted of robbery several years later. Bob Hacking was an outstanding point-to-point rider, while his son Paul has become one of the top amateur NH jockeys.

The one objective that completely eluded success was my attempt to write a publishable novel. I was writing a book, intermittently, between cricket, meals and watching horseracing on television. By the end of the year I had completed a document of a kind, but on reading it through was aghast at its mediocrity. It was just awful! I hid it away, showed it to no-one, and it remains to this day concealed in my 'sulk house' in Suffolk.

I left Rye after six weeks of wonderful hospitality from Sylvie and Adrienne. Despite my intellectual failure I felt refreshed and fit. Driving up to Scotland for a week's fishing at Whitebridge, I stopped on the way for a night with the Theodas family at Doonfoot in Ayr. Terry looked lovelier than ever. Eventually she was to marry a local racehorse owner called John Boswell. Together they now own and manage a country house-cum-restaurant in Devon, where the cuisine is as good as anywhere in the West Country.

In October I eased myself back into the social swing. I took Caroline Cadogan, sister of the erstwhile Lord Chelsea, racing at Sandown Park. I remember collecting her from the family home at the epicentre of the family's London estate, which encompasses the most valuable square mile of property in Knightsbridge and Chelsea. Lord Cadogan greeted me with the now familiar look that stated: 'You're not really what I've got in mind.' Nevertheless, it was a double delight taking Caroline to the races – partly for the pleasure of her company, but also for the asset of her Jockey Club ladies badge, which obtained her free entry to every racecourse!

It was around this time that I became especially friendly with Christopher Collins. Chris's father, Douglas Collins, had founded the Goya perfume empire and sold the business for a colossal seven-figure sum.

Chris lived with his mother, brother and three sisters in a large converted farmhouse with stables, near Great Missenden in Buckinghamshire. He had started riding in point-to-points, but was now branching out into NH. I met him first at a race meeting at Sandown on a Saturday and he invited me to dinner and to stay for the weekend. Typically, I accepted and drove down to Buckinghamshire after racing, with only the clothes that I was wearing.

Chris invited me to ride out in the morning. After dinner I embarked on a game of cards with Nigel Baring, another house guest, which lasted until 6.00 am. I was losing £50 which I could ill afford. As the sun rose, we walked out into the paddocks. 'Double or quits I can jump over that paddock rail,' I challenged. 'Done,' said Nigel. I estimated the height of the paddock rail as no more than four foot six inches, and I had jumped five foot at Harrow when finishing third in the school high jump. I sailed over the rail and breathed a sigh of relief, but poor Nigel, who had worked hard all night for nothing, was speechless. I was not, I am ashamed to say, on duty to ride out at 8.00 am!

That weekend was the foundation of one of my oldest friendships. Chris is godfather to my son Thomas and I am godfather to Chris's son Edward.

It had been an enjoyable – but expensive – year and, encouraged by my aunts, I acknowledged the wisdom of thinking in terms of returning to work. Obviously I had drawn a line through my career with the *Mirror*, so there was no going back. However, there was talk of the Jockey Club creating a public relations agency to improve communications with the press – to be called the Racing Information Bureau.

In January 1964, I went for an interview with a man called Kennedy Brown at Patrick Dolan Ltd in Bruton Lane, followed up by two further interviews in March and April. Broadly speaking I was suitable for the job, but the mix of individuals was the negative element. One of the early appointees spoke out strongly against me, regarding me as unsuitable for public relations. He was probably absolutely right and now, in retrospect, I am indebted to him. So the new year began as the previous year had ended, with a mix of parties, horseracing and, as the summer approached, cricket.

It was a wonderful winter of National Hunt racing. The Hennessy Gold Cup had brought together two quite exceptional steeplechasers – Arkle from Ireland and Mill House, the giant winner of the 1963 Gold Cup, from England. It was an evocative race, run in a heavy mist. What could not be seen from the stands was that Arkle had blundered badly at the last ditch, enabling Mill House to gallop on and win easily. The big horse looked majestic. In the Boar's Head at Ardington that evening some of us agreed that Mill House would never be beaten; but others who had watched the race on television ventured that Arkle just might better him on another day.

In the King George VI Steeplechase I bet the odds on Mill House privately and with bookmakers. Luckily, as it turned out, Arkle did not appear and Mill House won easily. It was not until the Gold Cup of 1964 that the two great horses were re-matched, in the greatest, most keenly anticipated head-to-head horserace that

I have ever seen. Staged, unusually, on a Saturday and attracting a crowd that stretched the Cheltenham enclosures to their limits, it was a sporting occasion that will always remain in the memory. Huge bets were struck. I, for one, remained convinced that Mill House was invincible.

In the race Mill House played the hare and Willie Robinson tried to stretch his rival to the limit running down the hill. They jumped the second last with a clear advantage, but suddenly the realization dawned that Willie Robinson's foot was hard on the accelerator, while Pat Taaffe, on the superlative Arkle, had his hands full. At the final fence it was all over: Arkle jumped majestically and galloped powerfully up the hill to win by five lengths.

We, the Mill House supporters, were stunned. We stood with open mouths. We could not believe that our hero was beaten – and not just beaten, but resoundingly. Our cash was lost and our judgement was in question. It was one of the most shattering, sobering and shocking experiences of my racing career. I just could not believe that it had happened. Mill House was a broken reed and was never the same horse again.

Arkle proved to be the greatest steeplechaser that anyone of my generation has ever seen. No-one will ever know how he would have fared against the 1930s hero, Golden Miller. It is my personal belief that no steeplechaser was ever foaled who had the beating of Arkle.

Three years later, through my job in television, I was to meet Arkle and the legendary names around him – Tom and Betty Dreaper, Pat Taaffe and Anne, Duchess of Westminster. They were wonderful people, worthy of a great horse, just as Arkle was proud to fulfil their expectations. When Arkle's chronic arthritis necessitated his being put down, I was one of the hundreds, no doubt, who wrote to the Duchess to commiserate with her loss. She wrote back the most delightful self-effacing letter, ending with the invitation of a day's fishing on Loch Stack – in the shadow of Ben Arkle – the next time that I was fishing in the north of Scotland. It was an invitation that I accepted on several occasions.

The Duchess was always surrounded at Benmore by fascinating and amusing people. One year I met Diana, Lady Delamere, the central figure in the murder saga in January 1941 in Happy Valley, Kenya. The victim was Lady Delamere's lover, the Earl of Erroll. Her husband-at-the-time, Sir Jock Delves Broughton, was arrested and tried for the crime, but acquitted, although the majority of Nairobi society believed him to be guilty.

Fascinatingly, a recent book suggests that Diana Delamere was very probably the murderer. Some years later she allegedly shot and wounded another lover who threatened to leave her. He survived after Diana had summoned a doctor, who insisted that her victim should be taken to hospital. Diana agreed grudgingly, adding: 'But not in my new Mercedes. I don't want his blood all over my car!' Her role was played by Greta Scacchi in the film *White Mischief*. On the basis of our brief acquaintance I find the accusations against her difficult to believe.

I seemed to harbour an insatiable obsession to take out every single attractive female under the age of 25 in London. I suppose that I could not bear to miss an opportunity to share the day with a pretty girl. During 1964, I took over 30 different girls to either lunch, tea, dinner, racing or a nightclub. I am aware of this statistic because the matter was raised at the end of the year: a bet was struck and a list compiled. There were 32 names on the list, and topping the league was a girl called Diana Maitland-Hume, a regular date during the spring. Diana was a talented interior designer, who lived in Radnor Walk, off the King's Road, close to the 'Chelsea Potter' public house. Ginnie Hutchinson – a regular racing companion – came next. Ginnie eventually married Major Johnny Lewis, a stalwart of the British Bloodstock Agency for many years. I was still seeing Harriet Smith, but the spark of commitment had not been rekindled since her debutante year.

I was overawed by a girl called Anne Dunhill, of the cigarette family. Anne was already doing some photographic modelling and was strikingly beautiful. It was she that I took to the Eton & Harrow Match – an accurate barometer of my admiration. Anne has led a colourful life and her high profile has made her passage through various relationships easy to follow through columns of newsprint.

Early in the year I realized that it was time to have a place of my own. I took the lease on a flat in Alexandra Mansions, in the King's Road, near the corner of Beaufort Street. I furnished, decorated and carpeted it single-handed and eventually asked my schoolfriend, Peter Ohlson, to share the flat with me. Peter was pursuing a career in marketing and we got on fine.

It took a while to recover from the impact of Mill House's defeat in the Gold Cup, but two weeks later it was time to head towards Liverpool for the Grand National meeting. I was invited to a weekend house party by an old friend from Cheshire, Sandy Gunning, whose brother Alistair had been a near-contemporary in West Acre at Harrow. It was a lively party with a high-rolling roulette game. One of the liveliest sparks was a girl called Liz Brewer. I doubt if anyone reading this book has not read or heard of the professional activities of Liz, a party-giver par excellence, whose public relations work has included 'marketing' Ivana Trump in London society. Liz and I hit it off, and I drove her back to London at the end of the weekend. She invited me for drinks or dinner a couple of times, but even in those days Liz's diary was jammed to capacity.

The 1964 National was a quite thrilling race, with the flat-race sized Team Spirit, ridden by Willie Robinson, getting up in the last few strides to beat the unfashionable Johnny Kenneally on Purple Silk. I wept for Johnny who had ridden an exemplary race, only to have what appeared an assured victory snatched from his grasp.

By the end of April, after Queen Charlotte's Ball, the new crop of debutantes were starting to feature in the gossip columns. I dined with the Boyd-Carpenter family before Juliet Aschan's dance, on the evening of 2000 Guineas day. John Boyd-Carpenter was a highly-regarded member of the Tory cabinet and his daughter was pert, sparky and fun. We were pictured together at the dance by Tom Hustler, the society photographer. I was not entirely surprised

My parents were married at Shellingford Church, in the grounds of Kitemore House.

Nanny welcomes a new generation. My mother (left) and Aunt Diana had both grown up with her benign discipline.

Whatever happened to those blond curls?

Dancing days. 'Sharing a joke' (as the gossip writers put it) with Simon de Zoete and Sarah Boyd-Carpenter, later Baroness Hogg.

A weekend in the West Country with Belinda Heathcote-Amory, Sir Rupert Mackeson, and members of the Howard de Walden family.

Alison and I were married at Chelsea Town Hall. It was the most important day of my life.

The regular viewer. Who says that we didn't appeal to a wide audience?

A chip off the old block? My son Thomas – a lucky talisman at Wembley.

The family group. Bates (my labrador) finds photography an exhausting ordeal.

Calling the horses, with Peter O'Sullevan at Chepstow.

Above: Early days at BBC TV, as 'the next Peter O'Sullevan'.

Below: The day of Frankie Dettori's 'Magnificent Seven' at Ascot. Sue Barker and I interviewed Frankie in rotation.

Above: The story of Whitebridge. His first and only hurdle race – he was ridden by New Zealand Champion jockey Graham Walters – ended in disaster at Ascot.

Below: Tumbledownwind – the bravest of the brave in the mud at York, in 1977.

Above: The toast is Tumbledownwind! The Gimcrack euphoria, shared with co-owners Norah Hunter-Blair (next to me) and Joë Farmer.

Below: My best friend (Tykeyvor), with possibly the greatest jockey in the world, the American Gary Stevens.

Partying with Steve and Amy Cauthen, and owner Walter Mariti (right) at Stetchworth Park, Newmarket.

The great Sir Garfield Sobers, partying at Robert Sangster's Barbados house on the eve of the match between the Newmarket Trainers XI, and Peter Lashley's XI, at the Kensington Oval.

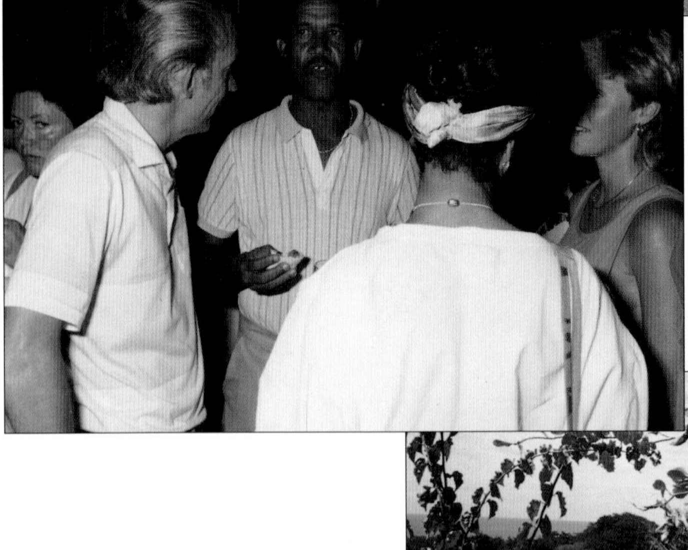

Rum punch at noon – overlooking the fourth fairway at Sandy Lane Golf Course in Barbados.

when Sarah became head of John Major's financial policy unit, and was eventually made a life peeress.

There were strange developments on the cricket pitch: the Blue Angels were starting to win some matches! We were beaten, as usual, by Littlehampton on 13 June, but the following day we beat Bognor and I scored 40 runs. I have no direct recollection of this, so can only surmise that I became paralytically drunk!

For Royal Ascot I stayed with a friend called Phyl Carnegie, whose mother, Lady Northesk, had a convenient home at nearby Shurlock Row. It was always fun staying with Phyl, although one weekend I was asked by a pale-faced girl, from a well-known Scottish aristocratic family, if I would take her back to work in London on Sunday evening. 'Work' turned out to be performing in two fairly adjacent strip clubs! I was acutely embarrassed as she climbed out of my car and felt like a pimp!

The Royal Ascot meeting of 1964 will always remain in my mind. For weeks I was convinced that the shrewd 'Towser' Gosden had prepared a horse for the King George V Handicap and that it would be the subject of a large gamble. The only drawback was that the horse needed soft ground. On the eve of the race it started to rain and I was thrilled. It rained all night, so in the morning, driving to the course, there were deep puddles by the side of the road. I rubbed my hands in glee! By the time we reached the course I was starting to become concerned – still it rained. It never stopped: the course was flooded, racing was abandoned, and a bet that I was convinced would win had gone up in smoke – or rather, sunk without trace!

Two weeks later I was invited to an interview with Mr Gerald Green, the chief credit controller of Ladbrokes, the bookmakers. My betting was continuing to show a healthy profit and I had ten bookmakers' accounts, to be assured of obtaining the best value in the ante-post markets. Usually at least one cheque would arrive from a bookmaker each week, but occasionally a large liability would build up with a different bookmaker. After a week like Royal Ascot with considerable overheads, for instance, it was possible that no resources would exist to settle the account.

Mr Green wanted to know when I was proposing to settle. It is one of those unanswerable questions. In principal, if bookmakers are owed money, they are anxious, with justification, that the client should not continue to bet until the debt is paid. But if the client depends upon betting for the bulk of his income, how then is he going to raise money to settle the debt? Mr Green and I reached a compromise, and I determined to have a 'working evening' at the chemin de fer tables at Pauline Wallis's Casanova Club!

I spent most of July and the first part of August playing cricket, but I was looking forward immensely to the Ebor meeting at York. I had been invited to stay by an enchanting girl whom I had met at a party, called Kathleen Starkey. 'Mops', as we called her, was really special. Her father, a retired Army Colonel nicknamed 'Cuckoo' owned the Huttons Ambo estate near Malton, where the ex-jockey Edward Hide has bred horses successfully for years. Her stepmother, formerly the Countess of Howe, was the mother of those two great society beauties, Mary-Gaye and Charlotte Curzon.

The colonel did not like the cut of my jib one little bit. He did not like my clothes (I confess that my lightweight suit was inexpensive and off-the-peg); he did not like the length of my hair; and he did not like the fact that, as he put it, I 'lived off my wits'. Mops was unconcerned by all this, but it was nonetheless an uncomfortable week. The highlight was the Ebor Hunt Ball, where the colonel's friends looked at me over their whiskies with disapproval. I have always treasured a piece of doggerel, which I claimed to have composed but did not:

*There was an Old Buffer called Starkey*
*Who had an affair with a darkie.*
*The results of his sins were quadruplets, not twins:*
*One black, one white and two khaki!*

Mops became a very dear friend over the next three years. It was to her flat that I went to watch the transmission of my first BBC programme recorded for 'Sportsview' – a Grand National preview – in March 1966. She was kind and sensitive and was adored by every one of my friends. Apart from my mother, I have never met anyone quite so unselfish. She eventually married John Jenyns, a solicitor based in Thirsk and steward at several Yorkshire race meetings. Sadly in May 1997 he was obliged to resign as senior steward at York racecourse after an incident with two executives from Channel 4 Racing who had met with his displeasure.

John was a perfect husband to Mops, but tragically she was struck down with multiple sclerosis in her early thirties. She spent the last years of her life in a wheelchair, but rarely missed a York meeting. When Pontenuovo won the Bradford & Bingley Handicap at York in 1991, I whispered to her: 'That one was for you.' She died two years later and I will never forget her.

Mops had joined our expedition to Whitebridge that autumn. Heaven knows how we obtained 'clearance' – we were a pretty disreputable group – but I suppose that Mops persuaded her father that there was safety in numbers!

It was an autumn of marvellous parties, not least the pyjama party given by the wild Diana Hallowes. But the need for a job was becoming acute. At the beginning of November the excellent *Evening Standard* racing correspondent, Peter Scott, moved to the *Daily Telegraph* where he was to remain until his premature death. I applied for his job at the *Standard* and was granted an interview by the sports editor, Peter Goodall, but a decision had been taken to make an 'inside' appointment. Jack Waterman was to move from another department to take over as racing correspondent.

I was disappointed at not getting that job. But that feeling was swept away by the need to plan for a skiing holiday in Engelberg in Austria, with Mark Saleby, Tim Cassel and a host of others. It was to be an expedition that all of us who went on it still talk about to this day.

# SEVEN

# *In Search of the Holy Grail*

A tall, shambling Old Etonian, irregularly shaven and with lank, untidy hair, was my best friend and most regular companion during 1964 and 1965. His name was Mark Saleby. We enjoyed a comparable lifestyle in that the cornerstone of our financial activities was a regular battle with bookmakers, but Mark had an undisciplined and unrealistic agenda, with the hint of a Dostoyevskian mentality lurking in the background. He was always in search of the Holy Grail.

He lived intermittently with Phyl Carnegie, on the top floor of a shortly-to-be-condemned block of flats, overlooking the Embankment, on the edge of World's End. It was Mark who introduced me to cannabis resin: I smoked it once but happily it did nothing for me and I never experimented again.

Mark was convinced that there was a magic route to beating the bookmakers. One evening he came to the conclusion that by reading a racing publication called *Timeform* whilst smoking pot he would see 'The Truth'. Unfortunately the following day he suffered reverses of more damaging proportions than usual.

His volatile girlfriend found his irregular lifestyle and unpredictable conduct difficult to cope with. On more than one occasion there were suicide threats and violent and devastating outbursts of rage. In retrospect, I can hardly blame her. At the time we christened her 'The Monster'.

Phyl Carnegie did not ski, so Mark was a loose cannon on the group trip to Engelberg. He was a good player to have on board. On the fishing trip to Whitebridge in the autumn he had discovered an unforgettable wine and spirit merchants in Inverness, managed by a once-in-a-lifetime character called Mrs Heraghty. This lady would invite clients into the back room, or parlour, for tasting. We left her establishment with several bottles of her unique 'curiously old Highland malt whisky' which provided unlimited pleasure, followed inevitably by pain, throughout our holiday.

We assembled at Victoria Station on Monday 28 December, a disparate group of about a dozen. There were serious skiers, party-goers, and husband hunters. Some were all three. There was an early blip when the sight of one girl, to whose bland and vacuous self-obsession I felt positively allergic, caused me to pull my cases off the luggage rack and walk back down the platform. I was forcibly restrained. During the following fortnight my ingenuity was stretched to the limits to avoid sharing a single journey on a chair lift or meat-hook with this girl.

It was the best holiday of my life in terms of raw skiing. We would leave our chalet soon after 9.00 am and ski almost non-stop until teatime. It was a long walk to the lower slopes and a long way home, so by the end of the day we were always exhausted. On the last day of the trip I was skiing with such confidence that I finished third in a British Ski Club downhill no-fall race. I was far from the best skier in our group, so I can only think that none of the remainder entered!

Two of the girls in our party, Harriet Pugh and Sally Scott, were strangely fascinated by Mark Saleby. He was, I suppose, a total contrast to the majority of men they met during their London season. Harriet, whose uncle Sir Francis Cassel had been secretary to the legendary owner of Golden Miller, Miss Dorothy Paget, was exceptionally intelligent, with an almost supercilious intellectualism. She was critical, quizzical and to Saleby, I suspect, alluring. Mark, despite his alternative lifestyle, was cultured and well-read and there is no doubt that they stimulated one another.

Harriet's cousin, Tim Cassel, now an eminent QC and the husband of Labour peer Baroness Mallelieu, was our team leader. Tim was the subject of close attention from Carolyn Lade, who the following year did some modelling and eventually married Anthony Speelman.

The fly in the ointment was Harriet's 10-year-old brother Oliver, whose personal pleasure was to conduct a door-to-door roll-call at about 7.30 am to discover who had been sleeping with whom. None of the doors had keys, although chairs and other substantial objects were employed to keep at bay the ubiquitous and talkative Oliver!

'Mops' was unable to come, so my partner on this trip was Belinda Heathcote-Amory, a petite and bubbly girl whose uncle, Lord Howard de Walden, was to fulfil his lifetime's ambition by winning the Derby 20 years later with Slip Anchor.

It was a magnificent holiday and we slept for ten hours every night. We made long-lasting friendships. Harriet, happily married, now sits as a local magistrate, while Tim Cassel is part of one of my racing syndicates. Young Oliver returned home with undreamed of wealth, having extracted 'hush money' from several sources.

I returned to England in mid-January for Penny Walker's marriage to 'Rocks' Oppenheimer. Ironically, they set up home in Park Walk a few hundred yards from my modest flat.

It seemed a good idea to capitalize on the fitness attained in Engelberg, and so I resolved to start riding again. I had a dream of riding in the Old Berks point-to-point at Lockinge on Easter Monday, a meeting that we never missed going to in the 1950s. At a higher level, I speculated about riding under NH Rules. My friend Jimmy Armstrong had achieved this with the help of a hurdler trained by Peter Walwyn; unfortunately, horse and jockey capsized at the final flight on the big day at Fontwell. But Jimmy had 'been there' and I was envious.

I went hacking a couple of times at Leatherhead and in Hyde Park. Lilo Blum, the sister of former Newmarket trainer Gerry Blum, had a successful livery stables in Grosvenor Crescent Mews, behind what is now the Lanesborough Hotel. Lilo had a mixed bag of horses, from an old 'schoolmaster' which independently stopped at red traffic lights and walked on at green, to a young hunter horse recently arrived from Surrey, which could take a good hold.

It was always hazardous riding in Hyde Park. One morning I was cantering on the north side, alongside Bayswater, when a pneumatic drill was fired off a few yards away. My conveyance took flight in terror, heading quite out of control towards Marble Arch. I became aware, to my horror, that unless breaks were applied we would carry straight on and down into the dark underground car park! Happily there was a very small metal railing at the end of the canter, which the young horse felt ill-disposed to negotiate.

At the beginning of April, I travelled to Moreton-in-Marsh to spend three weeks learning advanced horsemanship from Colonel Talbot-Ponsonby, a distinguished equestrian who was an experienced course-builder and had instructed the British Olympic Three-Day Event team. It was normal for a rider to bring his own horse, but since I did not have one I borrowed a mount for the period of my stay.

It soon became obvious that I should have taken a course before I went on the course. We were riding for six hours a day and it was exhausting. I was taught to sit properly on jumping, to exercise control over ridge and furrow, to instruct a horse to change legs, and other basics of serious advanced riding. It was an eye-opener and a shock to the system, there being many occasions when I yearned for the day to come to an end.

My accommodation and refuge was the Redesdale Arms in Moreton-in-Marsh, which doubled as a high-class hotel-cum-restaurant, with an academy for young ladies learning the art of catering. There was an exceptionally attractive trainee during my three-week stay, called Penelope Tindall, who later moved to London and became the *Evening Standard*'s 'Milk Queen'. However, I was far too exhausted even to *contemplate* mischief after a day's riding with Colonel Talbot-Ponsonby!

I carried on riding during the summer and then in the autumn bought a hurdle race winner called Regis, with a view to riding under Rules. My plan was to send him – and myself – to a friend called Noel Robinson, who trained at Haggerston Castle, near Berwick-on-Tweed. I would spend three months learning the different discipline of riding a racehorse and then – Bingo! – I would be ready to go. That was the plan, but other events were to intervene.

Meanwhile, my friend Christopher Collins had hatched an even more ambitious plan, to ride in the Grand National no less! At the time he had ridden just one winner under Rules, and he weighed over 11 st. Chris asked me whether I could find a horse for him to buy to ride at Aintree. Obviously the choice was limited, given Chris's heavy weight, but I had an idea.

I had taken out a girl called Clare van der Gucht, whose step-father was the racehorse owner Major Jack Lyons. He owned a horse called Mr Jones which looked perfect for Chris and had the right sort of weight. The horse was trained by Arthur Stephenson in County Durham. Arthur was renowned for having a complete phobia of the press – he hated having his photograph taken, and in all the years that we were friends he never once allowed a television camera anywhere near his stables. But he and I understood one another and always got on well. Chris and I travelled up to Co. Durham, we both liked the horse, and a deal was done.

This was to be the turning point of Chris's riding career. He had a fantastic ride in the 1965 National, finishing third to those two equine heroes, Jay Trump and Freddie. It was an amazing achievement by a rider of almost overcome limited experience. I had travelled to Liverpool with my father, who always reported on the race, and I stood overcome in the press box with tears running down my cheeks! The Grand National has always been that sort of race, but for the second year running emotion had overcome me. However, little did I guess that in 12 months time I would have a direct input into the mechanics of the unique occasion.

Tragically, Mr Jones broke his back in a subsequent race, but Chris was so fired up by his achievement that he determined to give race riding his very best shot. With the help of Arthur, he assembled a group of horses – mostly from Ireland – that enabled him to become champion amateur jockey in the next and following seasons.

Arthur had every reason to be grateful to me, especially as Chris was followed into the yard by our friend Peter Greenall (now Lord Daresbury), but he never once granted me a single interview on BBC television!

During this period I was spending some time with Sir Rupert Mackeson. He was serving in the Royal Horse Guards at Wellington Barracks near Buckingham Palace, and was having a few mounts as an amateur rider. We had spent a weekend the previous autumn with the Heathcote-Amorys in Somerset, after Rupert had ridden at Taunton races.

It is extraordinary how a person's life can undergo a complete metamorphosis, and Rupert's experience is a prime example. In the mid-seventies he created, with a mutual friend in Juliet Aschan, a company called 'Master Class', specializing in overseas cultural tours. However, early in 1978 he 'disappeared', leaving the company with debts assessed at £100,000. He was discovered 19 months later in Rhodesia, arrested and charged locally with assaulting a police officer. The following months were a mixture of embarrassment and farce. An attempt to deport him to Britain was aborted after his noisy sit-down protest on the airport runway. He was flown to South Africa, imprisoned in the Transvaal, and then driven back to Rhodesia, described as the 'most unwanted person in the world'. Eventually he was arrested again in Rhodesia, and in April 1980 flown back to Britain to face 19 charges of deception, relating to cheques. He was granted bail of £15,000 during five periods of remand. Eventually, after 15 months, he was formally discharged on the grounds that he had been unlawfully returned from Rhodesia, as Britain had no extradition agreement with the 'illegal' regime of Mr Smith. Thus he was deported as opposed to 'extradited'.

Rupert is now a bookseller in Hungerford, and by some accounts has scant regard for my literature: 'I've never liked any of Julian Wilson's books!'

My three weeks with Colonel Talbot-Ponsonby had made it difficult to keep on top of my betting activities, with the result that a period of cashflow problems ensued. I owed £116 to a bookmaker called Upex and gave them a post-dated cheque as a gesture of goodwill. At Sandown, on Whitbread Gold Cup day, I was betting with Laurie Wallis, with whom my credit was good. For this I was reported by Upex's course representative and received a strong letter from their head office. There was a hidden threat to have me 'warned off' if I didn't settle. If I could afford to go racing and bet, they demanded, why could I not afford to pay Upex? It was a delicate situation to handle: 'Cuckoo' Starkey was right – I was having to live on my wits!

My problems came within an inch of resolution at Royal Ascot. There was a new Tote bet, recently introduced, called the 'Quadpool', which required one to nominate the winners of the second, third, fourth and fifth races on the card. On the third day at Ascot I had a serious stab at the Quadpool. The first and third legs looked 'gettable', whilst I was convinced that Prince Hansel would win the fourth leg. It was just a question of solving the second leg, the Royal Hunt Cup, one of the toughest races in the calendar.

Hence I took six selections in the Hunt Cup, including Blazing Scent, drawn on the far side of the course. A furlong from home the scenario looked rosy. Three of my nominees were fighting it out on the stands side while Balzing Scent was clear of the field on the far rails. Then, a hundred yards from home, a big grey horse loomed up on the stands side with his jockey riding a furious blitz finish: it was Lester Piggott on Casabianca. My heart sank and I felt faintly sick, as Piggott got up in the last stride to win by a short head. I knew that he had won and no other jockey could have achieved it. Five of my selections in the race finished second, third, fourth, fifth and sixth. Prince Hansel won and the Quadpool dividend was £393 10s 0d – the equivalent of well over £4000 today. I took a long time to get over that experience.

I was taking out two terrific fun girls, Doonie and Bunny Herdman, who were full of laughter. Their father, Pat Herdman, owned horses in Ireland with Charlie Weld, the father of Dermot. The family lived at Strabane in County Tyrone, where Pat was Master of Hounds, but like many horse people they took a house in Dublin for the Royal Dublin Show. Angel (to give Bunny her correct name) asked me if I would like to stay for the week. So much for my fitness regime: Horse Show week is a rigorous examination of horse and man – and especially man!

Angel's dance was on the Tuesday night, clashing with the Tipperary Hunt Ball at the Shelburne Hotel. No doubt several revellers chose to take on both events. It was a brilliant party, lasting well into the dawn. On the Wednesday we raced at the now defunct Phoenix Park and dined with the Guinness family just outside Dublin. Meanwhile, in Dublin the Kildare Hunt Ball stretched well beyond midnight with the usual excesses and inevitable injuries. On Thursday I was due to fly back to London to write my column; but Dublin was a party I just did not want to leave, so I flew back on the Friday and carried on where I left off!

The Herdmans had a runner on the Saturday in the 'Phoenix 1500' (now the Heinz 57 Phoenix Stakes) and I joined the group in the paddock. They were magical people.

During the week I had met a girl called Venetia Turner, whose father was the Irish Turf Club handicapper, Major Dick Turner. It was a happy meeting and the Turners became great friends. Dick helped to establish my company Seymour Bloodstock, in Ireland, and became a director. When the family moved to England in the 1970s it was Dick who found me my cottage near Newmarket, which has been my country home now for 20 years. Venetia was engaged to a tall, fairly intense fellow called Archie Orr-Ewing, but the week following the Horse Show she wrote to tell me that she had broken off her engagement. Before long, however, she changed her mind again and she and Archie were married on 10 December. Sadly the marriage did not survive for a great length of time.

Back home the Sixties were swinging relentlessly. The hard

currency was pot, fame and free love. The King's Road was the epicentre of everything.

There was also the West End, which was my beat. Number-one spot was held by The Garrison run by Robert Mills, a club-cum-disco beneath Les Ambassadeurs Club off Park Lane. For the younger set, Sybilla's – one of the original light-strobing, ear-busting discotheques – was the tops. It was named after the beautiful Sybilla Edmonstone, with whose brother Archie I had stayed at Duntreath Castle in Stirlingshire the previous autumn. But eventually Annabel's in Berkeley Square, named after Lady Annabel Birley, trumped the lot. It became – and remains – the archetypal nightclub worldwide. By the late 1960s every girl in London wanted to be taken to Annabel's.

One evening I was dining with a girl whom I had known as a friend for two or three years. 'Will you take me to Annabel's?' she asked. 'If you will go to bed with me,' I replied flippantly. 'OK,' she said, and it was an exceptionally successful deal. Annabel's was good, and the rest was better – at least for me! Interestingly, that night enhanced rather than devalued our friendship.

At this time I became fully solvent for almost the first time in my life. When my mother died the terms of her will stipulated, wisely, that my inheritance should be held in trust until I was aged 25. I had passed the winning post, paid the bookmakers, and thought about buying a new car.

I had also been doing a job in the latter part of the year. Tom Blackwell, a member of the Jockey Club and a director of Turf Newspapers Ltd, invited me to work as assistant editor on a publication called the *Tote Racing Annual*. The offices were conveniently situated in Clarges Street, Mayfair, and the workload was not overwhelming. I was overdue to submit to a work discipline, but the drawback was trying to stay awake after a liquid lunch! In the end our *Annual* was well received, although there was one glaring omission: I just could not get hold of a suitable picture of Arthur Stephenson!

An office party was held at the Washington Hotel, during which my secretary, Jane Fenton – who had found me infuriating to work with – finally unleashed all of her repressions. We settled our differences in a way that appeared to satisfy both of us.

By the early autumn I knew that the time had come to think about a full-time job, after almost three years of a fantasy lifestyle. It was Peter Scott who drew my attention to a BBC advertisement in the *Sporting Life* during the St Leger meeting. I replied, mainly as a courtesy to Peter.

Television? I knew nothing about it. I had grown up with radio and the voice of Raymond Glendenning, whose commentaries I had often imitated at school. I was soon to learn.

# EIGHT

# *Cresta Capers*

The BBC's television coverage of the Coronation in 1953 introduced a vast proportion of the British people to the attractions of 'live' TV. The Coronation coverage was a triumph for the Outside Broadcasts department, attracting a vast audience of over 20 million. Sales and rentals of TV sets doubled overnight.

It was the first time I had watched television and my reaction was mixed. My mother did not buy a set until 1957, but I have no recollection of feelings of deprivation. When racing at Goodwood was on television I would go round to the Berners' butler's pantry! The other big televised race meetings, Cheltenham and Royal Ascot, took place during school term-time.

I began my career with BBC TV on 1 January 1966, but it has to be said that there was something of a false start. After being introduced to my new colleagues – mostly production staff – on the Monday morning, I was allocated a desk in the stage manager's office. Ron Pantlin took me under his wing: the immediate effect of that arrangement was that by the end of lunchtime on my first day I had consumed six bottles of Guinness in the BBC Club.

It was soon evident that a severe winter was imminent and that racing would be frozen to a standstill. After two weeks in my new job, therefore, I had the nerve to ask if I could take ten days' holiday! Sensibly the request was granted and I was off to St Moritz with Chris Collins.

When Chris had finished third in the Grand National on Mr Jones, the fourth horse to finish was Rainbow Battle owned by the champion point-to-point jockey and all-round sportsman, Bill

Shand-Kydd. Now Bill had challenged Chris to go down the Cresta Run. 'You may think you're Captain Magnificent after Aintree,' said Bill, 'but if you want a taste of *real* danger and excitement you'd better come out and ride the Cresta.' Chris had no option but to comply, and I was invited to provide moral support.

The Cresta Run is three quarters of a mile of hard ice, carved out of snow and watered nightly to create a fresh frozen surface, in temperatures as cold as minus 10 degrees. It was created in 1884 by an Englishman called Major Bulpetts, and both the course and sport evolved gradually until it became an Olympic event in the winter games of 1948. The run drops 514 feet over its passage from the village of St Moritz down to Celerina, at the foot of the valley. During its course, ten bends or corners of varying severity must be negotiated.

The toboggan (or skeleton) has no steering as such, so navigation is achieved by movement of the rider's body, adjustment of grip and use of the toe-end of the boot. A skeleton with extra lead screwed on can weigh up to 60 kilos. The more weight that it carries the faster it travels down the ice; equally, the more likely it is to carry its rider up the ice-bank and over the lip of the flattest and longest bend, Shuttlecock.

Riders travel head-first down the ice with face and chin no more than eight inches from the ice. On the lower banks, speeds rise to 70-80 mph. All riders wear obligatory protection – helmet, goggles, knee and elbow pads and metal handguards. These latter protect the unskilled rider from disfiguring damage on the hard ice wall. Thighs and shoulders receive tolerable bruising. The worst damage is likely to be sustained in falling off a skeleton during the run, notably during a 'Cresta kiss' – ice against the face.

No device protects against an awkward landing in the straw over Shuttlecock. The ultimate penalty is a broken neck. Fatalities are rare, but broken bones are plentiful, especially from falls on the less-well cushioned landing points on the upper banks.

The Cresta Run is unique. There are bobsleigh runs now world-wide and the 'bob' is an established Olympic event. But there is only one Cresta, and the St Moritz Tobogganing Club remains one of the most exclusive clubs in the world.

I knew none of this as I accompanied Chris on the flight to Zurich and on the four-hour train journey to the Engadine Valley village which, over the next 20 years, was to give me as much pleasure and excitement as any sporting activity in the world. I had agreed to come as a Cresta spectator, for just one morning, while the rest of the trip would be devoted to skiing. That 'one morning' was to change my whole winter sports perspective.

A novice rider is known as an 'SL' (supplementary-list rider). He is obliged to wait until no club member wishes, or is available to, use the Run. (Nowadays it is so popular that SLs are compelled to arrive and 'sign on' at 7.30 am so that they can use the run before the members arrive at 9.00 am.) The beginner is obliged to ride from Junction, a starting point about one-third of the way down the run, opposite the clubhouse and changing room.

The riders from 'Top' are already travelling at 40-50 mph by the time they pass Junction, while a beginner, starting from a prone position from Junction, has a far better chance of negotiating Shuttlecock. As Chris was introduced to the club by Bill Shand-Kydd, I took position on the spectators' ledge at the famous bend.

It was awesome to behold – an experience similar to watching a steeplechase from the last fence. A rider's arrival is signalled by a gentle crescendo of metal against ice, bursting into a sudden explosion of raking, clouded by ice-dust and followed by a rapid-fire adjustment of hands and sliding seat. Within seconds the rider is a fading, departing vision, accelerating into the lower banks. It is violent, and it is enthralling. A shiver passes through the body, just as a spectator. Sometimes, of course, the rider does not disappear into the distance; instead the sound and ice-spray stops suddenly as the rider hurtles over the edge. Then there is an eerie silence until the bell rings from the control tower and the unhappy individual is invited to indicate that he has no broken limbs and is able to return unassisted.

This, then, was the challenge that faced Chris on Monday

7 January 1966. The fastest time recorded from Junction in those days was around 44 seconds; Chris travelled down the run, very cautiously as advised, in a time approaching a minute and a half. 'Well,' said I jokingly, 'I wasn't very impressed with that!' 'All right,' said Chris, 'you go down and we'll see how impressive you are!'

I made every excuse under the sun, but not one of them was viewed as remotely acceptable. Bill would introduce me; riding kit was available from the club; my credit was good; and there were several club skeletons available for use by beginners. Almost before I could draw breath I was changed, kitted out and standing by the ice wall awaiting the brusque summons of the legendary secretary, Fairchilds McCarthy: 'Wilson to the box'. It might have been 'Wilson to the gallows' – that was how it felt.

A sickening, hollow, aching feeling in the pit of the stomach overwhelms the first-time rider. There is also a prickling flush of heat, followed by clammy cold. Instructions are issued by a senior rider which are impossible to absorb. Is your kit in place (helmet on, goggles down, chinstrap fixed, handguards on, . . .)? And then – 'Don't forget to rake . . . don't go too fast . . . keep your seat back . . .'. The bell rings and your instructor removes his boot from the front of the skeleton. You are about to ride the Cresta Run. One thing is certain: there is no stopping, or turning back.

My first passage to Shuttlecock was, in fact, reasonably controlled, with the help of boot-rakes speared into the ice. It was after Shuttlecock – a reasonably safe period in terms of lateral banks – that the exhilaration began. The first shock was on slamming into the ice wall opposite to Shuttlecock with my metal-protected left hand: that was like crushing a hand in a car door. From the left wall you bounce to the right wall and slam the opposite hand. But the pain was overriden by the exhilarating speed, the awareness of the ice rushing by and the escalating wind-roar in the ears. By the lower banks I was happily out of control – there were more scrapes and minor bumps, but speed was the overriding sensation. At the end the feeling was of breathlessness and the instant analogy of having boxed three rounds with Sonny Liston!

Chris never went down the Cresta again, but I was addicted. For the rest of my holiday I checked in at the clubhouse each morning at 9.00 am sharp. On some days an 'SL' would have two rides, sometimes three; and on very quiet days for members, even four. By the end of the ten days I was posting respectable times and applied to become a member of the club. I was accepted and paid my annual subscription of £5.

How times change! My list of bankers' orders the following year read as follows:

| | |
|---|---|
| *The Apron Strings* [gambling club] | *1 guinea* |
| *The Casanova* | *2 guineas* |
| *Les Ambassadeurs* [Garrison] | *3 guineas* |
| *AA* | *3 guineas* |
| *BUPA* | *£4 7s 0d* |
| *St Moritz Tobogganing Club* | *£5 0s 0d* |
| *Sybilla's* | *7 guineas* |

Thirty years later, in 1997, the AA charged £88 for their services, while the Family Health Plan cost £1841.24! Inflation, or what?

I was enslaved by the Run and returned to St Moritz each year until 1971, when my bride suggested that the Cresta was an inappropriate location for a honeymoon!

In 1967, I formed an attachment to a particular skeleton belonging to the club, called 'Hotblack'. It suited my style of riding ideally and the balance was perfect. Evidently it had belonged many years earlier to a Major Hotblack. That year I stayed in a hotel called Caspar Badrutt in the centre of St Moritz. In the adjacent room was a fascinating old racing figure called Chris Jarvis, whose son – also Chris – worked for the Press Association gathering news of riding arrangements, before the days of overnight declared jockeys. Chris senior had spent holidays in St Moritz with Sir Gordon Richards, who spent many winters in the Engardine, skiing and curling. Chris revealed that he had helped Gordon to choose and organize his outside rides, as well as helping with certain other activities connected with betting!

I was obsessed with the Cresta, but would ski for a couple of hours after taking lunch at the Sunny Bar in the Kulm Hotel. The Cresta Run was closed at mid-day when the high sun melted the ice, but the Bob Run, on the other side of the road, was protected and remained open in the afternoon.

One morning I met a Cresta 'follower', Carolyn Michael. She was in St Moritz with an Old Harrovian called James Manclark, who rode the Cresta in the morning and spent the afternoon on the Bob Run. Carolyn was visibly bored and wanted to ski, so we became skiing companions on several afternoons. When we returned home we exchanged telephone numbers but I did not contact her until July.

We had dinner together on 10 July, and three and a half years later we were married. Carolyn became the mother of my son.

On returning to St Moritz in 1968, I was determined to have a crack at winning a race. 'Hotblack' was flying, but the one blot on the horizon was a friend called Richard Wrottesley ('Old Rotters') who also had fallen in love with that skeleton. Inevitably it created a problem if we were both riding in the same race.

We both entered for the Lady Ribblesdale Cup, in which I was given a very fair handicap mark off which it was felt that I had a reasonable chance. It was snowing on the day which slowed up both the run and the faster (scratch) riders, whereas I could take risks on the slower surface. It was Rotters' beautiful wife, Georgina, who solved the problem of the skeleton. Normally, they would be returned to the clubhouse from the bottom of the run on a large lorry (the 'cameon'), in batches of 10 or 12, but Georgina drove her car up and down the hill frantically, to ferry 'Hotblack' after each of our rides.

After two rounds of the race I was comfortably clear and looked certain to win. But Rotters pulled a remarkable final ride out of the bag, so that, incredibly, we dead-heated over the three rides, to one-hundredth of a second! Under the rules we were expected to 'ride off', but the combination of worsening conditions and the extraordinary situation over 'Hotblack' – it would have meant a gap of several minutes between rides – made the obvious decision a 'dead-heat'. We had made history: it was the first-ever dead-heat in the history of the Run.

The celebrations afterwards in the Sunny Bar were explosive. Rotters was hugely popular and it was his first win after several years of trying. The snow had now set in and the high jinks were taking root. But my celebrations were brutally curtailed as a telegram arrived from Harry Middleton which read as follows:

DIMMOCK AND COWGILL AND ALL THE RESTA
WISH YOU THE VERY BEST OF LUCK ON THE CRESTA
WE ALL HOPE THAT YOU'LL BE TRIUMPHANT ON SUNDAY
BUT IT'S THE SALT MINES FOR YOU IF YOU'RE NOT BACK ON MONDAY

I was to fly home that evening for a meeting the following day. Since the previous November, following a major outbreak of foot-and-mouth disease, horseracing had been banned, first in agricultural areas and finally over the entire country. Now there was to be a vital meeting with the Ministry of Agriculture, with the possibility of a recommencement of racing at Newbury at the weekend. Old Rotters was planning a major party – and so was I – but I would not be there. On reflection it probably saved me a fortune!

There was, however, a tragic sequel to the story of 'Hotblack'. Richard Wrottesley was killed in a car crash in Ireland two years later. He had bought 'Hotblack' from the club and in his will he requested that our beloved skeleton be buried with him. I thus said 'goodbye' to two special friends. In all the subsequent years at St Moritz I never did find a skeleton that suited my style so well.

It gives me great delight to see the name of Wrottesley amongst the top British Cresta riders of today. Richard's son Clifton, the

Sixth Baron Wrottesley, won no fewer than six races in 1997, including the Grand National.

Despite the 'Who's Who' list of members, there is nothing snobbish or élitist about the Tobogganing Club. As a Cresta joke, there is an annual race between the aristocracy of England and Europe (the Hon's and Von's Race). Rotters was an active supporter of the race. But Cresta riding, like so many dangerous sports, creates a brotherhood bound by courage and danger. On the ice all men are equal. The experience and exhilaration of reaching Celerina is an accomplishment that breaks down barriers of class and nationality. On that basic precept, the St Moritz Tobogganing Club remains, in my view, the friendliest, most companionable club in the world.

It was to be 18 years before I won my second race on the Cresta. I had only returned to St Moritz once in the interim, in 1973. This visit occurred because in 1972, Sandy Gall, the ITN newscaster, had produced a magnificent film about the Cresta Run. I arranged for the BBC to buy transmission rights, re-edited and dubbed it, and transmitted it in 'Grandstand'.

Clement Freud was on the telephone to me that evening: 'Is there any reasonable expectation that I could survive that experience you described today?' he queried in that familiar mournful manner. 'I think you'd enjoy it,' I replied. The consequence was that Freud was commissioned by the *Daily Telegraph* magazine to do a picture story of his personal battle with the Run. It was a courageous enterprise – Freud was 49 at the time.

We travelled over on 21 January. It was a terrific trip, climaxed by Freud taking over a small but delightful restaurant in St Moritz-Bad, where he prepared a memorable dish for all who had helped him in the previous ten days. He had progressed from an initial ride on which he almost, historically, came to a halt – such was the strength of his legs and thus breaking power – to a final run of conspicuous respectability. His published feature was a masterpiece, memorable also for a front cover of the author with toboggan, looking balefully – or resignedly? – down the run, and his now widely quoted description of the Run as 'the ultimate laxative'! Certainly, the dressing room lavatories are not the most sweet-scented area of St Moritz on a race-day morning.

My next return to St Moritz came as a sequel to Steve Cauthen's house-warming party at Stetchworth in April 1985. Steve had arrived in Newmarket to ride for Henry Cecil's stable after six years as contract jockey to Barry Hills at Lambourn, and he had been offered a stud cottage at Stetchworth Park by the owner-breeder Bill Gredley. Earlier in the day there had been a Vodaphone promotional lunch at the Bedford Lodge Hotel. After lunch we were invited to Stevie's, where a case of champagne had been delivered as a moving-in present. We were joined by Jimmy Lindley, Walter Swinburn and finally Bill Gredley himself.

By 6 pm little remained of Stevie's present. In the circumstances it is not easy to be specific as to how the subject arose, but I became aware that Walter was regaling his audience of his experiences that spring on the Cresta Run. 'That sounds a promising start, Walter,' I said patronizingly. From that harmless remark developed a challenge that was to take us to St Moritz the following January.

It was 12 years since I had ridden the Cresta, but I firmly believed, in the rosy glow of champagne, that it was an art that stayed with you. A bet of £500 was struck with Walter, the winner to be the fastest rider over three runs. Stevie said dryly: 'I'm backing Walter,' and his bet was the same. Bill Gredley looked at the greying, good-living, fantasy rider in front of him and saw the easiest £500 that he had ever earned. 'I'll have a monkey,' was all that he said. Jimmy Lindley, mindful of the possible folly of irritating his BBC employer, bit his tongue.

So it was that on Saturday 28 December 1985, I returned to my beloved Engadine Valley. There were, of course, many changes at the club – new people, new hotels, a new secretary (Digby Willoughby), and a computerized results and performance bank.

It was so long since I had been to St Moritz that no record of my previous riding existed: I was starting from scratch. There was no trace of my old boots, and my helmet was condemned! Its shallow comfort had long been outdated by stringent new safety standards. I was profoundly unhappy.

For the first three days I slipped around in the launching box, wearing club boots with an almost flat surface. What spikes they possessed had been worn almost level by the passage of time. I was flopping on to my skeleton from almost a standing start! Swinburn's spies no doubt fed him the encouraging news that my times were poor. Clearly, I was yesterday's man.

On New Year's Eve I went out to buy a new pair of boots, with sharply honed spikes, and entered for the Escalante Cup on New Year's Day.

At teatime in St Moritz a sheet is available in the Kurverein (the Information Centre) listing the handicaps allotted for a race the following day. My posted handicap caused me both amazement and embarrassment: I had been given a handicap which merely required me to turn up, ride and stay in the run!

We saw in the New Year at our hotel, the Steffani, run superbly (and with special terms for Cresta riders) by the Marki family. There was a glittering dinner/dance and a spectacular 'Welcome' to 1986. We shared a table with Johnny and Phillipa Winter and danced into the early hours.

I also had a companion in my second wife, Alison, who remarked, jokingly, that Johnny Winter's heart had been racing when he danced with her. To our horror, we heard in the morning that Johnny had been taken to hospital with a seriously raised and irregular heartbeat which was difficult to control. That put a damper on the entire trip.

There was a huge field of 35 for the Escalante, but I won the race with embarrassing ease, by over half a second. My new boots had improved my practice times by two or three seconds and I received some old-fashioned looks. But the runners up, Alex Meyer and Aris Ziros, were genuinely pleased for me. It was a fairytale return. I had almost forgotten how to conduct a 'Firework' – the collective victory ritual – but the magic that I had largely missed in 1968 was all the sweeter the second time around.

Walter Swinburn arrived the following day to the dramatic news that he was about to face the winner of the Escalante! He brought with him a lively party, including his boisterous brother Michael and the trainer James Fanshawe. They interpolinated with a group of army riders and there were some extremely noisy evenings at the Steffani and surrounding areas. The patience of the local gendarmerie was finally exhausted by a snowball fight at 4 am in the entrance to a leading hotel!

If Walter's preparation for the race was unorthodox, his times were improving by the day. A small element of doubt crept into the outcome. Nigel Dempster wrote, in a preview of the event: 'The smaller man may win because of less wind resistance!'

The great day finally arrived – Tuesday 7 January. I was still ahead in practice, but would Walter, with his celebrated big-race temperament, come good on the day? The story of the race had swept around St Moritz and there was an unusually large crowd, including several Swinburn 'groupies', on the terrace of the clubhouse. It was all over fairly quickly. I clocked 48.82 seconds on my first run, while Walter failed to break 52 seconds until his third and final run.

I was amazed at the interest and publicity that the event generated. Back at the Steffani, after a celebration at the Sunny Bar, I was interviewed 'live' on BBC Radio, while several press men telephoned from England. Now it was just a question of collecting the money. This was the hard bit!

Bill Gredley, to his credit, settled on the day of my return and Steve Cauthen delivered not long afterwards. Walter, who has an erratic accountancy policy, was less prompt. By the start of the Flat, on 20 March, settlement was yet to arrive. Walter rode a winner at Doncaster on day one and was interviewed by Brough Scott, who referred to his winter activities, the race on the Cresta, and Walter's defeat. 'Yes, but Julian cheated. He went out earlier than me to practice!' he claimed. The next day he received the following letter on the headed notepaper of a well-known firm of local solicitors:

*Dear Mr Swinburn*

*DONCASTER/CHANNEL 4 – 21ST MARCH 1998*

*I am instructed by our client Mr Julian Wilson, to institute proceedings against you for alleged libel and defamation of character following your broadcast with Mr Brough Scott at Doncaster on Friday March 21st.*

*Our client has drawn to our attention certain intemperate comments made by you, suggesting a lack of integrity on the part of our client.*

*This suggestion was extremely damaging to our client, who enjoys an unparalleled reputation for honesty and fair play in the eyes of the British public. In view of the seriousness of the matter, I am instructed to take immediate action against you, and press for substantial damages.*

*We would ask you please to send Mr Wilson a written acknowledgement of receipt of this letter.*

*Yours sincerely*

*PS. Mr Wilson instructs us that he may consider settling out of Court in the sum of £500.*

The letter was opened by Walter's mother, Doreen, who read through it, ignored the 'PS' and telephoned Walter and his trainer Michael Stoute in horror. 'How could Julian do this? I thought they were friends!', wailed Doreen. When the spoof became public knowledge Walter was shamed into settlement, and he has waged a war of attrition ever since! We spent the winnings on a memorable dinner for about two dozen at Au Jardin des Gourmets, in Soho.

A re-match was arranged for the following year, but was cancelled when I pulled a muscle while skiing. It was generous of Walter to accept my withdrawal. He was closing on me all the time.

The next year, David Gower and Allan Lamb came out to St Moritz with a friend, Simon Strong, who introduced them to the

Run. Their riding proved a fascinating character study. 'Lamby' started cautiously and clocked a first ride almost as slow as Clement Freud! From there on he improved gradually and consistently. Once he had 'sussed' the bowling, he went out and played some shots! Gower, meanwhile, went 'gungho' into a fast first time, and then was slower his second time down. On day two he went for gold and crashed at Shuttlecock on his second ride! Both men live life to the full and are marvellous companions. It was inevitable that Gower would make his mark on St Moritz, but four years later he did so in an unexpected way!

Nowadays, cricket is played on the lake during February and teams come from all over the world for the annual 'Cricket On Ice'. It is an unusual variation, played on an artificial surface with a rubber-like ball, but the outfield is all ice. At 5000 metres the altitude seals the bowler's breath, so few bowl off a long run.

Gower had heard about the impending cricket and long after midnight decided to drive his car across the lake to inspect the wicket. While he was at it he simulated the driving at Hendon Police College, spinning the vehicle all over the ice. Unfortunately he attempted to drive off the ice at an unsuitable spot, to find his wheels first of all skidding and eventually sinking into the shallow ice. The following morning his car was totally immersed!

I was to visit St Moritz just twice more, each time with my son Thomas, now an enthusiastic and skilful skier. There was a small problem: Thomas was having more fun in the evening than his father!

The first year, because my wife Alison had become disenchanted with skiing, I brought a 'minder' – Pippa, the daughter of a friend – to ski with Thomas and get him into bed at night. Fat chance. Thomas is a night-owl, so it became a battle of wits. Thomas was immovable and simply refused to leave a scene that was his idea of Eldorado. Pippa was dying to join the 'young' while I was yearning to slip away for a quiet whisky and soda at the King's Club.

The final straw came in 1989. Thomas, now 15, had become almost unmanageable. On our last night I gave up the unequal battle with my son, who was drinking happily at the bar with a companionable middle-aged lady, whose worst vice appeared to be an addiction to smoking. I went to bed, cursing the Wilson heritage of nocturnal stamina. In the morning I went to thank our hosts for their usual kindness and to pay the bill. 'I am afraid,' said Peter Marki, 'that we will have to charge you for the fire damage.'

'What?' I demanded. 'There hasn't been any fire damage!' 'Oh yes,' said Peter, 'last night, in your son's room. The fire brigade were here at 3 am We were very concerned.' I was speechless – my son! 3 am! Eventually the miscreant appeared, bang on departure time, white as a sheet and mumbling assent to the charges as laid. We had almost reached Chur on the train before I demanded to be told what had happened. 'Well Dad,' he offered, 'it was an accident. I was just flicking that lighter that I had bought for mother, when it fell out of my hand and set fire to my duvet. Then the table caught fire, and . . . ' At that point I stopped him, thinking that it was the best story he was likely to come up with. He has never confessed the truth of the conflagration, but for some reason the expression 'toy boy' keeps recurring in my brain.

How I loved that wonderful place, but I knew that it was time to stop. A heavy fall at Shuttlecock – while wearing a new 'approved' helmet – had damaged my neck so severely that I was unable to serve overarm at tennis for 18 months. I had broken 47 seconds from Junction riding an old club toboggan in my final year. It was a good time to finish.

The following year I would be 50. I said goodbye to the Toboggan Club staff for the last time and surrendered my locker. It was a misty moment – I shall think about the Cresta on the day that I die.

# NINE

# *Under Orders*

Towards the end of that first trip to St Moritz the weather back in England had relented and racing resumed on 24 January 1966. I returned home on 27 January. The BBC, understandably, were anxious to avoid throwing me in at the deep end. Unlike the other television racecallers, I had no experience of racecourse commentary. I was starting from scratch and needed practice. For several weeks, when the BBC had a Saturday fixture, I would undertake a couple of 'mock' commentaries in broadcast conditions on the Friday. For the time being Peter Bromley – who had rejected my job, preferring to stay with BBC Radio – was Peter O'Sullevan's understudy, while Michael Seth-Smith was the interviewer.

By the end of February, Dennis Monger felt that I was ready, so on Saturday 5 March my name appeared in the *Radio Times* for the first time – 'Racing from Newbury. Commentary: Julian Wilson and Clive Graham'.

Meanwhile my plan to race-ride was on the back-burner. I had sold Regis to a gentleman called Mr Lake from Norwich for £50 profit and the promise of two rides in point-to-points. Mr Lake sent him to Albert Ketteringham, one of the top point-to-point trainers in East Anglia. Then on 15 February I received a letter from Ketteringham:

> *We are running Regis at Moulton point-to-point course near Newmarket on Saturday week the 26th. All being well you can have the ride if you wish, but any alteration I will let you know . . .*

I had just ten days to get fit, gather together some kit, and acquaint myself with Moulton, so I started running furiously and booked myself in with Lilo Blum. Then, during the week of the race, Albert Ketteringham telephoned: 'He's not quite ready, that horse. I'm waiting a week with him. You can ride him on 5 March if you wish.' And that was the beginning and end of my career as a putative amateur rider. On 5 March I had a prior engagement, and I was to have similar engagements on most Saturdays for the next 32 years. Regis performed capably in point-to-points, but the following season reverted to hurdle racing and won at Fakenham. What might have been!

On Friday 4 March I rehearsed for my big day at Newbury races and then joined the production team at the Bacon Arms in the evening. Dennis Monger was determined to keep me relaxed. He poured burgundy down my throat during dinner and, to enhance my confidence, related repeated anecdotes of the incompetence and inadequacy of other commentators. I could not claim to have eaten robustly, nor indeed did I sleep soundly. The vision of a tight-rope walker, on a narrow piece of wire, high above a circus ring, with no net to be seen, was a recurring nightmare.

The great day arrived and Dennis's suggestion was to have a quick sharpener to settle the nerves. I had a vodka and orange juice, which I sipped half-heartedly. For the second time in six weeks I was almost rigid with terror. It is hard to equate the fear of facing the Cresta Run, and your first broadcast, but in this case I had had a great deal longer to think about it. That did not help.

I remember very little of the three races that I called, but there appeared to be no catastrophic mistakes and the first three home were nominated in the correct order. With genuine amazement I received a charming letter from Dorothy Herdman, the mother of Doone and Bunny, the following week:

> *I thought your commentary was first class and you sound like a veteran with years of practice behind you.*

Well, the Irish were always prone to exaggeration! Peter Dimmock, however, was less eulogistic: 'You'd better go down to tele-cine and look at the recording.'

The essence of television commentary is to balance what is evident to the naked eye with the image that appears on the viewer's screen. It is hopeless describing a scenario which the viewer cannot see, or which looks different on screen. From a racecaller's standpoint there is a sharp conflict between the perspective that he views from the grandstand and the image transmitted by cameras shooting from a different angle in the country. The secret is always to keep one eye on the television monitor. It is not an easy technique to master, especially on day one. Furthermore, in 1966 the pictures were still in black and white.

But I was on my way! Ten days later I recorded the first race of the Cheltenham Festival as a sound test for BBC Radio. David Coleman was presenting the television coverage for the final time. I was then used as a 'gopher', but my turn would come.

My relationship with Coleman was always uneasy. He felt, with some justification, that he had a standing in the horse world. His daughters were successful competition riders and, apart from Cheltenham, David presented the Grand National coverage, with considerable skill, until 1976, when he chose to seek his fortune abroad.

Coleman was certainly comfortable in the company of the National Hunt jockeys. What I resented was that he would always offer his opinion as definitive fact on a racing matter, rather than ask for my view. Our silent antagonism came to a head in the autumn of 1970.

The previous Sunday, Nijinsky had been narrowly beaten in the Prix de l'Arc de Triomphe. It was a heart-breaking defeat, but not entirely unexpected. The great horse had suffered severely from ringworm in the autumn; had a rushed preparation for the St Leger – his owner was anxious to win the Triple Crown; and boiled over alarmingly in the paddock at Longchamp as photographers flashed cameras at him from every angle. Lester Piggott rode an exemplary race and came to lead 100 yards from the finish, whereupon Nijinsky veered from a straight line and was caught in the shadow of the post by Sassafras, ridden by Yves Saint-Martin.

In racing, backing a loser is never the fault of the punter. He has invariably been robbed by (a) jockey error, (b) an incompetent trainer, (c) unbelievable bad luck, (d) a conspiracy to defraud him, or (e) all four. In this instance the bar-room critics picked on Lester and claimed that he gave Nijinsky too much to do in the straight.

On the Tuesday evening John McNicholas, the 'Sportsnight' production assistant, telephoned me at home and requested me to 'put some words' on the Arc coverage for transmission the following night. 'What sort of words?' I asked. 'Well, David wants you to illustrate that Nijinsky came from a long way back,' was the reply. 'He didn't come from that far back,' I countered, 'he only had half a dozen lengths to make up in the straight and is capable of doing that in a furlong. He just wasn't himself.'

'David would like you to dub it anyway,' said John.

'Well, don't expect me to criticize Piggott,' I said, 'he did nothing wrong.'

The following morning I voiced over the pictures, prompted by John, but provided no more than a factual description. To my horror, when 'Sportsnight' came on the air, who should be with Coleman but the controversial ex-jockey Charlie Smirke, retired for a decade and now bloated in appearance. Charlie spent much of his time on the golfcourse – and notably the 19th hole – around Epsom. Now Charlie had always had the green eye for Lester since the Irish 2000 Guineas of 1957. Smirke had won the Classic on a colt called Jack Ketch, trained by Eddie Quirke. After the race Lester joined the winning owner, Mary Annesley, and in his inimitable way muttered: 'Nice horse, that. I'll ride him for the rest of the year.'

Now, live on television, it was payback time for Smirke. He claimed that Lester had given Nijinsky far too much to do and that it was obligatory to be in the first six turning into the straight at Longchamp. He and Coleman concluded that Nijinsky should never have been beaten and that it was entirely Piggott's fault. I was livid, because my reportage had been used at the 'top' of the item so it appeared that I was in collusion with Coleman and Smirke.

The following morning I stormed into the office and fired off a memorandum to the editor of 'Sportsnight', copied to every other relevant individual, expressing my disgust and concluding that I would never work for the programme again. It was a hard-hitting document, including expressions like 'editorial integrity', 'betrayal' and 'deception'. It was even suggested by someone that I might care to sleep on it. I did not care to.

Within minutes of its delivery I received a summons from the head of sport, Brian Cowgill. Cowgill was a volatile, irascible individual, with a broad Lancashire accent and an exceptionally short fuse. He had worked his way up from teaboy at the local newspaper in Clitheroe, to the highest level of television. He was a remarkable achiever, but not a man to call a spade a garden implement.

'What the hell's this?' he said dryly, pointing at my memo. I reiterated my grievance but did not get very far. 'Who the f---ing hell do you think you are? You dare write this stuff and circulate it round the entire f---ing department. Do you want to work here or not?' I did, and furthermore, my contract was due for renewal within two months. So: 'Yes, Brian.' 'Well f--- off then. I'll tell you who you're f---ing working for, not you. You'll do what I f---ing say. Now piss off.'

Brian had been economical in his use of words, but his meaning was reasonably clear. I seethed with anger and Coleman and I avoided one another for the rest of the year.

Two weeks later Nijinsky ran in the Champion Stakes at Newmarket. Once again he boiled over in the paddock and, at long odds-on, was comfortably beaten by Lorenzaccio. This time there were no excuses.

All this was a long way ahead from that first Cheltenham Festival. Coleman asked me to find the legendary Michael O'Hehir for an interview. To my shame, although I was entirely familiar with his rich brown voice, I had no idea what O'Hehir looked like! It was a bad start.

I was to play only a peripheral role in the Grand National coverage, but my 'Sportsview' feature, on the amateur riders featured in the race, was fun to film. The BBC's coverage of the race was submitted as an entry for the Eurovision Outside Broadcast Festival, but unluckily it was a dull race and so missed the Golden Rose.

It was at Royal Ascot that I was given my head for the first time. In those early days the majority of programmes were introduced by commentators out of vision, presenter-led outside broadcasts being still years away. So Peter O'Sullevan would welcome the audience and set the scene without ever being seen on the screen. I was to conduct interviews between the races.

The first day went reasonably well. We were a friendly team, and Dennis Monger, Judith Chalmers (our fashion expert) and I shared a bottle of champagne after the show. On the evening of the second day Chris Collins gave a fabulous party at The Garrison to celebrate his becoming champion amateur jockey. It was a terrific achievement. Chris stood 6ft 2in in his socks and spent 20 hours a week in Turkish baths to keep his weight down to 10st 10lb. While he had studied accountancy he weighed 13½ st. He was driving over 1000 miles a week between his home in Buckinghamshire, the races and Arthur Stephenson's stables in County Durham. 'Noel Day' had pointed his readers in the right direction the previous December; I had backed him to win the title at 8/1!

The Garrison was bedecked with the blue and white of Chris's racing colours. The dinner was superb and the wines of top quality. We danced into the night. After midnight I smooched with the attractive wife of an elderly baronet. 'Why don't we go to Annabel's?' she whispered. 'What about your husband?' I replied. 'Oh don't worry, Billy and I always come home separately from Annabel's.' But I did not want to leave Chris's party: I stayed far, far too late.

For the remainder of the week I was below par. Fighting Charlie won the Ascot Gold Cup and I interviewed his trainer Freddie Maxwell.

But on Friday I ran into a brick wall. George Cadwaladr rode a 440/1 double and I interviewed him after his success on My Audrey in the Wokingham Stakes. I had been briefed that George's father worked as head lad for the Tarporley trainer Eric Cousins. Unhappily, as I was eventually to learn, this was not the case.

'Do you come from a racing background?' I asked. 'No,' replied George. So I followed with: 'Is your father in any way connected with racing?' 'No,' was the terse response. Desperation crept into my voice. I was pleading: 'So your father is not, for instance, a head lad?' to which he said simply 'No'.

Thus was a harsh lesson brutally learned. Unfortunately it was learned rather publicly in front of three million viewers. It was an interview that was remembered – at least by my critics – for years to come.

The following week 'Lorimer', the anonymous columnist in the *Horse and Hound*, wrote of 'the unconvincing young interviewer . . . with long curls tumbling on to his stiff collar . . .' It was not for many years that I learned the identity of Lorimer: it was the legendary Dorian Williams, whose commentaries adorned show-jumping while the sport was at its peak. Dorian wrote to me a charming letter after Cheltenham one year, revealed his identity and we became friends.

It was during the week after Royal Ascot that I bought my first racehorse for the Flat. I had talked my way into it at the wedding of an old friend, Aubrene Hobbs, earlier in the year. Aubrene had been a wide-eyed 14-year-old when I was in Newmarket in 1961. Her father, Bruce, was assistant trainer at the time to Captain Cecil Boyd-Rochfort. Now, in February 1966, she was a beautiful teenage bride. Bruce had been set up as a trainer in the historic Palace House Stables in Newmarket.

Several glasses into the reception, I asked rashly: 'Bruce, if you've ever got anything in the yard that should be bought, let me know.' These are magic words to a racehorse trainer – words that he will not allow himself to forget! Four months later, Bruce was on the line: 'Listen, I've got a horse here that might suit you.' It was an unraced chestnut two-year-old colt by St Crespin III, and had been given the name Tenth Man. A dispute with the owner had resulted in the colt being on the market, but it remained in the yard. Bruce liked him so I bought him. It was an investment that I came to regret in trumps. But Whitebridge (as I renamed him) was to teach me more about racing and owning racehorses than 16 years of reading about the sport.

Towards the end of 1966 I bought my first house. I had inherited a relatively small sum from my mother after death duties and I invested the balance in a two-bedroomed house in First Street, Chelsea – bolstered by a hefty mortgage.

First Street, which runs between Milner Street and Walton Street, is an interesting area of real estate. The houses were built in the nineteenth century to accommodate workers on the Great Exhibition. Now the 18 houses closest to Milner Street were freehold properties, while the others remained in the ownership of the Cadogan Estate and were leased to council tenants, at a rent of £2 a week. Inevitably, there was a loophole in this arrangement and some of the council leases were acquired by shrewd property entrepreneurs who refurbished the houses and sold on the leases for six-figure sums!

My house was enchanting, with two storeys, a bathroom at half-way house and a further bedroom and bathroom in the basement, which led out into a medium-sized garden. It was a perfect area in which to live. There were high-class restaurants within walking distance, two popular pubs in The Australian and Admiral Codrington, shops in Walton Street (including a laundry and dry-cleaner), while my delightful daily woman lived in no. 52 so was on hand in a crisis!

There was also a property nearby which housed four attractive and helpful girls, all of whom were to marry into racing – Sue Balding (who became Sue Perkins), Jane Adams (Sheppard), Penny Greenslade (Pope) and Emma Hastings-Bass, who became Mrs Ian Balding. Emma and Penny would come to 'waitress' when I gave a party. Jane, married to breeding-industry regulator Sam Sheppard, has been a near-neighbour in Suffolk for 20 years.

BBC television covered 89 days' racing in that first year of 1966. I was allocated 11 commentary days (while Peter O'Sullevan was elsewhere, or on holiday), 10 paddock commentary days, and 29 days of interviewing.

On the day of the Cesarewitch, I was to learn another discomforting lesson. Newmarket was one of the six long-term contracted racecourses covered by BBC-TV; the others were Ascot, Cheltenham, Goodwood, Liverpool and Newbury. Kempton had slipped the net for a couple of years, opting for a financially disastrous contract with Pay-TV. The Derby was covered by the BBC in competition with ITV on the basis of its status as a 'national event'.

We also covered – on an *ad hoc* basis – racing at Ayr, Chepstow, Haydock, Lanark, Lingfield, Newcastle, Stockton, Stratford, Uttoxeter, Wetherby and Windsor. Two of those meetings, Chepstow and Haydock, were to become long-term contracted courses, under the vibrant management of the late John Hughes. It is sad to reflect, however, that seven of the remaining courses are no longer covered by the BBC, while Stockton (Teeside) is defunct.

We covered just ten days a year at Newmarket, thereby excluding the Craven and July meetings and two days of the second October meeting. On the July course, where the runners are out of sight from the grandstand over distances beyond a mile, we used two commentators. Then I was positioned four furlongs down the course. On the Rowley Mile course we had the same system for all races beyond six furlongs. During the mid-week, while I was interviewing, Michael Seth-Smith would be sent to the Devil's Dyke, while on Saturdays I would take over as 'country' commentator.

No-one warned me about the Cesarewitch. I was to cover the first mile-and-a-half of the race, which entailed standing in a small, badly sited hut on the Devil's Dyke, looking straight into a low, shimmering, autumn sun, attempting to locate and identify 30 horses that were the best part of a mile away. The black and white monitor, skilfully located so that the sun shone straight into it, showed small specks in the far distance!

I have never listened to a recording of that 1967 Cesarewitch and hope never to be invited to do so. The winner, Boismoss, made almost every yard of the running. It is to be hoped that at some stage in the race I was able to identify his pale grey colours in the grey haze of the sun. The only consolation was that, with a colourless picture, the audience would have had difficulty in identifying my many inaccuracies.

The following year I made a plan. This entailed researching four or five runners who were likely to lead, or be prominent, in the early stages, and inventing a 'script' for the early part of the race. When the runners finally became identifiable, after a seemingly endless first mile of the race, I was ecstatic that four of my five 'leaders' were correct.

I had mixed feelings when the BBC lost the Newmarket contact in 1968, fearing that I might be indirectly responsible. When I interviewed Clement Freud on the draughty Rowley Mile course, his opening shot was along the lines of: 'When Sir Robert Scott of the Antarctic cried "Good God, this is an awful place", I think he must have meant Newmarket.'

But there was a deeper agenda. The Jockey Club wanted more money and Peter Dimmock was calling their bluff. At the time there existed an agreement between BBC and ITV not to bid for each other's racecourses, so as to depress the value of contracts. But ITV were punching below the belt: they offered Newmarket 20 days' coverage of racing, against the BBC's 10 days, and were thus able to almost double the BBC's financial offer.

To Dimmock's horror, he was advised that the deal was a *fait accompli*. Thus we had lost our last two Classic races and the 'autumn double'. Dimmock was stunned. It was the start of a 'dirty war' between BBC and ITV. Two or three years later, when Brian Cowgill learned of a football match arranged with ITV Sport, he gave instructions that under no circumstances was the match to be played. I was telephoned to that effect at 2 am. These were the days of fierce, head-to-head rivalry with the competitor, and I loved it! By contrast, in 1997, we were blithely giving away events to Channel 4 Racing as if we were a charitable organization.

There was a bitter-sweet ending to 1966. With Kempton – and therefore the King George VI Steeplechase – covered exclusively by Pay-TV, we were obliged to go elsewhere. Perversely, we chose the two-day meeting at Wolverhampton. While Arkle was breaking his pedal bone, and suffering defeat by Dormant in the shock story of the year, we were spending the festive season in the shadow of a railway embankment in the Black Country. But some good came out of it for me. Clive Graham was working at Kempton for the *Daily Express*, and I took over his paddock duties at Wolverhampton. There was a delay at the start of one race, so I had the chance to broaden my commentary. Brian Cowgill, for the first time, expressed himself as satisfied with my work!

Towards the end of December I rang Brian Venner, the producer of 'Sportsview', in a state of excitement. I had heard that George Moore, the legendary Australian jockey, would be coming to England in 1967 to ride as contract jockey for Noel Murless. He was to replace Lester Piggott, whose bluff had been called by Murless. Lester wanted a non-exclusive deal with Murless, so that he could take better rides if they were offered. Murless, who paid Lester a large retainer on behalf of his owners, found that unacceptable. Lester was playing brinkmanship and thought that there was no-one who could replace him.

But the international bloodstock agent George Blackwell put up George Moore, and brokered the deal. George was to arrive in England on the eve of the Craven meeting the following spring. Lester announced that he would be riding as a freelance in 1967.

The arrival of George Moore was a major story and I was determined to be in at the top. I contacted George in Australia, collected him off his Qantas flight on Friday 14 April and delivered him to the Westbury Hotel. The following day I drove him to the

Lime Grove studio for an exclusive interview on 'Grandstand'. We became friends and George asked my advice over a driver and a handicapper.

George's big problem – or rather his wife Iris's problem – was with his accommodation. Noel Murless had arranged for the family to stay in a cottage on the Eve Stud. It was perfectly pleasant and comfortable, but its size was in sharp contrast to the Moore's magnificent mansion overlooking Sydney Harbour. Iris Moore was blonde, glamorous and incompatible with English country life – especially when the cold April winds blew from the east. Iris saw them as royalty living in a garden shack. Before long the family had moved to London, where George rented a comfortable flat in Cadogan Square.

Meanwhile, on the racecourse, George was making a sensational impact. The Murless horses had taken the Craven meeting by storm. It was an historic week. On Monday the Queen had visited the new National Stud adjacent to the July course, and Tuesday saw the official introduction of starting stalls, at Newmarket. But for the rest of the week the headlines belonged to George. Every winner he rode was a winner forfeited by Piggott. By the end of the year the champion jockey's total had dropped to 117, from 191 in 1966.

There was Moore-mania and the following Guineas meeting was a major triumph. He won the 2000 Guineas on Jim Joel's Royal Palace, who was having his first race of the season, and the 1000 Guineas on Bob Boucher's Fleet. Both winners were trained by Murless. Fleet was to feature in an unhappy episode when she was hit in the face with Lester Piggott's whip in the Eclipse Stakes. Noel's wife Gwen thundered: 'That so-and-so will never ride for us again!'

Now George was to ride Royal Palace in the Derby and Fleet in the Oaks. Bookmakers were laying serious bets against George winning all five Classics. Lester, meanwhile, was banking on Ribocco, the improving Charles Engelhard-owned colt, to revive his season.

Derby Day was a memorable occasion. Royal Palace shot into the lead well over two furlongs out and looked set to win comfortably.

Suddenly, there was a moment of unease. Piggott was storming up the centre of the course on the 22/1 shot Ribocco. Could the Old Fox destroy George's ultimate moment of glory?

He could not! Royal Palace held on to win all-out by 2½ lengths. Jim Joel had won his first Derby and both he and George had fulfilled a lifetime's ambition. Royal Palace returned to an emotional reception and George took off his skull-cap and waved to Iris in the grandstand.

To the relief of the bookmakers, Fleet was only fourth in the Oaks. The dream was over, but the Murless/Moore winners continued to roll in.

It was in the late summer that rumours began to suggest that all was not well. There were stories of mysterious telephone calls in the middle of the night. One evening all of Iris's clothes were found to be shredded in the Cadogan Square flat. There was talk of a gang of Australian punters hassling George, and more and more it became clear that Iris was anxious to return to Australia and the comfort of her Sydney home. George suddenly went missing: no-one, including Noel Murless, had the faintest idea where he was.

I was sent to France by 'Sportsview' to track him down. I flew to Paris and took a taxi to Alec Head's house in Chantilly. No-one had heard from George. Eventually, 24 hours later, he turned up in the Hotel Meurice in Paris. I filed a report from the BBC's Paris office, but George's activities in those 48 'missing' hours remained a mystery.

By the autumn the Murless horses were no longer invincible and lads in the yard were complaining about aspects of George's riding. Meanwhile, Lester won the Irish Derby and St Leger on Ribocco. The faltering autumn came to a head at Newmarket in October. George was due to ride Royal Palace in the Champion Stakes and return to Australia on a flight from Heathrow the following Monday. I asked George to record an interview with me on the morning of the race, but for the first time since his arrival he failed to show.

In the Champion, Royal Palace finished third to Reform, ridden by Scobie Breasley. Murless was deeply disappointed and thought he should have won. No-one saw George again. He caught an evening flight to Australia and did not, as expected, return in 1968.

George's career continued to be dogged by controversy, but he was a truly great jockey and turned out to be a highly successful trainer in the Far East. I treasure his 'annus mirabilis'.

George Moore was not the only sensation of 1967. The success of Hill House in the Schweppes Gold Trophy was the most controversial and evocative of all my years in racing. Never before, or since, have I heard a horse being booed as he passed the post. It was my first major commentary race for the BBC. What a baptism of fire!

Hill House was owned by Len Coville and trained by the larger-than-life ex-commando, Captain Ryan Price. No-one was indifferent towards Ryan. You either liked and admired him, or felt that he sailed unacceptably close to the wind. In the case of Hill House, he was caught up in a hurricane!

Ryan had already been 'warned off' the Turf following a previous success in the 'Schweppes' with Elan. He was shattered and felt that he had been hard done by. The 'Schweppes' was the most valuable handicap hurdle of the year and a terrific betting race. Ryan loved the race despite the trouble that it brought him.

In 1967 he trained two horses for the race, Hill House and Burlington II. Hill House had a 'prep' race at Sandown a week earlier and there were suggestions that he could have finished closer than fourth. In the week leading up to the big race the press were heaping coals on the furnace. Many were convinced that Hill House had been laid out for the race for months and was the subject of a major gamble. Others took the view that Hill House was a smokescreen and that Burlington II, owned by Major Derek Wigan, was the stable's main fancy.

It was magnificent intrigue – plot and counter-plot – and the racing public flocked to Newbury expecting a major event. They were not disappointed. Hill House ran away with the race by 12 lengths and all hell was let loose! The crowd booed and harangued

Ryan Price in the winner's enclosure, while the stewards held an enquiry and ordered a dope test. It was a major news story – and my longest contribution to the evening BBC News!

The following week I negotiated an exclusive television interview with Hill House's owner for 'Sportsview'. There was one condition: I must not ask how the horse had managed to improve 21lb within a week! If I did, he would stop the interview. The following Tuesday I travelled down to Coville's manor house in Lower Slaughter, near Cheltenham, and filmed the interview. I was pleased enough. The story was still red-hot. Ryan Price, needless to say, was speaking to no-one.

That evening, in the cutting room at Lime Grove, David Coleman viewed the interview. 'Why didn't you ask him about the improvement?' he complained. I explained, but he retorted: 'Yes, but you still should have asked him.' He was right in a way, but at that early stage I was building the trust of the racing world. There were plenty of 'exclusives' to chase and favours to be asked in the years to come. And there was more to follow up in this particular sensational story.

Two weeks later, the dope test taken on Hill House following the 'Schweppes' proved positive. There followed the most extraordinary train of events, during which it was claimed that Hill House manufactured his own cortisone. Exhaustive tests were conducted – Hill House spent more time at the Equine Research Station than at Findon – and eventually Ryan was absolved from wrong-doing.

I can reveal that the benefactor who saved his career was Lord Weir, who elicited expert evidence from some North American veterinarians. Ryan was grateful to Lord Weir for the rest of his life and repaid the debt to the family by training What A Myth to win the Cheltenham Gold Cup two years later.

## TEN

# *National Nightmares*

The Grand National has been the BBC's most important and prestigious outside broadcast since Peter Dimmock won the contract to televise the great race in 1960. It is a remarkable event, which involves a remarkable television operation.

The sheer engineering logistics are awesome. It is a shop-window production and something of which the BBC can be very proud.

There will never be a more extraordinary race for the National than in 1967. Michael O'Hehir's magnificent commentary on the events at the twenty-third fence will remain a television classic.

In one respect Michael was fortunate. As his son Tony and I know, having covered many Nationals from the same site, there was no better spot for the pile-up to occur. The twenty-third fence is directly beneath, and less than 50 yards away from, the Bechers commentary point. If the catastrophe had happened at Bechers, Michael would have been in serious trouble. Until the landing side of Bechers was levelled out and spectators prevented from standing by the fence, it was impossible to see into the 'drop' from our commentary position. If you missed a horse hitting the fence at Bechers, you missed the fall and could only hope that the jockey would be thrown back into view.

I once arranged for my commentary position to be moved to the outside of the course, facing Bechers, but the head-on vista made commentary difficult over the remaining fences. Nowadays, since the modification of Bechers, there is rarely a faller at the once-awesome obstacle, so the commentator can concentrate on describing the race.

Race-calling the Bechers area was incredibly difficult. There was no time to look at the monitor – too much was happening with up to 40 runners. For this reason a race-reader was indispensable, to call out fallers and horses that had refused or pulled up, beyond the mainstream. Every horse had to be accounted for to the viewers. So, just as your commentary was developing a flow, your race-reader would shout 'Spanish Steps pulled up,' and your rhythm was broken by an interjection, as you repeated the information. Moreover, if his 'call' was wrong it was your head on the block.

I spent Foinavon's Grand National in the BBC's videotape control room at Television Centre, with a view to editing highlights of the race for the end of the programme. In those days there was no such thing as mobile videotape units, so all editing and re-dubbing had to be done at base. I was more use there than at Aintree and I remained in the videotape centre in 1968.

In 1969 I was given my chance and covered the first three fences. Michael O'Hehir was covering Bechers, but had the bad luck to call Highland Wedding, the eventual winner, a faller. Peter Dimmock, in his wisdom, took Michael off the team the following year. The entire race was now to be covered by two commentators, Peter O'Sullevan and myself. I was to cover fences 1-11 and 17-26. From a mile away I could barely *see* the runners at the first fence, let alone identify them. Luckily, there were only 28 that year.

In those days I would stay at the Golden Eagle Hotel, Kirkby. Awaking on Grand National morning and browsing through the newspapers, it was impossible to avoid being overawed. '18 million viewers in Britain . . . 500 million viewers worldwide . . . multimillions of pounds bet on the race . . .' It made chilling reading. To quote Cash Asmussen on the Breeders Cup: 'It's the type of race that gets you damp under the arms!' It was that Cresta feeling all over again: 'Help! I'm in the middle of all this!'

Happily, sanity was restored in 1971 and we settled on having three commentators for the race. John Hanmer was eventually added to the team and covers fences 1-3 and 9-13 to this day. The mix was right and there were some outstanding race commentaries during the 1970s and 80s.

In the early 1970s, Mirabel Topham jeopardized the entire future of the race by selling Aintree to the Walton Group, whose principal was a bearded, former building merchant, Bill Davies. It was tragic to see Aintree, and the great race itself, rapidly disintegrate. The attendance dropped to no more than 10,000 and the police presence, formerly 400 strong, was decimated. Aintree was falling to pieces.

There was even talk of running the Grand National elsewhere. I recommended on BBC-TV that it should be run at the point-to-point course at Larkhill and turned into a picnic and purely television event. The traditionalists were horrified and I was widely castigated.

The ensuing campaign by the Jockey Club, largely financed by Lord Vestey, was heroic. The course was bought for the nation, the race saved. Under a progressively vibrant management, Grand National day – and notably also its two preceding days – have gone from strength to strength.

The day itself is an exhilarating and exhausting broadcasting experience, but in editorial terms it is the icing on top of the cake. Our first programme meetings for the National would follow hard on the publication of the big-race weights at the beginning of February. From there on in we would plan and activate our various ideas to build up to the race.

It was always the fences that made the Grand National unique. So, in 1969 we decided to persuade two erudite jockeys to jump round the course in cold blood, describing all the while the excitement and pitfalls. It was my project, and I chose the soon-to-retire Brough Scott and the heroic Freddie's regular jockey, Pat McCarron. It was not so easy finding suitable horses whose owners were prepared to let them loose around Aintree, even at a price, but after hours and days of telephoning I eventually succeeded. Brough and Pat were quite superb, the operation went without a hitch, and the item was voted a huge success.

The following year some bright spark wanted to go one step further by suggesting that we get Harvey Smith to jump around. Oh dear, I could see nothing but difficulties! Nevertheless Harvey was approached and surprised me by agreeing – at a price.

There was a problem in that he had nothing at home to jump around on, and this time I found it harder to find suitable mounts. We ended up taking a tremendous risk. We booked a horse called Cashel Fort, who was a light of days gone by and was lacking a little size, and the 12-year-old Limetra, owned by Harry Lane. The drawback was that Mr Lane decided to run Limetra in the Topham Trophy just two hours before the scheduled jump-around. There was no other day on which we could film because all the outside broadcast resources were needed to make it work and the racecourse would not allow us to record before racing started lest the fences were damaged.

So twenty minutes after racing ended, the jockeys – Pat McCarron had volunteered again – were microphoned up and the horses saddled. Harvey was to ride Limetra who, despite his earlier exertions, was clearly the safer conveyance. Pat fearlessly had the leg up on the unimpressive Cashel Fort.

They decided to jump the Chair while the horses were relatively fresh. It was not a good decision. Cashel was 'cold', terrified by the sight of this monstrous 5ft 3in obstacle, and crashed straight into it. He landed in a heap of mud, fir and spruce and detached and damaged the microphone. At least this had the effect of waking Cashel Fort up! Inevitably there was a delay while the battered McCarron was re-assembled and the sensitive sound equipment repaired and re-checked.

We moved on to the first fence. It was just one demand too far for old Limetra. He had jumped round once already today; he had jumped the Chair again quite happily; but now he had been standing for 20 minutes in the chill of the evening and he wanted to go home. Nothing that Harvey could do – while the television cameras were rolling – would persuade Limetra to move. He planted with a vengeance. He had had enough.

My whole life passed before me in those few minutes. Brian Cowgill and the editor of 'Grandstand' were sitting in Television Centre watching this expensive and widely publicized débâcle unfold before them. Harvey was becoming increasingly disenchanted. One comment will always remain with me: 'I've got an appointment in Leeds at 6.30 you know.' Barry Brogan and other jockeys were effusive with free advice.

Just as my career seemed to be ebbing away before my very eyes, I clutched at a final straw: 'Harvey, why don't you have a sit on that little horse and let Pat ride the old horse?' Harvey went for it and Pat saved my life. The combination of a fresh pair of hands, and a jockey's seat and communications, encouraged Limetra to re-enter the fray.

They streamed away over the first three fences by Fazakerley Bank, with Cashel Fort jumping for fun, and with Harvey becoming more and more confident and – just as important – more verbose. By the time they reached Bechers, Harvey reckoned the game was easy. He steered Cashel Fort towards the inside of the fence and jumped Bechers at its steepest point, on the descent. Within a split second Fleet Street had the front-page picture they wanted and we had a story for 'Grandstand' that no-one would want to miss. Harvey picked himself off the floor unharmed.

'Thank you God,' I mouthed, 'and thank you Pat McCarron!' Harvey was late for his appointment in Leeds, and I slept all the way back to London, in a fierce storm, with lightning and hail, in our six-seater aircraft.

I was only to invite one more celebrated equestrian to jump round the famous fences. I travelled to Gatcombe in 1979 with producer Fred Viner, in an attempt to persuade the Princess Royal to take her life in her hands. We enjoyed a pleasant lunch, the Princess was interested and charming, and afterwards Mark Phillips showed me his event horses. But the answer was in the negative, which was a shame because I am certain she would have loved doing it.

In 1973 the editor of 'Grandstand', Alan Hart, had a bright idea: 'Let's follow one horse – one with a chance – all the way to the race,' he said in February. 'We'll call it "Follow the Favourite".' The horse that I chose for this purpose was Red Rum, trained on the beach at Southport by the little-known car-trader 'Ginger' McCain. He was 20/1 at the time.

All through my racing life I have been amazingly lucky, but this was one of my luckiest breaks. The footage that we shot in the following weeks, with producer John McNicholas and cameraman Ian Hutchinson, has been the backbone of the Red Rum legend. The shots of 'Rummy' in his strong canters on the sands, pulling the powerless Billy Ellison's arms out of their sockets, have been used countless times in tributes and eulogies of the great horse. They were a running theme in the 1995 film *Red Rum – A National Treasure*, so brilliantly produced by Gerry Morrison.

That first year we shot him from the dunes, between the rushes, from the sands, focused upwards, and in tracking shots from Ginger's or my car. At the time I was driving a BMW. Our only mis-cue was when Ginger said 'go' one morning and my smart car sank gently into the soft sand! With the incoming tide imminent, a tractor was required in double-quick time.

There will never be a more emotional, enthralling and simply unbelievable Grand National than the 1973 version. It is one of the inevitable shortcomings of television that great moments are condensed into a convenient 15-20 seconds. The 'highlights' of this race occupied the first eight and a half minutes, during which the Australian horse Crisp gave an exhibition of jumping never before seen at Aintree. He just flew the fences. He was breathtaking. He stood back and defied the laws of Aintree gravity.

But Red Rum kept him in his distant sights. Like a terrier he went in pursuit from the last fence, and as his rival faltered and started to wobble he put his head down and reeled him in. It was thrilling or heart-breaking, depending upon your allegiance. To the neutrals it was both.

If hard evidence were needed that this was the greatest National of all time, the official time of 9 minutes and 1.90 seconds confirmed it. It shattered the existing record, established by Golden

Miller 40 years earlier, by almost 20 seconds. There have been faster times since, but only since the course was modified and made substantially easier to jump round.

The story of Red Rum evokes many happy memories: my friend Tommy Stack's role in the record-breaking third win; partying with the Stacks at Linton Springs and riding a finish on Liz Stack's washing machine at 2 pm; the friendliness and hospitality of Ginger and Beryl McCain; and my interview with his octogenarian owner, Noel le Mare, which began, unforgettably: 'In 1906, on a Friday afternoon . . .' and ended ' . . . I thought, by God, I'd like to win that race.'

In December 1977 we asked Ginger McCain the impossible – would he bring down 'Rummy' to appear live on the stage at BBC television's 'Sports Review of the Year' on 14 December? 'No problem,' said Ginger. So he and Beryl travelled down the previous day, reconnoitred the theatre and the lift in which 'Rummy' would have to travel, and stayed the night in Chelsea with my wife and myself.

The show was a triumph. 'Rummy' behaved impeccably, without a hint of stage-fright, in front of bright lights and a large studio audience. The highlight was a 'live' link-up with our studio in Leeds where Tommy Stack, recovering from a broken pelvis, had been driven by ambulance. When 'Rummy' heard Tommy's voice from Leeds, he pricked his ears in a cameo that will live forever.

Only one other Grand National in my lifetime could compare on the Richter scale of emotion – the triumph of Aldaniti over crippling lameness and of Bob Champion over cancer in 1981. Sometimes on National day you feel that God has written the script. Sometimes – as in 1997 – it is the Devil. Aldaniti's win, from 57-year-old John Thorne riding Spartan Missile, wrenched every string of emotion in the human frame.

I had filmed both horses and riders the previous week. The fitness regime of John Thorne would have stretched a commando to the limit. The story of the race, quite rightly, became the subject of a feature-length film, starring John Hurt as Bob Champion and

Edward Woodward as trainer Josh Gifford. It was a race that Josh, one of the best ever NH jockeys, had never won in the saddle. Now he was rightly immortalized.

The following year John Hanmer suffered the ultimate broadcasting nightmare. When he reached his commentary position half an hour before the National, he discovered that the area in his line of vision to the first fence had been allocated as a parking area for double-decker buses. There were scores of them, and no-one was going to move them! In the event, the worst possible scenario came about. Ten horses fell at the first fence, including Aldaniti. All that John could see was an escalation of fallen horses and bodies on his monitor and an army of loose horses galloping into sight towards the second fence.

I was lucky enough to avoid a major professional catastrophe during my 24 years commentating on the race. One year I did call a horse 'a faller' at Bechers – he *had* fallen and slid along on his belly, but he then proceeded to get up again!

My worst crisis came one year in the early 1980s. As the morning progressed, I developed a blinding headache and felt increasingly unwell. This was worse than the usual Grand National nerves – for some reason I invariably had a headache on National day. As the race drew closer, I felt worse and worse. The half-hour leading up to the race, spent isolated in my commentary hut 50 feet above the ground level, was a nightmare. My headache, if anything, got worse, and I felt increasingly sick.

The power of adrenaline is remarkable. Somehow it drove me through the race as if everything were normal, but afterwards I climbed down my ladder and was violently sick. A friend, Sally Hindley, drove me back home. I slept most of the way and went straight to bed. Whether I had eaten something unpalatable, or whether the problem was gastric, I shall never know. But the following year I made different hotel arrangements.

My final Grand National commentary was in 1992. It had been decided that Peter O'Sullevan should be succeeded by the Australian, Jim McGrath, and that I should focus on presentation and paddock commentary. So Jim McGrath took over my position at Bechers. It was just as well.

On the Thursday evening, after a successful first day, I started coughing. I coughed for half the night, barely slept, and woke up feeling tired and unwell. I telephoned the production team and Richard Pitman to alert them that I was unfit to work. I faxed Richard my script and left the Friday programme to him. I dosed myself with medicine and throat lozenges and wrote my scripts for the following day.

As National day dawned, I was aware of a major problem. The 'fancied runners' story was waiting to be dubbed and I had all but lost my voice! I dressed, packed my case and drove to Aintree. It took almost an hour to voice over a story which would normally have taken me ten minutes. Just as I came to the end of a link, my voice would crack. My colleagues were unbelievably patient. At the end of it I felt dreadful, but once again adrenaline had got me through the dubbing session. Having been driven home and gone straight to bed, I managed to stay awake until the start of the National, although I was dying to sleep.

It is hard to describe my feelings as the start was delayed, the tape was broken, and finally the grotesque nightmare of the second false start unfurled. A thousand thoughts raced through my mind: What a disaster! Surely the jockeys realize what's happened. I should be *there*, describing it! I should be there, *reporting* it! And above all . . . Oh God, I do want to go to sleep!

I had to sleep, so I asked my wife to put on the video recorder and slipped into a deep slumber. Five minutes later the telephone rang: 'Niall here. I'm editing 'Match of the Day', will you come into the studio and deal with this shambles?' I tried to explain to Niall Sloane, as politely as possible, that he was missing the point. The reason that I was absent from Aintree was the fact that I was dying of influenza. It was not, as one press room 'well-wisher' had suggested, because I was miffed at no longer being part of the commentary team.

Thereafter I slept for several hours. I found it hard to believe that

I had missed one of the biggest stories in the history of the Grand National. It was a day for reputations to be made, before a national audience. I was absent . . . and impotent.

My fever raged over the weekend, but I was determined to return to work at Ascot on the following Wednesday. I was still coughing on Tuesday, but managed to script the programme, arrange the videotape editing and prepare for an early night. I had already arranged for the presentation position at Ascot to be moved from the notorious 'windy corner' of the first-floor balcony – designed with pneumonia in mind – to a sheltered area at the top of the grandstand. Then the telephone rang.

'Peter Scudamore here. I thought I'd let you know that I'll be announcing my retirement tomorrow.' Aaargh! I telephoned this news to the long-suffering assistant producer, Gerry Morrison, who was just finishing a long and complicated session of editing the Grand National coverage. Could he try to beg, borrow or steal a further three hours of editing time to produce a complete summary of Peter Scudamore's career?

Not for the first time, Gerry did an amazing, life-saving job. For my part, I tore up my script, started all over again, and was still working – and coughing – at 10.30 pm. In the event it was a terrific programme, with Peter riding a winner on his final ride, just before we went off the air.

We had already arranged, months earlier, that Peter should join our commentary team. He has had his critics, but in my opinion he has brought to television a unique insight into the art of race-riding. He is honest, articulate and not afraid to criticize his former colleagues when necessary. He was by far the most successful NH jockey ever, and there is no-one that I would prefer in his role. I would also trust him with my life.

The three days' coverage of the Grand National meeting was always exhausting, and one of my favourite moments of the year was either getting on the London-bound train at Lime Street station or, in later years, driving away from the racecourse on the journey home. National day was not just the culmination of several weeks' hard work, it was also the climax of the National Hunt season. Now there was the Flat season and the Craven meeting at Newmarket to look forward to in two weeks' time.

It was the aborting of this time-honoured procedure – the 'Leaving of Aintree' – that made the events of April 1997, at a personal level, almost doubly grotesque.

There was no indication whatever that the IRA would consider disruption of horseracing's greatest worldwide showcase. Apart from the controversial kidnapping of Shergar – widely accepted as the work of a splinter group – the Republicans had no record of harming a sport which creates so much employment for Irish people in both England and Ireland. Nor was there ever a history of damage to Liverpool, where a vast number of the population are of Irish extraction. So, despite the bomb damage to bridges near the M6 motorway early in the week, no-one had seriously entertained the possibility of any threat from the IRA; from the Animal Liberation fanatics perhaps, but not from those whose supporters did, in many instances, profit from the horse racing industry.

How wrong we were. Two 10p telephone calls, from public call boxes, achieved the evacuation of 52,000 racegoers, watched by a worldwide television audience of 400 million.

When the alert was made known, I joined Desmond Lynam. We were ordered to leave the weighing room area and were ushered out to the BBC compound, where the various control vehicles and production caravans were parked. Before long, in one of the most arresting and real sequences of 'live' television ever in a sporting arena, we were commanded by the racecourse manager, Charles Barnett, to leave immediately – 'including you, the BBC, now!'

There was a total evacuation, on to the street, on to the Melling Road and, initially, into the centre of the course. No vehicles were to be moved from any car park within the boundaries of the racecourse. The race was abandoned and we were marooned. We waited in hope that the ring of steel would be lifted, but by 6.00 pm it was clear that the police and anti-terrorist squad would not relent. All 6000 vehicles must be left on the course overnight and be searched individually, in the presence of the owner, the following day. It would be wrong to reveal how I extricated my car from the Owners and Trainers' car park, but I did.

We had been sitting in a small cabin in the car park. We were cold, frustrated, disillusioned and hungry. Peter O'Sullevan, who had been looking forward to commentating on his fiftieth Grand National, looked exhausted and far older than his 79 years. I was yearning to drive home, have a hot bath, and put the nightmare out of my mind. I was free! My Mercedes purred gently down the M56, when the mobile phone rang.

It was Dave Gordon, the editor of 'Grandstand'. 'Where are you?' he demanded. 'I'm going home, Dave,' I replied, 'I've had enough.' 'Oh no you're not,' he replied, 'you're turning round and going to the press conference at the Merseyside Police Headquarters at 7.30. We'll send you a camera and you can do a report for 'Match of the Day'.'

I could have wept! Bloody car phones! I was just so tired, after two exhausting days on the Thursday and Friday and a bad night's sleep on Friday night. I checked in with BBC Radio Merseyside, recorded an interview for radio, and then walked over to the press conference, which turned out to be at 8.30 pm. BBC News cameras were there and there were statements from Paul Stephenson, the Assistant Chief Constable of Merseyside, and Charles Barnett.

Two things emerged, off the record. Firstly, of the two telephone calls, one had been accompanied by the recognized IRA codeword and the other by a close approximation. I wondered, secretly, whether somehow the code could have been 'leaked' after the M6 bombing. Secondly, it was clear that the racecourse and the police were determined that the race should go ahead on the following Monday. I was told privately that it was scheduled provisionally for 5.00 pm.

I returned to the television studio at BBC Radio Merseyside and eventually recorded an interview with Gary Lineker for transmission at midnight on 'Match of the Day'. We talked about the effect on the horses, many of whom had been released from the racecourse stables at 6.15 pm, and the plight of the jockeys whose clothes and possessions were sealed in their changing room. At that very moment a dozen jockeys, wearing just silks and breeches, were sharing a room at the Adelphi Hotel! More important, they had eaten and drunk well, and those who had weighed out at 10 st at 3.00 pm were now turning the scales at four or five pounds overweight.

Most important, I stressed the resolve of everyone in the racing world to whom I had spoken that the race should go ahead. Lord Daresbury, the Aintree chairman, and Charles Barnett were watching the broadcast with Paul Stephenson and the chief constable. The Home Secretary, Michael Howard, and the head of the anti-terrorist squad were kept informed of every development.

The broadcast had a notable impact. By all accounts it played a significant role in the courageous and controversial decision, made at teatime on Sunday, to stage the Grand National the following day.

The day was a triumph. Racegoers travelled from all over Britain for the unique occasion. Entrance was free, and a crowd of 20,000 gave voice to the defiance of the British people. I drove back to Liverpool from Newmarket on the morning of the race and a photograph was flashed round the world of my arrival at the course with arms hoisted as the security guards did their work.

Charlie Barnett had scarcely slept since Saturday. The 1000-strong security force had been tireless. But the nightmare was, of course, far from over. On Monday there were no fewer than 25 calls, many of them correctly coded and several from the same individual, as the day progressed. At one stage the caller is said to have raged: 'For God's sake get them out, I'm trying to avoid a tragedy here.'

The decision to go ahead was approved at the highest level. Prime Minister John Major endorsed the judgement of the police and the security forces and, under a cloak of secrecy, flew by helicopter, with his wife Norma, to support this unprecedented act of defiance.

Never before had a massively attended public event gone ahead in the face of a coded IRA warning.

Meanwhile, the BBC's head of sport, Brian Barwick, had persuaded the Chief Executive and the Controller of BBC1 to clear the schedules for a one-hour 'live' transmission and a 'highlights' programme at 6.30 pm. Brian was asked what audience he would expect to achieve at early teatime. 'About eight million,' claimed Brian, assessing the optimum viewership on all known data. Incredibly, 12 million switched on.

Since the Saturday night, I was playing with a loaded deck. Everyone was tense. I went to see Dave Gordon, shortly before we went on air. 'The Prime Minister's coming and I think I could get an interview,' I offered. 'If we interview Major, Des will do it,' snapped Dave. I seethed with anger.

In the event, I was in the paddock interviewing Stan Clarke, the owner of Lord Gyllene, and Charlie Brooks, the trainer of Suny Bay, when John Major appeared. Martin Hopkins, the producer of 'Grandstand', shouted: 'Julian, go and interview the Prime Minister!' With the general election just weeks away it was a sensitive encounter, but John Major pitched it just right. As events were to show, nothing could have rescued the Tories' cause at that stage!

It was a surreal scene as Lord Gyllene won the great race by 25 lengths from Suny Bay. It was the only time, however, that the occasion was arguably more significant and memorable than the result. There were many heroes, including of course the team associated with Lord Gyllene. Charles Barnett, Lord Daresbury and Paul Stephenson, too, were heroes. Des Lynam was unflappable as ever and Peter O'Sullevan called his fiftieth National in impeccable style.

What no-one else knew was that I, too, was driving away from Aintree for the last time as a BBC broadcaster. It was a memorable day for the final broadcast, but at the time my thoughts were more down to earth: 'Thank God I shan't have to go through all that again!'

# ELEVEN

# *Restless Spirits*

Flicking through my address book in early July 1967, I came across the name of Carolyn Michael. I called her and we had dinner the following Monday. Presumably we enjoyed each other's company, as we dined again three days later. Thereafter, the romance became a slow-burner. I was due for one of those.

In the early part of the year, Caroline Dyson, an enigmatic blonde girl with a sense of adventure, was living in my house. Caroline was an excellent horsewoman, whose brother Tim trained National Hunt horses under a permit. I bought Tim a horse called Codswallop for £500, with which he was extremely successful. Caroline rode Nearumba in the first-ever race under Jockey Club rules for lady riders. While we were together I arranged a point-to-point ride for her with Albert Ketteringham – in lieu of my forfeited ride – on a horse called Paul Douglas. Unfortunately, the horse was badly in need of a run and the ride was not a success. Caroline later became secretary and work-rider to the Lambourn trainer, Peter Walwyn.

Caroline and I remained good friends and I was delighted when, in 1972, she married an old friend, Julian Lewis, a former assistant trainer with Henri van de Poele, in France. Julian (or 'Screamer' as he is affectionately known in the Lambourn valley) became a successful bloodstock agent, specializing in trade with France.

Caroline had moved out of my house and I had just finished an affair with an extremely pretty girl called Harriet Hubbard, whose uncle Ralph was clerk of the course at Goodwood. She was to marry another very good friend – and my eventual best man – Michael

Bailey, a successful former amateur rider and brother to the trainer Peter Bailey.

Carolyn Michael was a different type of girl. She had no real interest in racing, or in country pursuits, but she was intelligent and enjoyed good food and wine. She was sensible, efficient, and both helpful and understanding when I was working intensely. When we were married I would often work until 1 am in the morning, building up my bank of owners' racing colours, drawn with crayons and felt pens on pocket-sized cards. I still have over 3000 cards in long files. What a waste!

This was a period of professional consolidation for me, and I accepted every job offered. I worked for BBC's News, Radio, and even Drama. I recorded dialogue and commentaries for 'Z Cars' and 'Take Three Girls' with Jimmy Bolam and Susan Jameson, and a light entertainment show with Terry Thomas. I was available, eager and inexpensive – in fact, a producer's dream!

They were exciting times. Peter Dimmock, at the helm of outside broadcasts was enthusiastic and valued horseracing. Most importantly we had a realistic budget.

When the foot-and-mouth epidemic broke out in November 1967, Peter was quickly on the phone. His message was straightforward: 'Find me some racing!' I pointed out that there wasn't any, but he was insistent: 'Well, find some abroad. Don't just sit around doing nothing!' So I arranged a transmission from St Cloud on the outskirts of Paris on 9 December, the last day of the Flat season in France, and from Cagnes-sur-Mer on Boxing Day. Peter O'Sullevan and I were the commentary team.

On 16 December we staged the world's first electronic horserace at London University. The Massey Fergusson Gold Cup should have been run at Cheltenham the previous Saturday. Instead, an Atlas 1 computer was fed with data, duly spewed out reams of papers which I handed to Peter O'Sullevan, who converted what was printed into a racing commentary. The winner of the 'race' was Arctic Sunset, ridden by the young Irish jockey Barry Brogan. Barry had travelled to London for the event at the invitation of the BBC, and I took him to dinner followed by a night at Pauline Wallis's Casanova Club. Barry took to casino life like a duck to water.

Pauline Wallis was a wonderful 'nanny' to all the rash young men who were inclined to gamble more than they could afford. She was precision-accurate in the amount of credit that she was prepared to extend. But Pauline – sister of the hugely popular Colonel Tommy Wallis, who became a Member of the Jockey Club in 1989 – was clearly unhinged by Barry's good looks and gentle Irish charm.

Barry was playing roulette and quickly won about £500. Thereafter his luck changed and by midnight he had lost almost £2000. Pauline had allowed him initially £200 credit, but against her better judgement extended his credit time and again. To everyone's relief, at last his luck changed and he won back everything that he had lost, plus £180 profit. I took a deep breath and wiped my brow – I had visions, as his sponsor, of being invited to make good his losses!

Barry was alive with the excitement and stimulation of casino life – he was hooked. The following day he went to the Knightsbridge Sporting Club where the house were rash enough to extend him £1500 credit, which he promptly lost. To the best of my knowledge he has never settled. Unfortunately he became addicted to gambling, and eventually also to alcohol. These addictions destroyed his life, and I have always felt partly responsible. Barry had been a brilliant jockey and one day at Wolverhampton rode five consecutive winners. In the end he had lost all his money and all his friends.

The sequel to that first successful broadcast of a simulated horserace was the 'Computer King George VI Steeplechase' at the English Electric headquarters in Queensway, on 30 December. This event was far less satisfactory. Who wrote the computer program I do not know, but one of the outsiders for the race was a horse called Master Mascus, ridden by Mr John Lawrence (now Lord Oaksey) at 50/1. John was covering the event for his newspaper and foolishly I laid him £50-£1 against Master Mascus. Absurdly, the no-hoper 'won' and I was obliged to pay up!

Earlier in 1967 we had switched our outside broadcast unit, on the morning of racing, from Lingfield (which was frozen off) to Warwick. The following Saturday I was installed on standby with a unit at Sedgefield, in case racing at Windsor – notably prone to flooding – was called off at the eleventh hour.

All in all, at the BBC we were providing a service that ITV could not match. Dimmock was a bully, but he was dealing us good cards and we were winning with every hand.

By 1969, my betrothal to Carolyn was almost sealed. In April, I bought her a Yorkshire Terrier from a breeder in Newmarket, the jockey Alan Burrell. We named him Josh Gifford. Josh (the jockey) had ridden my first-ever winner, a horse called Partlet, bought from Michael Bailey, at Folkestone in 1966. Josh was a splendid dog. I would take him running in Battersea Park and taught him to juggle with a lightweight football. We were deeply upset when he met with his demise in the jaws of a friend's Golden Labrador, in Newmarket in 1977. It was on the day of Barry and Penny Hills's wedding in Leicestershire and I raced back to Newmarket to console Carolyn, missing a magnificent party.

I was also running a racehorse in Carolyn's name, called Qalibashi. I bought the mare at the December sales from the extraordinary and eccentric John Meacock, who trained on a cinder track near Alresford in Hampshire and called all his horses unpronounceable Arabic names. He wore a battered trilby hat, smoked incessantly through a cigarette-holder, scattering ash indiscriminately, wrote unintelligible poetry and was quite the dottiest man that I had ever met!

I sent Qalibashi to be trained by Neville Dent in the New Forest. She had an educational run at Wincanton and showed promise. Indeed, she appeared to possess the ability to win a small race, so we prepared her for a gamble. For D-day we chose a conditional jockeys' novices hurdle at Southwell on 3 April, the day before Good Friday. The going was suitable, the opposition was moderate, and the mare was well. I arranged a 'starting price job' with a leading bookmaker. (The essence of an SP job is that the commission is placed off-course and no money should find its way back to the course.) I was concerned about one thing only: when I walked the course I discovered that the hurdle course was now inside the steeplechase course, as opposed to outside, and was therefore sharper. Furthermore, the 'cushions' of the hurdles had been painted a bright shade of orange.

Qalibashi looked well. She was owned by the unknown Miss C.A. Michael, trained by the unfashionable N. J. Dent, and ridden by a little-known claiming jockey called D. Elsworth. On the course she opened at 20/1, and I had on £200 to win – the equivalent of almost £2000 nowadays.

Two things went wrong. There was a delay at the start and the skilfully placed commission haemorrhaged back to the course. Qalibashi shortened from 20/1 to 7/1 during the delay. The other mishap was caused by the brightly coloured hurdles – the mare galloped smoothly to the first flight, took one look at the luminous orange paint and said 'Help!' She propped at practically every flight of hurdles, but still finished second. I had not backed her each-way. That was to be her day, and she never did win us a race. Ultimately, a heart murmur was detected.

Carolyn came with me to Scotland that July. Whitebridge, our wonderful old fishing pub between Inverness and Fort William, with fairly primitive facilities and a variable dining room – I'm sure it's different now – was not quite her scenario, so we checked into Knockie Lodge.

Loch Knockie is situated about five miles from Whitebridge. It was always my favourite loch to fish in Inverness-shire and I caught my first big fish there – a 2½lb brown trout – at the age of 11. The lodge dates back 200 years and was built as a hunting base for the Chief of Clan Fraser. It is a beautifully sited old house, with views of Loch Knockie and Loch Nan Lan, which harbours the most savage and vituperative horseflies that I have ever encountered. Fishing off the bank at Nan Lan is a suicidal venture.

Now the lodge had been converted into an attractive and comfortably furnished hotel, with an ambitious dining room and cellar. The fishing, I felt, had slipped into decline, but the cuisine was excellent. Carolyn was reasonably happy. We were unmarried and in Scotland – so, of course, we had separate rooms.

On the first night, Carolyn came rushing down the passage. 'I've just seen a ghost!' she gasped. Some might regard this statement as a device to lure a man, minding his own business, into a cold and lonely bed. But Carolyn was truthful and not prone to hysterics, so I accompanied her to her room and slept most of the night there. Nothing happened. Presumably the spectre had glided through the door, passed through the room and disappeared out of the window.

I made enquiries in the morning. Evidently there was indeed a ghost that came up the back stairs and visited that particular room. As I recall, he dated back to the visit of the Duke of Cumberland's red-coated army who passed by after their victory over Bonnie Prince Charlie at Culloden Fields.

This was not the only occasion on which a companion had experienced the supernatural. On the night of the previous year's Cambridgeshire at Newmarket, I took a friend for dinner and a weekend at Great Fosters, near Egham, a rambling old country house/hotel dating back to the period of Henry VIII. We stayed in the Queen Anne suite which, for some reason, had twin beds. In the morning my companion said: 'Ju, why were you sitting on the end of my bed during the night?' I assured her that I had not, but she was quite insistent that someone had sat there for several minutes. Once again I asked a member of staff if there was any history of restless spirits at Great Fosters. 'Which room were you in?' he asked. I told him. 'Oh yes,' he replied, 'that would be old so-and-so. He often passes through there.' It remains fascinating that some individuals are aware of and attract the spirits of the departed, whilst others, like myself, are insensitive.

Although Carolyn came on that trip to Scotland, it was normally my aunts Diana and Sylvia who accompanied me on the fishing holidays. My aunts and I decided to explore further north-west because the lochs around Whitebridge were in gradual decline and in need of being re-stocked. We moved beyond Inverness-shire to Sutherland and a splendid fishing hotel called Altnacealgach, between Ullapool and Oykel Bridge. There was excellent sea trout fishing at the nearby Ben More estate.

Altnacealgach was a brilliant operation, ahead of its time, run by a martinet called Mrs Attwood. At dinner there was a magnificent spread of two joints – beef and pork, say – on a help-yourself basis. The starters and puddings were serene. The breakfasts, likewise, were unmissable, notably kippers, or trout, specially prepared, which you had caught the previous day. There was a loch directly opposite the hotel, so after dinner you could enjoy a further hour-and-a-half's fishing. It remained light until almost 11 pm.

Insatiable, I attempted unsuccessfully to seduce one of the waitresses. I shall always believe that it was her fear of Mrs Attwood, rather than any other factor, that conspired to frustrate me!

My aunts and I moved further north and west. We fished at Torridon; Achiltibuie, from the magnificent Summer Isles Hotel where they grow their own produce and have a private smokery; and from Scourie, Lybster and as far north as Tongue. The Tongue Hotel had wonderful views overlooking the Kyle of Tongue and Ben Loyal, the so-called Queen of Scottish Mountains. We fished on Lochs Craggie and Loyal with variable success. We finally came to rest, as our north-west headquarters, at Kinlochbervie. There were splendid hill lochs and we were close to Loch Stack, with its views of Ben Arkle and Foinavon, where the Duchess of Westminster was such a wonderful and generous hostess.

It was on Loch Stack that I had my only experience of a salmon. We were fishing for 'brownies' and sea trout, when a fish rose unusually to me and took my fly very late. Within seconds my reel was screaming, and the fish pulled the boat, literally, from one side of the loch to the other.

I was fishing with a conventional 12ft trout rod, with a standard nylon cast and three flies. Eventually the fish ran deep in a bay on the road side of the loch. By now it was clear we were into a salmon. After half an hour my wrist was beginning to ache, but this was the fish of a lifetime; the ghillie guessed him at 12-15lb. I felt that we were winning – he was trying to lean underneath the boat – but with the ghillie's help we avoided mistakes.

The tension was unbearable, and then suddenly he was gone. I thought the cast must have broken, but that was not the case. In fact the hook had snapped on a new fly that I had bought in Inverness just a week earlier. I was distraught and inconsolable. Nonetheless, it was a magnificent and enthralling three-quarters of an hour.

Sutherland is a magnificent county of mountains and moors, lochs and rivers and generally the most romantic of scenery. In the 1970s, when I was working more intensely than at any time of my life, nothing gave me more pleasure than to sit tranquilly in a boat on a Sutherland loch, casting a fly and knowing that the nearest telephone was at least five miles away. That is a *proper* holiday. Now that I am released from the burden of television, I look forward to renewing my love affair with Scotland.

Carolyn was not one of life's natural fishermen. Normally, when my aunts and I went to Scotland, she would visit her parents, David and Denise, in Switzerland. Carolyn came into her own, though, on the two *tours gastonomiques* that we undertook. Although slight of stature, she had a remarkable capacity for doing justice to a five-star meal!

Our most celebrated expedition took place in August 1972. It was skilfully designed to embrace a tour of France's best-known regional racecourses. It was memorable in every way and bears relating in detail.

We started in Bordeaux, travelled the 'wine route' and had lunch at Margaux. Dinner on Wednesday was at La Sourire in Gradignan. On Thursday we drove to Cap Ferrat to lunch at Forestière. On Friday we stayed and dined in Blaye and on Saturday drove on to La Rochelle. I backed a good-priced winner in England and dined on oysters, lobster and tarte-aux-fraises!

On Monday we lunched in Chenhutte, and on Tuesday moved on to Angers. We dined at Les Rosiers, Jeanne de Laval. On Wednesday we drove to Tours, lunching on the way at the Auberge du Mail at Amboise and dining at Le Lyonnais.

The highlight of the trip came on Thursday when we lunched at the magnificent Charles Barrier, a Relais Gourmand, in Tours. We ate salade tourenaise; mousseline de brochet, sauce d'ecrivisse; agneau roti, legumes à la crème; and finally a mouth-watering gateau d'orange. It was quite superb. We travelled on to Orleans and to Saumur, but our lunch at Charles Barrier was unquestionably the highlight of the trip.

There was also a shorter tour to accommodate the great restaurants of the south of France. In this instance the schedule included: L'Oasis at La Napoule; Le Cagnard at Haut de Cagnes; La Colombe D'Or at St Paul de Vence; Pavillon Eden-Roc at Cap D'Antibes; and Le Moulin de Mougins. Unfortunately I fell ill on arrival at Le Moulin and missed out!

By the summer of 1970 I was definitely becoming committed to Carolyn. There were still other girls in my life, notably Joanna Marshall, the daughter of the Northumberland racehorse owner Johnny Marshall; the delectable and amusing Anne Baring, now an MFH; and the divorcee Pamela Drury-Lowe, whom I took to Wimbledon. But on 1 October Carolyn and I announced our engagement – we were to be married on 29 December, the day after the Kempton Christmas meeting.

The question was – where were we going to live? Carolyn had a two-bedroom flat on the top floor of Chelsea Towers, an elegant modern block behind Chelsea's town hall, while I was more than happy in First Street. Carolyn, however, was not over-enamoured with my bachelor house. She felt that it was unsuitable as a family home and that Chelsea Towers was the best interim option.

We were married at St Mary's The Boltons at 3.00 pm and the reception was held at 30 Pavilion Road. My best man was Michael Bailey, who made an excellent – if slightly provocative and indiscreet – speech interspersed by bouts of stuttering! The following day was spent consigning most of my furniture to storage: I was not encouraged to clutter up our open-plan, Designers Guild-decorated residence!

On 31 December we flew off on honeymoon. The destination was a little-known West Indian island, where cricket was exceptionally popular and the climate idyllic. We were going to Barbados.

## TWELVE

# *Barbados*

Barbados was, in 1970, an almost unspoilt Caribbean island with 300 years of British tradition. It is a small island of 11 parishes, small rural villages, and country lanes. Magnificent white-sanded palm-fringed beaches face either the wild Atlantic or the gentle Caribbean seas. In the 1970s the main industry was sugar cane; now it is tourism, a multimillion pound international bonanza.

The climate is stunning, the air warm, soft and luxurious. The temperature for most of the year is between 79 and 85 degrees, day and night. Now Barbados is a tourists' paradise: around Bridgetown, the capital, and the south coast of the island, cheap package tours abound, while on the west coast, between Sandy Lane and Speightstown, it is possible to spend thousands of pounds a week.

I am indebted to Carolyn's parents, David and Denise Michael, for the magnificent honeymoon that was their very special wedding present. I was to visit Barbados a dozen times in the following 20 years and made friends on the island who will be friends for life. At the same time, our holidays became legendary!

That first year there were no more than a dozen people on the island who were known to us. Tourism was undeveloped and the English colony was small and centred around the polo ground at Holders Hill, the home of Lord Beaverbrook's daughter, the Hon. Janet Kidd. Carolyn and I were booked into an elegant new Aparthotel called Greensleeves. It was composed of a dozen or so self-contained apartments, with kitchen and balcony, in a crescent overlooking the hotel swimming pool and dining room.

It was conveniently sited away from the main road, but no more than 150 yards from the beach house, with its bar and lunchtime restaurant. It was idyllic. The hotel was run immaculately by Jack Teller and his son Nick. Nick had been married to the singer Susan Maugham.

The beach restaurant was *the* place to have Sunday lunch. It was a perfect scenario: a couple of rum punches, roast beef from the carvery, followed by a sleep, a swim, or quarter of an hour's water-skiing. Or all three.

In Barbados there are certain lessons to be learnt. The first of these is not to step on small, black, prickly objects on the sea-bed. They are called sea urchins and they leave a deposit of poisonous spines in the sole of your foot. It is extremely painful, especially if you tread on several at the same time.

Greensleeves boasted a magnificent waitress-cum-matron called Dulcie who was the best sea urchin treater on the island. The secret involved lemon juice, candle grease and a naked flame. It was important to achieve the correct balance and technique, otherwise the pain was quite excruciating. Dulcie came to know the soles of my feet quite intimately.

At the polo ground we met the genial Yorkshire trainer, Sam Hall. He was staying with one of his owners, the arms-dealer Geoffrey Edwards, at the house below Holders. Geoffrey, whose companion was the actress Aimi McDonald – the archetypal 'dumb blonde' – was giving a party and invited us. It was a magnificent affair, with many of the island's glitterati present. There was torchlight, soft music and tables elegantly positioned around and below the swimming pool and garlanded with beautiful flower decorations.

I was chatting to Gary Sobers when I felt something on my right leg. I shook it vigorously and a large insect fell on to the grass. The effect was as if it were a grenade with the pin removed. There was bedlam. Everyone around jumped up and a man sitting next to me picked up a chair and started belabouring the creature. The women had beaten a hasty retreat. The interloper was a giant centipede whose bite was an automatic ticket to hospital and a passport to injections of morphine for 24 hours!

The party was, sadly, distinctly disrupted and one or two guests drifted away. When we came to leave and to thank our host and hostess, if looks could kill we would have been stone dead. You would have thought that I had brought the beast in my pocket!

We flew to Trinidad for the day to go racing. It was delightfully colonial. The ladies were separated from the men at an early stage and remained at their end of the Governor's box, sipping tea and talking amongst themselves. I was shown the stables and security areas by the local vet, Steve Bennett. The urine samples were packaged and sent to Florida for analysis, in the constant fight against doping.

At the end of racing I collected a rather underwhelmed Carolyn and we dined at an excellent Indian restaurant in Port of Spain, before travelling to the airport for the flight back to Barbados. The plane, due at 11.00 pm, had not taken off from its point of origin so we were obliged to stay overnight at the Airport Hotel. It was awful. The hotel was just beyond the main runway and planes seemed to take off all night. Each one shed a spray of fuel which floated like oil on the surface of the swimming pool, the smell permeating even through our bedroom wall. Above, a rodent was scratching the roof from an early hour. Carolyn slept barely a wink. Our companions on the trip, Graham de Vere Nicoll and Jane Kidd, had a similarly restless night. We were pleased to get back to Barbados.

Despite that experience it was a wonderful holiday and the first of six that Carolyn and I were to share on this paradise island. In the following year and for the rest of our visits we gathered together a team of friends to share a rented house. There was a changing cast of characters from year to year, which included Nigel Angus, Tony Murray, Hamish Alexander, Tony Collins and Gavin Pritchard-Gordon – all engaged in the racing industry and accompanied by the wife or girlfriend currently in favour. We rented a number of different houses, but all were on a 400-yard stretch of the coast on Gibbs Beach.

As the years passed, more and more friends and others from the racing world flocked to Barbados. It began as a trickle and ended as a flood. Eventually the island was dubbed 'Newmarket-by-the-Sea', but by then we were exploring pastures new.

Barbados was a holiday with a well-regulated ritual. At mid-day, on the dot, the first rum punch of the day was served. It was vital that this be properly prepared, with the correct ingredients and in the precise measures. This objective occasionally took days to achieve, but some maids had a formula handed down from mother to daughter, which was sheer perfection. Eventually our rum punches were widely acclaimed. It was wise to drink just two – a third would entail a lengthy post-luncheon siesta. Only Harvey Smith, a regular visitor on one trip, insisted on drinking four!

We slept or water-skiied in the afternoon and played beach football in the early evening. We would dine at home and play cards, or go drinking and dancing later on. Greensleeves was our favourite after-dinner stop-off and rum and coke was the evening drink. Despite regular breaches of 'discipline' I attempted to regulate the household, but with little success. For some reason I was dubbed 'The Führer'.

Of many memorable episodes, a week spent with Oliver Reed stands out. We had rented a house called 'South Winds' and were walking down the beach on our first day. There was a shout from the trees. It was Simon Reed, whom I had met in the Sports Room at BBC Radio. His father was the freelance racing journalist, Peter Reed, and his brother the well-known actor. Ollie had been working and almost 'dry' for six weeks. That had made him like a caged animal, and we were the excuse that he needed to break free. We had several beers and Ollie was on his way.

While we dined, Ollie moved on to the Mullins' Beach Bar. He sat down heavily at the bar, ordered a Banks beer and boomed in the general direction of a group of locals: 'It's a pity you bastards don't know how to play cricket.' Mullins was closed that night soon after sunrise. Ollie looked round defiantly as the locals drifted away in disarray.

The following evening we dined, in our separate groups, at Greensleeves. Ollie's girlfriend was firing eye missiles in my direction. He himself had been water-skiing, misjudged his drop-off and ended half-way up the beach, leaving a major abrasion on his thigh. He was thus under restraint, but looked like a balloon waiting to burst.

Sitting at a table next to the pool was a beautifully dressed woman picking delicately at her dinner. Her husband looked taciturn and disinterested. Ollie could contain himself no longer. He rose to his feet, stepped over to the elegant lady's table and, in his best Shakespearean voice, boomed: 'Madam, if you will join me in the swimming pool, I shall order you a bottle of Dom Perignon champagne.' She looked at Ollie coolly, with a faint smile on her exquisite features, and continued to eat. Ollie bowed theatrically and moved back to his table.

A few minutes later, the elegant lady stood up and hush fell on the restaurant. She very slowly removed her earrings and bracelets and placed them on her table. She took off – with comparable aplomb – her tunic and unfastened her skirt in a single movement, which she passed, like a matador's cape, to a passing waiter. She kicked off her diamante shoes and, clad in what passed for a super-elegant bikini, dived with perfect poise and timing into the pool. To a man, the restaurant rose to its feet in a standing ovation.

Ollie was as good as his word. The Dom Perignon was chilled and served, as Ollie dived, less elegantly, into the pool. Thereafter, the evening went into decline. Diners dived off the roof of the restaurant – a favourite personal act of exhibitionism – and others were immersed fully-clothed. Carolyn, unhappily, misjudged her dive, hit her toe on the lip of the pool and broke it.

The following morning the local doctor was subjected to a lengthy surgery. Among his clients were Ollie with a lacerated thigh, my wife with a broken toe, and a boy from the water-ski boat with an undefined venereal disease!

A regular guest of my friend Jeremy Hindley, who had converted a beach cabin into a charming house on Gibbs Beach, was the racing columnist Charles Benson. Charles is a remarkable 'collector' of people and an adept party-organizer. Whether it be a Derby-winning celebration at Annabel's, or a pop concert at Earl's Court, he is a master planner. For years, until a widely publicized affair in years to come – between Robert Sangster and Jerry Hall – he was extremely close to Mick Jagger.

It was to be some years before Mick 'discovered' Barbados, but Charlie Watts was an early pioneer. Charlie dropped by for a drink one evening and was charming. I had one big surprise: I had always believed that, like jockeys, drummers would have wrists of iron, but Charlie had the limpest of handshakes.

I spent a couple of evenings at the Greensleeves bar with another pop legend in Alan Price, who had recently split with Eric Burden and the Animals. Alan was fascinating about the Animals' early days and how the fortunes that we imagined they earned had been siphoned elsewhere. Otherwise, for some reason, we spoke mostly of Fulham FC!

It was Charles Benson's habit to spend half of his holiday with either Jeremy Hindley or Robert Sangster in Barbados and the remainder as the guest of David and Diana Heimann on the enchanting island of Mustique. Close to St Vincent in the Windward Islands, Mustique is no more than five miles long and was bought in the 1950s by Princess Margaret's old friend, Lord Glenconner. When we first visited the island there were no more than 20-odd houses; now there are more than 50, some worth over $20 million. There are 100 shares in the Mustique Company, Hans Neumann – the former top tennis player – owning 25 per cent of the action. It is a massively valuable piece of real estate.

Every year Benson would invite a team from Barbados for a day-trip to Mustique. We would fly in a small private plane from Barbados and land steeply, over a mountain, on to the short landing strip at the end of which was the relic of a plane whose pilot had been only partially successful. We would be collected in a minibus from the strip and Charles would entertain us at The Ginger Bread

House, built by Rory Annesley, the brother of the Irish trainer Richard.

On our first visit, Nigel Angus fell for the esoteric charms of the beautiful Charlotte Curzon, the stepsister of my old love 'Mops' Starkey. Nigel swum a mile from Basil's Bar to a yacht on which Charlotte was reclining. Charlotte was impressed with his ardour, but not his line of chat, as he was too exhausted to say anything!

On our second visit, Benson was entertaining Brian Ferry, lead singer of Roxy Music, and his fiancée Jerry Hall. Jerry was a 20-year-old Texan with a shock of blonde hair, a deep southern drawl and a dry, sassy sense of humour. With her height, style and exceptionally long legs, she had taken the world of modelling by storm. Now she was in holiday mood and was to prove that devouring the cat-walk was far from her only talent.

Charles drove us to the elegant Cotton House, Mustique's only hotel, but the bar was not open. We sat in front of the house by the old cotton mill, with its old-fashioned grinding machinery and furls of bougainvillaea smothering the walls. Benson, always with an eye for the main chance, suggested a bet: 'Now, you see this rather undernourished, weak-looking girl here,' he said, pointing at Jerry. 'I will bet any of you $50 that she can beat you at leg wrestling'. 'What's leg wrestling?' I asked. 'It's the same as arm wrestling, but with your leg – you lie on your back.'

Every one of us had a go, and every one of us was turned over! She completed the workout by rolling over, without effort, the bulky, 16-stone frame of Benson himself.

Jerry was good fun, but I felt there was a slight tension between her and Brian Ferry. Sadly for Brian, within weeks of their impending marriage, she fell in love with Mick Jagger in New York and broke off the engagement.

Some years later, in 1984, our team switched from Barbados to Mustique for our full holiday. At the farthest point of the island we rented the beautiful and exotic house called Obsidian, the property of the Earl of Lichfield, a contemporary of mine at school when he was known as Patrick Anson.

Obsidian was a house with a fabulous view out to sea. When Selwyn, our major-domo, delivered our rum punches at mid-day it was a moment sublime. The only house between ourselves and the ocean was Les Jolies Eaux, the property donated to Princess Margaret by Lord Glenconner. There was a long staircase hewn into the rock down to a private beach in a sheltered cove. We never once saw another soul on our beach. The sea was warm and buoyant and I would swim for 45 minutes on a featherbed lagoon.

Tony Murray, the top jockey, was our team captain in Mustique. Tony was engaged to a wonderful, bubbly girl in Margaret O'Toole, the daughter of the legendary Irish trainer Mick. I was deeply sorry when the relationship was broken off, although events were to prove that this may have been a partial blessing. Tony was to die in 1992 in tragic circumstances.

Our cove was in total contrast to Pasture Bay, a beach on the opposite side of the island. Pasture Bay had a severe undercurrent and on my first visit there I was almost swept out to sea. I was badly shaken. Even Charles Benson, a strong swimmer, was once in trouble for 20 minutes off Pasture Bay

The 'royal family' of Mustique were Virginia, Countess of Royston, and her lover Basil Charles, the local entrepreneur who ran the world-famous bar. 'Basil's Bar' was, quite simply, the only pub on the island. Every Wednesday there was a lively 'Jump Up', and Virginia staged marvellous picnics and was the spirit of Mustique. Tragically, she was struck down by cancer. I visited her in hospital in London and knew that she would never see her beloved island again.

The following year we arranged a game of cricket against the locals, but it was an embarrassingly one-sided affair. Our scratch side contained an Italian who had never played cricket (Luca Cumani) and several players the worse for rum. Our batting collapsed and we bowled badly. It was a black day for English cricket. We blamed the pitch.

We had a wonderful welcome from our major-domo that second

year. As we arrived at Obsidian from the airstrip, Selwyn was waiting with a tray with two jugs: one was filled with his own special rum punch and the other with Bloody Mary!

It was Tony Murray who had placed me in a deeply embarrassing and unenviable position in Barbados a few years earlier. Tony's girlfriend at the time was Wendy Cousins, the petite and engaging daughter of Eric Cousins, who had the distinction of being Robert Sangster's first-ever trainer. On this occasion Tony had gone missing down the beach. We all knew where he had gone, with whom, and what they were doing, but we expected him back before nightfall. At 10 pm there was still no sign of Tony, and 'Maudie' (as we called Wendy) was becoming emotional. I don't know what she was drinking, but it was strong stuff and there was plenty of it.

We were at Greensleeves and we tried to remove Wendy to a quiet corner. No corner was 'quiet' enough for Wendy in this mood. She was alternately berating Tony and then his companion, in terms that were becoming progressively colourful. The management, understandably, lodged a complaint, after which I was nominated to escort Wendy home.

Wendy is quite small and I was, at the time, reasonably strong, but try as I might I could not get Wendy down the steps of Greensleeves. I thought deeply about using my boxing experience to knock her out but I didn't dare risk it. In the end I was rescued by an angel of mercy who appeared at my shoulder in the form of Edna Tate, the mischievous wife of the Midlands trainer Martin Tate.

'Now Maudie, what's all this about?' she asked sympathetically. Wendy launched into another tirade of abuse against Tony, using language not widely understood by the female sex. 'You're quite right, darling,' said Edna, putting her arm around Wendy, 'you are absolutely right. *All* men *are* bastards. Every one of them.' 'And he's a bastard, too!' shouted Wendy, pointing at me – whereupon they went home happily, sharing the joy of abuse of the master sex.

I am not certain at what time precisely Tony attempted to slip into their room, but the slamming of doors, and subsequent dialogue, would have woken the whales. In the morning Tony was wearing the most savage black eye I have ever seen on a man in civilian life.

I incurred the displeasure of another jockey's girlfriend in 1982. It was the year after Willie Carson had suffered his crashing fall at York during the Ebor meeting. Willie's injuries were horrific and there was a suspicion of brain damage.

Willie and I were good friends and during the 1970s would always dine at Pontevecchio, in the Old Brompton Road, on the night of the Derby. The previous year I had matched him with the 'Generation Game' hostess Isla St Clair, who was living in my London house. (They were photographed at Epsom by the Dempster Diary, but the relationship was entirely innocent.) Nigel Angus had been dating Isla in Scotland and asked if she could stay with me in Chelsea now that she had broken into the big time. I was Isla's chaperone and our friendship was entirely platonic.

Meanwhile, Willie had ended an affair with the amateur jockey and breeder Suzanne Kane and was now courting Elaine Williams, a shy, petite girl with a hunting background, from Cheshire. I asked Willie and Elaine to join us in Barbados as part of his convalescence after the York incident. It was almost five months after the fall, but Willie had not thought about sitting on a horse. He was still uncertain of himself, and the Bajan climate was made-to-measure for his convalescence. We stayed in an elegant Venezuelan house called El Refugio, and in the evenings we played racing quizzes. Willie was still shaky and could not remember certain names.

One day we took Willie and Elaine on a trip to the south side of the island, to Crane Beach, in St Philip. There the sea was very different from the calm of the west coast. There was a fierce wind, and huge rolling waves crashed in from the Atlantic. The beach was therefore a surfer's paradise. Our sport was jumping and riding the waves: if you got it wrong you were smashed, cartwheeling into the surf, to emerge dazed and shaken and covered in sand.

Willie, fearless as ever, insisted on having a go, but Elaine was concerned. As she pointed out, Willie was barely five feet tall and some of the waves were eight feet high. Furthermore, there was a fierce undertow as the waves receded. Within minutes Willie was in trouble: he was swept out to sea and was swimming frantically to stay in touch with the shore.

Poor Elaine, whose eyes had never left him, panicked. She rushed into the sea, determined to swim out to save him. In her confusion she missed seeing a huge wave, which tossed her like a feather before pile-driving her head-first into the surf. Now it was Elaine who was in need of help. She was stunned, had swallowed a gallon of water, and lost her bikini-top. Willie, meanwhile had found a wave and surfed back into the shore. We dragged Elaine on to the beach, where she gasped and choked quite alarmingly. It took her some days to recover mentally. It was thoughtless of me to have suggested the trip.

Three years later I dealt myself and my second wife, Alison, a dose of the same medicine. It was our second year in Mustique and we had been told that there was a wonderful walk around South Point. We took that to mean that the walk was on the beach, on the rocky foreshore, in the shadow of the towering and craggy cliffs. Four of us embarked on the 'adventure' walk – David and Fiona Gibson, of Barleythorpe Stud, Oakham, and Alison and myself.

As we edged closer to South Point, with the sea now washing around our ankles, it struck me that the promontory was still some way distant. By now, in some bays, the waves were swirling up to our knees and waist. Something was wrong. Had we miscalculated the tide? There was talk of turning back. Suddenly a huge wave powered over the rocks and smashed us into the cliff-face. The crash of the furious sea against rock was deafening. Then there was silence.

There was silence because we were underwater. We had been tossed against the cliffs, like a piece of flotsam, and dragged backwards in the ebb-tide. Eventually, after a few seconds, when I was resigned to death, the wave receded and I jumped to my feet. I looked to my left, where Alison had been standing – she wasn't there. It was a second that lasted a lifetime, then I heard a voice on my right. It was Alison. We had somehow crossed over in mid-swirl.

We were all four alive. It was a miracle that none of us had smashed our heads against the rocks. We beat a retreat down the beach and re-grouped. Alison had several bruises, while David had bruises, cuts and abrasions. I had an open wound on my thigh, a suspected broken toe and had lost one rubber-soled shoe. Fiona was the worst casualty: as well as the inevitable bruises, she had a badly gashed elbow, pouring blood, which eventually was stitched – without the aid of an anaesthetic.

To their credit, the other three continued their walk above sea level, but I retired from the fray with the lame excuse that I could not continue with only one shoe! It transpired later that the expedition had been a suicide mission – the scenic path that we were supposed to take was 100 feet above sea level.

I have always respected the sea. I am not an especially strong swimmer and would never, for instance, dream of water-skiing without a lifebelt. It was in Barbados that I discovered another personal weakness. It came about when Duncan and Candy Sasse dined with us one evening on the beach. Duncan had recently trained Coup de Fer to win the Eclipse Stakes, while Candy was a devil-may-care tomboy behave-alike.

Candy had been parasailing off the west coast. 'You should try it,' she said, 'you'd love it – it's great fun.' The following morning, although I was first in the queue for a new experience, I viewed with misgivings the deep rope burns on the arms of dull-eyed locals in charge of the equipment, and was not encouraged by a stench of stale rum in the air.

I was ferried out to a floating raft in the calm bay. The harness was strapped to my body and orders passed on. I was to adopt a certain position, hold on to the supports in line with my shoulders and, as the boat set off and the parasail unfurled, allow myself to be lifted into the air. Thereafter, I should push the belt-support at my back to the seat of my bottom.

I took to the air without difficulty, but the task of slipping the belt beneath my bottom was beyond me. Instead of sitting in relative comfort, I was hanging on for dear life, with legs dangling. It was then that I discovered the other weakness in my make-up. As I looked down from 80 feet above the azure sea, I discovered that I was not blessed with a head for heights. I was utterly terrified: a shuddering frison overwhelmed me and I directed my gaze straight ahead. My knuckles turned white and my overworked arms began to ache. The wind buffeted me from side to side. I was more and more convinced that I would slip through the harness and plunge to a watery grave. 'I wouldn't do that again for a thousand dollars,' was all I could gasp on sinking eventually to the raft.

The next sailor, Gavin Pritchard-Gordon, was less fortunate. The wind dropped and he sank, parachute on top, into the sea. It transpired that, in the past, the guiderope had once broken and a 'passenger' had been blown halfway to Trinidad. Not long afterwards, following various insurance claims, parasailing was discontinued!

We had behaved progressively badly in Barbados during the 1970s, but 1979 was the year that everything came to a head. It was 12 months after Carolyn had left me and I was holidaying without a companion. Our team comprised Hamish Alexander and his girlfriend Serena Ainsworth, and Tony Collins. It was the first – or one of the first – years that the Irish 'boys' had honed in on Barbados. There was a lively group down the beach – Timmy and Trish Hyde; Demi and Kathy O'Byrne; and Bobby and Sarah Barry; all legendary names now in the racing and breeding world.

I got on especially well with Kathy O'Byrne, a sensitive girl whose interests were far removed from racing. While the rest of our two groups talked endlessly about horses and racing, Kathy and I explored a wider spectrum. We enjoyed each other's company and it was entirely innocent. But the 'boys' clearly felt that I had been over-familiar.

The following day they invited us water-skiing. Their hotel was facing a choppy bay and they had a boat and driver unknown to me. We set off, outside of the reef, on a journey that was to prove quite terrifying. No sooner had I kicked off my second ski than the boatman accelerated to a speed never before experienced. I bounced off the top of waves, went dry in my throat with apprehension, and felt my arms and wrists aching and becoming weaker. There was no sign of the driver returning to the beach, and something told me that if I dropped off I might be left to swim back to shore. At last the agony was over and I flopped into the sea. 'Did you enjoy it?' laughed Timmy. Evidently they had told the boatman that I was the British champion and 'needed a workout'!

On that day I was innocent of wrongdoing. On a later occasion I deserved retribution. We had gone to lunch one weekday with Robert and Susan Sangster ('the Sheilah') at Jane's Harbour, Robert's beautiful and exotic house next to Sandy Lane. Robert's guest was the international bloodstock agent Billy McDonald, who three years earlier had bought the eventual Arc winner Alleged for Robert, as a two-year-old. Billy was in favour and was accompanied on the trip by his 'fiancée', a Los Angeles model and part-time actress, whom I shall call 'Julie'.

After lunch the boys – Robert, Billy, Hamish and Tony – went off to play golf. Julie had nothing to do, so I invited her to have a look at our house and to do some water-skiing. We travelled back to Bel Air Annexe, had a couple more drinks and spent the afternoon skiing and in other pleasurable activities. We were in the shower when Serena, who had been swimming and sunbathing with some friends, returned to the house. 'Julian, the kettle's boiling,' she shouted. It was. That became a catchphrase for the rest of the trip.

In the evening we wandered down to Greensleeves bar after a good dinner with plenty of wine. Billy McDonald was there – not with Julie, but with a strapping amazonian woman with colossal forearms and the hint of a moustache. There was clearly a feeling that I had overstepped the acceptable limits of hospitality to Julie. 'This is Betty,' stated Billy. 'She is champion Brandy Alexander drinker and she is going to drink you under the table!' he challenged.

Betty was a formidable sight. The challenge could not be refused, but brandy was not exactly my specialist subject. We drank three Alexanders and then I took a gamble: 'Let's do some proper drinking now – let's drink tequila.' Tequila is not everyone's cup of tea. My former friend Simon Smith – Harriet's brother – came to a messy end once in my father's house after we had consumed over half a bottle, and was not invited again.

'OK,' said Betty. The full works entails a bite of lemon, a swallow of salt, and a shot of tequila. We did three and Betty was rocky. At this juncture I took my chance: 'I've enjoyed your company,' I managed to enunciate, 'but I've had a tiring day and I think I'll go home.' So I slid off my bar stool, walked accurately to the door, and set off towards home with as much dignity as I could muster. Fifty yards down the road I fell flat in the ditch.

Billy did not mention the episode again but, probably quite wisely, the 'engagement' was terminated soon afterwards – although Julie did have a remarkable talent.

Nick Teller, who had taken over Greensleeves from his father, was facing a quandary. There was no doubt that the bar takings from our group were beneficial to the business, but other customers were becoming annoyed. We were noisy, offensive and occasionally bad language was used. My attempts to impose authority as 'Führer' were increasingly ineffectual. During daylight I was deeply embarrassed, especially as the Tellers had always greeted me so warmly. I felt that a special relationship was being abused.

On two successive weekends there was unacceptable behaviour at Sunday lunch. It must be said that Susan Sangster was as boisterous as anyone and quite liable to dance on the table. There was an unhappy incident with some Bajan coffee. In the end Dulcie was tipped $100 to clear up the mess!

All this came to a head on Saturday 20 January. We were dining at Greensleeves after drinks with Martin and Edna Tate. There was a large and inglorious cast involved in this evening of shame, but the principal players included Charles Benson and the Lambourn trainer Anthony Johnson. There were the usual high jinks in the pool after dinner and perhaps the diving and splashing got out of hand. Whatever the cause, Nick Teller, polite and elegantly dressed, went over to Anthony Johnson's table to ask him to tone it down. Anthony stood up, said 'F--- off, Nick,' and pushed him in the pool.

Nick was beside himself with rage. He climbed out of the pool, stormed out of the dining room and returned a few moments later with a gun in his hand. 'Right! The lot of you – everyone out!' he raged. 'Now, every one of you!' Nick had snapped – his eyes were bulging, his hands trembling, and clearly he was capable of anything at that point.

Charles Benson tried to reason with a man beyond reason. Nick pointed the gun at him. Caroline Benson, failing to grasp the extent of Nick's crisis, shouted 'Shoot the bastard!' As Nick was screaming at his staff to phone the police, I slipped out of the dining room and disconnected the telephone wires from the hotel exchange. One by one Nick coerced his guests out of the dining room. We re-grouped in a house that Nick would not suspect if the police were involved.

It was a sad end to a wonderful chapter of Barbados life. Before long Greensleeves was closed and Nick left the business. When I last saw Greensleeves it was lying derelict and overgrown – a fading reminder of a lost corner of paradise.

# THIRTEEN

# *Family Feuds*

When Carolyn and I had been married for almost three years she was anxious to have a child. I had adopted a 'domani' approach, but in the end nature took its course and our son Thomas was born on 24 September 1973.

We had moved into our new home at 58 Seymour Walk, off the Fulham Road, only two weeks earlier. Carolyn had been rushing around looking at houses almost since she became pregnant and I let her get on with it. When she found the property she thought was ideal, I was happy to concur.

It was a tall, four-storey house, with a small garden, at the end of a fashionable cul-de-sac. The kitchen and dining room were in the basement, the drawing room on the ground floor, the master bedroom and bathroom on the first floor, my study and the nursery on the second floor, while Thomas and his nanny had adjacent rooms on the top floor. It was ideal and, as always, Carolyn made an excellent job of the decorations.

It was hard to find a diary 'window' for Thomas to be born, but that was Carolyn's affair, with the help of nature. In the event she chose a busy day. The servicing of my car, due at 10.15 am, had to be cancelled. I had an appointment with a solicitor at 10.45 am, a dentist appointment at 12.00 pm, and a lunch appointment with Russell Twisk, the editor of *Radio Times*, at 1.00 pm.

I drove Carolyn to the Westminster Hospital at breakfast time and asked her to 'hold on' until after lunch. In the event, lunch dragged on very pleasantly and I did not get home until 3.45 pm I phoned the hospital and was told the good news: Thomas had been born at 2.45 pm, weighed 7lb 8oz and appeared perfectly healthy.

At Leicester, Rapid River had won the Barleythorpe Stud Stakes. That's how a racing man remembers dates.

Carolyn stayed in hospital for eight days, which I took to be normal. I went to see her each day – in the latter part of the week, after racing at Ascot. On the following Monday, 'Nan,' who had brought up Carolyn, moved in, while mother and son reappeared in state the following day. The name Thomas was Carolyn's choice and I was happy to go along with it. The only victim of the whole procedure was Josh Gifford (the dog) who had been boarded out during all the excitement!

We had settled into a gentle rhythm of marriage. I worked ferociously hard during the week, we generally dined at home, and I drank little alcohol. On Saturday evenings we would dine well, in Chelsea or the West End; and on Sundays I would play football, or we would have friends to lunch. Now we were a family unit, and the balance of life changed perceptibly, but not drastically.

Thomas would join us for tea in the nursery if I was working at home, and if there was no football on Sunday we would go for a walk in Kensington Gardens.

My son was baptised in November, with an interesting choice of godparents.

They were Chris Collins, most of whose family are atheists, Nigel Angus, who has rarely found the energy to go to church, and Venetia Turner (or rather Warner, having divorced Archie Orr-Ewing and married again). Venetia and Carolyn had been friends at finishing school. Chris came up trumps with a case of Warre 1970 as a christening present. It was greatly enjoyed.

Seymour Walk was quiet and sociable. We had some pleasant neighbours, one of whom was the former model Vicki Hodge, who was married to Ian Heath, son of the owner of the top-class steeplechaser Charlie Potheen. At the same time she was enjoying a scandalous on-off relationship with the gangster-cum-actor, John Bindon.

Vicki would walk her Yorkshire Terriers past our kitchen window each morning, wearing no more than a thin nightie and a silken or lace dressing gown. We became friends and I took her racing at Sandown one day. She was looking for 'personality girl' work, and so I introduced her to the special events manager of a leading firm of bookmakers. Afterwards we had a drink at her home. Vicki had fabulous legs and as we spoke she crossed them in a way that was later to be made notorious by Sharon Stone. I finished my drink and walked home.

Some years later, in 1983, the Duke of York was to have a widely publicized encounter with Vicki on the beach in Barbados, and I can empathise with any temptation that he may have been subjected to. The following year Vicki sold the 'story' to a Sunday newspaper for £40,000.

Carolyn was not greatly involved in my work, but took an intelligent interest. We would rent a house on the beach at West Wittering, near Chichester, during Goodwood races and Thomas would have a week at the seaside.

It was broadcasting that led to our sharing a visit to Buckingham Palace to be received by the Queen in December 1974. Ivor Herbert had made a film about the Queen's racing interests, which we were shown in the Royal cinema. Personally, I did not feel that it was suitable for television transmission, although later it was broadcast by ITV.

I have been honoured to be presented to Her Majesty on three occasions and my admiration is unbounded. Last year I felt a deep empathy when, during a state visit to Pakistan, she commented: 'I sometimes sense that the world is changing almost too fast for its inhabitants, at least for us older ones.'

Three weeks after the birth of Thomas, Carolyn and I went to visit my father in Majorca. Earlier in the year he had moved to a hill-top house called Nido de Aguilas (Eagle's Nest), near the village of Capdella. Father was suffering from cancer of the lung. It had afflicted him first in 1969 and he had won the initial battle, but now he was advised to leave his beloved Fleet Street and to live amidst the clear, clean air of Majorca, to assist his breathing.

We travelled via Paris – and the Grand Criterium won by Nonoalco – flying on to Palma on the Sunday evening. I have one vivid memory of that expedition: of listening to the radio commentary of England versus Poland on top of that Spanish hill! England had to beat Poland to qualify for the 1974 World Cup, but were thwarted repeatedly by the Polish goalkeeper.

My father was, as always, an excellent host, but beneath his bonhomie and genuine pride at grandparenthood something was troubling him. It was only years later that I discovered the cause of his concern.

My stepmother Sally had two children by her marriage to 'Tommy' Thompson – a daughter Susan born in 1947 and a son Raymond born in New York in 1949. Raymond was educated at Douai and left that worthy Roman Catholic establishment to go to law school in 1967. He worked for five years as an articled clerk, before joining the well-known and reputable firm of solicitors, Clifford Turner. He moved eventually to Cumbria to practise in Whitehaven, but returned south again in the early eighties when his first marriage was dissolved.

Raymond set up his own practice in Diss in Norfolk and eventually sold it for a substantial sum. He and his second wife, Amanda, now live in a village near Thorndon, in Suffolk. They have three lovely children and Raymond has led an exemplary life. His mother was extremely proud of him.

Sally's daughter Susan, however, took a different path. Her accommodation on leaving school was in the north London suburb of Finsbury Park. From thence at weekends she was drawn to the black culture of south London. At the Ram Jam Club in Brixton she became friendly with the lead singer of a group called Juicy Lucy. At the same time she met a character called Lincoln Johnson. They were a colourful collection of individuals: Lincoln's brother Ben had recently been released from jail.

In March 1968, Susan gave birth to a daughter by Lincoln,

whom she called Sharon. Soon she was pregnant again, but this time lost the child after a particularly severe beating. Susan then moved back close to her mother and stepfather, renting a flat in Hampton Hill. Like her mother, she was subject to severe migraines and gradually her life fell apart. She suffered from paranoid schizophrenia, developed a phobia for her brother and stepfather, threatened her family with violence, and tried to kill herself. Eventually she moved to Norfolk with her daughter in the late 1970s and remained there until her death in 1988.

Sally was beside herself with worry and guilt. After my father's death she moved to Swaffham to be close to Susan and spent fortunes on treatment to alleviate her suffering. It was all to no avail. Sharon, meanwhile, was to fall pregnant at the age of 21 and has a daughter called Francesca. It was only recently that I became aware of this traumatic and unhappy saga.

While this nightmare was unfolding in the 1970s, Sally's constant concern for her daughter and her feeling of impotence so far from home was inevitably shared by my father. It cast a dark, brooding cloud over his retirement, while Sally was split between two people she loved. It was a constant concern. Susan was no longer accountable for her actions.

It was this spectre that hung over Nido de Aguilas when we visited in October 1973. Of course, it was not discussed. My father and I had a restricted agenda and Sally's family and emotional affairs were not included. I suppose father regarded me as too selfish to express the sympathy and comfort that Sally deserved. Perhaps he was right: I was self-centred and focused obsessively upon my career.

My career. There is no doubt that the 1970s were the golden age of programme-making at the BBC, and especially in outside broadcasts. We were filming stories of which I remain proud. I had won the trust of many of the great names in racing, who had previously been suspicious of television.

We produced two feature films on the legendary Noel Murless, who had hitherto been exceptionally publicity-shy. One of these proved the inspiration – and provided much of the text – for Tim Fitzgeorge-Parker's book *The Guv'nor*. Noel, along with his blunt-spoken Scots wife Gwen, became good friends in his retirement and I spent several pleasant evenings sharing a glass of whisky with Noel in his bungalow near the stud that he managed in Woodditton.

We also filmed a memorable documentary entitled 'Aintree Iron', on the life of the doughty Mirabel Topham. The executive producer was Ray Lakeland, a genial Lancastrian who had a remarkable skill of mollifying the formidable Mrs T. Ray, like a lion-tamer, would go into her cage while the rest of us stood with knees shaking outside. 'Now then, old duck, what's all this fuss about?' he would ask. Within minutes she was eating from the palm of Ray's hand, chastened like a petulant schoolgirl. Now filming could go ahead!

Brian Cowgill had taken over from Peter Dimmock as head of outside broadcasts. It was sometimes difficult to divorce fantasy from reality with Brian, but he was convinced that he had 'invented' one-day cricket in England and now he was determined to revolutionize television coverage of racing.

ITV had launched a strong competitor to our Saturday racing coverage in the 'ITV Seven'. Every weekend they transmitted from two race meetings, covering seven races at quarter hour intervals, over an hour and a half. The ITV Seven was a seven-horse accumulator bet, and every few weeks a punter would come up trumps and be presented with a huge cheque, 'live' on TV. The racing was mostly moderate – Catterick and Sedgefield were often involved – but the idea was a winner. I recall vividly that Susan claimed to bet on the ITV Seven. In retrospect one can appreciate the environment that led to this interest!

Cowgill was determined to confront the ITV Seven head-on, but did not want to cover two meetings. Said Brian in his broad Lancashire brogue: 'I want to stay at the races for an hour and a half, with no breaks. Non-stop racing! That's what I want!' I tried to explain that it was impossible to reduce the time between races to less than half and hour. I explained saddling, weighing out and weighing in, stewards enquiries, paddock and parades, ambulances and safety procedures, and most important – the mechanics of betting. Brian was not interested in any of this: 'I want to stay at the races and I want non-stop action. Lord's said that one-day cricket wouldn't work and it bloody does. So go and do the same with racing!'

It was obvious that the only means of increasing the number of races within an hour-and-a-half period was to include some 'novelty' or extra races that did not involve professional jockeys. So, as an intermediate measure, I devised a series of 'match' races between well-known personalities. They were run a quarter of an hour before our first race on the chosen Saturday. These were limited handicaps with a weight range of 14lb at official Jockey Club ratings.

The heats took place throughout the summer, and the riders were a mixed bunch: the Duke of Alburquerque, Ian Balding, Chris Collins, Ted Edgar, Hugh Fraser (the owner of Harrods), Clement Freud, Bill Shand-Kydd and the Earl of Suffolk. Some riders found difficulty in doing the weight; I, in turn, had difficulty in finding them horses to ride.

Clement Freud was so dehydrated, after losing about 21lb to ride at Bath, that he demolished three bottles of hock – with little help – in an extremely short time. 'Mickey' Suffolk took his training seriously and would land on Barry Hills' gallops in the morning by helicopter or light aircraft. Ted Edgar, to put it mildly, was an unusual shape for a jockey.

The final was staged at Haydock on the 'great day'. John Hughes, the enterprising clerk of the course, agreed to stage five races within an hour and half and obtained the Jockey Club's approval. This was the programme we devised:

| | | |
|---|---|---|
| *1.15* | *Ladies' race* | *1m 2f* |
| *1.40* | *Apprentices' race* | *2m* |
| *1.55* | *Match – Final* | *1m* |
| *2.15* | *Vernons Sprint Cup* | *6f* |
| *2.45* | *Tote Roll-Up Race* | *1m* |

The day could be viewed as a qualified success. The races were 'off' fairly punctually – we had fulfilled Brian Cowgill's requirement – and 'Grandstand' *could* have stayed at Haydock, had they so wished. However, the experiment was never repeated, which was probably just as well. For the record, 'Mickey' Suffolk, to his huge delight, won the Match Final. We presented him with an extremely modest 'Grandstand' trophy of which he is inordinately proud.

The previous year we had added Chester to our portfolio of racecourses. This was a thrilling meeting to cover, both for the quality of the pictures available – the race coverage was unmatched at any other meeting – and for the hugely enjoyable social aspect.

The May meeting at Chester is one of the great social events of the north-west. The local landed gentry have magnificent house parties, and the hotels in Chester and the surrounding countryside are fully booked. Willie Carson was married during Chester week, while the households of Robert Sangster, Bobby McAlpine, Lord Daresbury, Lord Leverhulme, Basil de Ferranti and many others are all nearby. It is a wonderful week, so it was heartbreaking when, in 1986, following the cutbacks imposed by Michael Grade during his period of management at the BBC, we were obliged to discontinue our coverage. It was ironic that, when Michael Grade moved to Channel 4, Chester became one of the flagships of their racing coverage.

In the autumn of 1972 'Mickey' Suffolk gave a magnificent party that was to bring a change to several relationships. The most important was the relationship between Mickey himself and the girl who was taking the photographs at the dance. She was Anita Fugelsang, who the following autumn became the Countess of Suffolk. Sadly, that marriage did not survive and Anita is now the Viscountess Petersham and stepmother to the Viscountess Linley.

Another relationship that changed for ever was that between myself and Pat O'Sullevan, wife of my colleague Peter.

Enjoying a successful year as Peter's understudy, I had commentated on 23 days' racing against 67 days covered by Peter. Peter was only 54, but I *was* looking forward to the time when I would take over his microphone. He suffered badly in the winter from bronchitis and the cold winds of Newmarket had caused him particular discomfort.

For Mickey's party I was staying with a lugubrious and larger-than-life character called John Irwin, who lived in a beautiful mill house in the village of Little Somerford. John's dinner party before the dance included the famous designer Nina Campbell, and Victor Barclay, the man whose features inspired the name 'Señor El Betrutti' (Mr Beetroot). I had been racing at Ascot and before we dined John and I cracked a bottle of champagne. After dinner we drank some superlative port and to Jane Irwin's understandable annoyance we arrived at the dance extremely late.

One of the first people I saw at the dance was Pat O'Sullevan. 'When's your husband going to retire?' I demanded, in what I regarded as a good-humoured way. 'It's very nearly my turn you know!' Pat's features froze. 'He's nowhere near ready to retire,' she said icily, 'and you're nowhere near ready to take over from him.'

That was that. It was an exchange that coloured our relationship for the following 25 years. I, for one, never again felt comfortable in her company. I have little doubt that her account of our dialogue to Peter influenced his attitude towards me – of which more later.

For all that 'false start,' it was a memorable party at which we danced until the early hours. I had dozens of conversations with racing guests, very few of which I could remember the next morning, except for a hilarious chat with a well-known bloodstock agent who was convinced that I was Jeremy Hindley and had trained a horse called The Go Between. I had a chronic attack of hiccups on the way back to Little Somerford and a savage hangover in the morning. What a party!

A couple of years later, on the train from Warrington to London after a day at Haydock, I asked Peter: 'When *are* you actually going to retire?' 'Oh, when I'm 65,' he replied. That remark was the basis of a misunderstanding that had a major effect on my life.

Two weeks after 'Mickey' Suffolk's party I voiced a commentary that was unique in my broadcasting career. BBC-TV had planned to show a recorded coverage of the Prix de l'Arc de Triomphe at between 5.30 and 5.40 pm on Sunday evening, but the programme was cancelled and the only coverage was to be on the evening TV News. Since Peter Bromley was covering the race for BBC Radio it was decided that his commentary would be recorded and laid over the pictures. I was not required, so I invited my father and grandmother to lunch. It was a classic family Sunday lunch and I served the best port.

The telephone rang at about 4.30 pm: it was BBC-TV News, and there was a crisis. The commentary on the 'Arc' had not come through because there had been some technical foul-up. They wanted me to go immediately to Television Centre to dub a commentary.

Having apologized to my guests I took a taxi to White City, but on the journey severe misgivings surfaced: I certainly was not fit to drive, so was I fit to describe 19 runners in Europe's championship horse race? On arrival I looked at the race recording and told the producer that I was ready. The first 'take' was good but the second was brilliant – it was probably as good a commentary as I had ever recorded! At least, that was my opinion when I saw it transmitted later.

In the early 1970s I built a good working relationship with Lester Piggott. Lester was never the easiest man with whom to communicate because he was liable to be preoccupied and monosyllabic. He has always had difficulty in hearing if there is extraneous noise, so the secret is to speak clearly and one-to-one. The best way to explain his hearing problem is that sound has to be processed on the way to his brain – this is why sometimes he has been misconceived as slow on the uptake. I developed the formula of typing out my basic questions and delivering them to him – either at home or in the weighing room – before we did an interview. The system worked well and we had some good interviews.

In the years when the BBC was covering the Derby in competition with ITV, I would be sited on a rostrum by the Rubbing Horse public house, about 100 yards beyond the winning post. Talk about boxing with your hands tied behind your back! Nonetheless, I got the first interview post-race with Lester after his wins on both Nijinsky and Roberto. We had an arrangement and Lester delivered. He was totally professional and reliable.

My luck ran out when Brian Taylor won the Derby on the 50/1 shot Snow Knight in 1974. I interviewed Brian the previous morning at Epsom after he had ridden his horse round Tattenham Corner. He was reasonably bullish about his chances, and I told him that the interview was to be shown on 'Newsnight' later that evening. Brian sat in front of his television all evening and the interview never appeared – it had been dropped for another late item, supposedly because someone thought Snow Knight was a 'no-hoper'. Brian was bitterly disappointed, and when he won gave his first interview after the Derby to John Rickman on ITV. Now it was my turn to be disappointed. It was the first of a long line of personal grievances against BBC News.

I was far from overwhelmed when News and Current Affairs Department asked me to report from Ladbrokes' headquarters in Harrow on the night of the 1974 general election. In my view our contribution was less than satisfactory. In a fast-moving scenario they were switching to us two or three minutes too late for each change in the odds. I was finally released at 3.00 am and was due to commentate at Haydock – 200 miles north – in less than 12 hours' time. After the excitement of the election and the experience of an entirely new style of broadcasting, I was unable to sleep. As luck would have it, the fields were small, and I cruised through the broadcast in third gear.

It was during 1974 that our colleague Clive Graham, a man universally liked and admired, died. He was someone almost impossible to replace and his partnership with Peter O'Sullevan – both on the *Daily Express* and on BBC-TV – was legendary. Clive was dry, off-beat and self-effacing. His 'homework' was done substantially in the Members' bar before racing, with pink gin in hand. The little titbits of information he received from his many friends pinpointed plenty of winners. Charles Benson succeeded him as 'The Scout' at the *Express*, while Jimmy Lindley and John Hanmer eventually took over his BBC paddock role.

There was one event in 1975 which towers above all others in the context of racing history, and that was the stable lads' strike. I was involved at two levels, as a broadcaster and as an owner. It was a profoundly unhappy episode which exploded at the Guineas meeting at Newmarket and simmered on for over two months. Enemies were made and resentments developed that persisted for many years. Most of the high-profile stable-lad strikers – who worked for Sam Armstrong, Clive Brittain and the owner David Robinson – have long since left racing. Only one, to my knowledge, still works in Newmarket.

The activists who caused chaos and divided racing at the Guineas meeting were flying pickets who had arrived in coaches from the docks and elsewhere. Their union spokesman, Sam Hardcastle, was a passenger on a wave of cynical violence.

In the week after the disgraceful scenes at the Guineas meeting – where jockeys were pulled from their horses, and conscientious stable lads, anxious to tend their charges, threatened with violence – I did a broadcast about the strike from Chester races. I tried to be as objective as possible and illustrated my exposition with hard facts and statistics.

This effort enraged a group of Labour MPs – harangued, no doubt, by my 'friend' Lord Wigg – who laid down an early-day motion criticizing my broadcast and claiming that my comments were 'inaccurate, adverse and prejudiced.' They called upon the BBC 'to restrain sports commentators from commenting on industrial disputes of which they obviously had so little knowledge'. This attracted a riposte from 16 Conservative and Liberal MPs . Their amendment to the commons motion regretted that the 14 Labour MPs appeared to spend their working afternoons watching racing on television! The affair was referred to the Director General of the BBC and entailed a great deal of paperwork, but by and large I received loyal support from my superiors.

I was also involved in the strike at a personal level, as a racehorse owner. To the horror of everyone in Newmarket, the strikers turned to arson and burnt down the Dutch barn at the back of the stables of Bruce Hobbs, my trainer. It was completely gutted, with the loss of 90 tons of hay. If the fire brigade had arrived a quarter of an hour later the entire stables would have been destroyed. As with almost all stables, Bruce had some union members in the yard and others who were working normally. One of the striking lads assisted his 'working' colleagues in containing the fire and moving the horses out of the yard. The remainder stood at the end of the road, cheering the flames.

The strike dragged on towards Derby Day and there were threats that 'industrial action' would prevent the great race from taking place. There was talk of picketing the racecourse stables and of the TGWU calling out horsebox drivers, starting-stall handlers and others whose labour was essential to the mechanics of a day's racing.

Now the most alarmed group of individuals were the bookmakers. Derby Day was a colossal betting bonanza, with turnover of upwards of £30 million. It was unthinkable that the Derby should be sacrificed. So Lord Wigg – who had two years earlier completed his term of office as chairman of the Horserace Betting Levy Board, but was still involved in racing politics as president of the Betting Office Licencees Association (BOLA) – was persuaded to travel to Newmarket to arrange an 'amnesty' with the lads for Derby Day. He was successful, and the Derby, 'the People's Race,' went ahead.

I was standing outside the weighing room during the day's racing – for some reason the BBC decided not to cover the Derby in 1975 and 1976 – when a leading bookmaker passed by. 'Congratulations,' I said, 'I gather that we owe this afternoon's racing entirely to you!' The bookmaker acceded and added: 'In the end I practically drove Wigg down to Newmarket.'

It was common knowledge what had happened, and the following day Nigel Dempster wrote an item in his *Daily Mail* diary identifying my bookmaker friend as the '*eminence grise* behind

Wigg's peace mission'. Within hours Wigg, a regular litigant, was threatening legal action. Two weeks later I saw Dempster at Royal Ascot, and having heard of the libel threat offered to give evidence in court in light of my personal conversation with the bookmaker. I felt that the *Mail* article was fireproof, but with the might of the former Paymaster General and his legal ally, the redoubtable Lord Goodman, in opposition, the *Mail*'s lawyers ran scared and settled out of court.

Unhappily for Nigel, *Private Eye* ran an item in its 'Grovel' column – with which Nigel was associated – suggesting that Wigg 'owed a favour to the bookmaker; had incurred excessive gambling debts; and, as a Minister of the Crown, had gambled beyond his means'. This was an accusation less easily defended and the publication was obliged to make a complete withdrawal and apology, as well as paying damages.

Wigg's luck ran out the following year. He was arrested and tried for using insulting behaviour likely to cause a breach of the peace, after it was alleged that he had approached six women between 11.00 and 11.20 pm in Park Lane on 17 September. The case was dismissed for lack of evidence as the police had failed to interview any of the six women allegedly accosted. The magistrate, Leonard Tobin, said that he did not accept the 76-year-old labour peer's account of events, but concluded: 'Kerb crawling itself is not an offence against the laws of this country. It may be objectionable, but it is not an offence.' Wigg was acquitted, but was publicly disgraced.

Sadly, the saga of the stable lads' strike was not over. The dispute dragged on until Royal Ascot, when ABS members working for the BBC were instructed not to cross the stable lads' picket line and the television coverage was aborted. Happily, normality was restored by the time of the King George VI and Queen Elizabeth Diamond Stakes, otherwise viewers would have missed the 'Race of the Century' – the enthralling duel between Grundy and Bustino, in a time that smashed the course record by almost three seconds.

The following month I had an unusual encounter with the late

Pinturischio, the potential champion ruthlessly destroyed by the dopers.

The Princess Royal's biggest flat-race win came on Ten No Trump's in the diamond race at Ascot – followed by an ingratiating interview by the author!

Royal Palace (black colours) winning the 2000 Guineas under a brilliant ride from George Moore.

Bill Shand-Kydd – Champion point-to-point jockey, and a regular at the Cheltenham Festival.

Who on earth was Bernard Parkin lampooning?

'The bigger they are ...' Harvey Smith takes a tumble at Bechers Brook with Cashel Fort.

Red Rum (left) blazing a trail on the harrowed strip on Southport Sands. 'Ginger' McCain (in car) checks his speed.

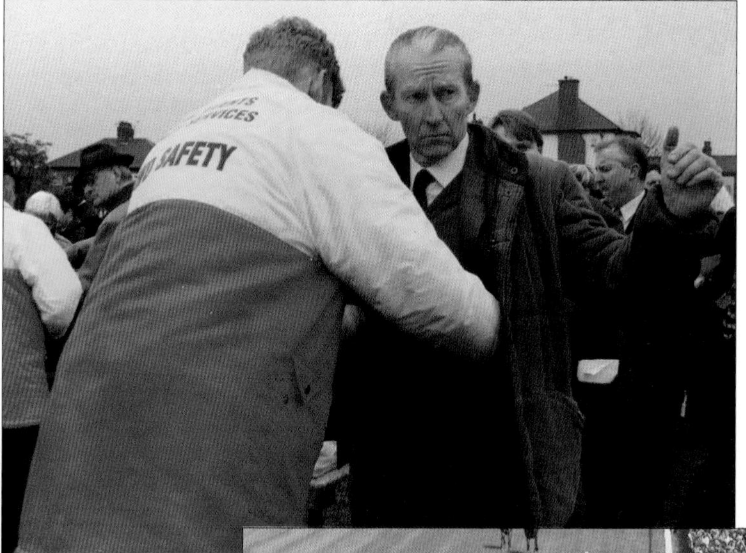


The Monday Grand National. 'Frisking' a suspicious character.

Shergar and Walter Swinburn winning the Derby by a record 10 lengths – and paying for Alison's engagement ring!

Pontenuovo (right) winning the Royal Hunt Cup at 50/1 – a dream that took shape 18 months earlier.

Nifty at Fifty. A memorable birthday lunch, after a hard week's work at Royal Ascot, in 1990.

The Royal Hunt Cup won by Pontenuovo, was the icing on the cake!

Above: A day to remember. Peter O'Sullevan's 50th and final Grand National – and my Aintree swan-song – shared with Des Lynam.

Below: My final BBC broadcast, at Chepstow. Clerk of the Course Rodger Farrant made it very special.

Dennis Waterman's XI. Spot the stars – Sexton, Jago, Mullery, Dodgin, Gubba, Armstrong and ... Wilson(?).

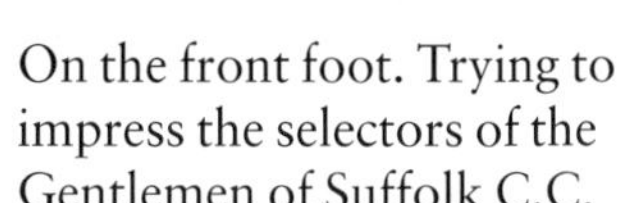

On the front foot. Trying to impress the selectors of the Gentlemen of Suffolk C.C.

Riding Battledore, the ice-wall before the world-famous Shuttlecock on the Cresta Run.

Above: Team-talk with Tarrant. Chris Tarrant talks a good game before Lord Taverners vs Lord Vestey's XI at Cheltenham, in July 1997.

Below: Lou Macari. At Swindon, his 'red and white army' marched onwards and upwards.

Jumping at Ascot. It's a serious game for the 'pros'.

Robert Maxwell, who was planning to launch a new newspaper in Scotland. He telephoned personally from his country house in Oxfordshire to ask whether I would write for it. We spoke for several minutes and he asked me to think it over, finally leaving me with two personal, direct-dial telephone numbers. Evidently this was typical of the man, in that he would exclude even his closest confidants from his decision-making. In the event, nothing came of it. As with several other offers of work, notably from the *Independent on Sunday*, it was vetoed by the BBC on the grounds that I was their correspondent.

I began 1976 with a 'Sportsnight' scoop. My friend Tony Murray, then one of Britain's top three jockeys, had decided to turn his back on Great Britain and ride for a leading stable in France. I flew to the south of France where Tony was riding at Cagnes-sur-Mer, on the first Sunday in March. The following 48 hours were amongst the most traumatic of my life.

Charlie and Wendy Millbank, for whom Tony would be riding, invited me to a party on the Sunday night. For some reason I got involved in a fierce argument with Julian 'Screamer' Lewis (not about his wife) and challenged him to a fight in the garden. Luckily, he did not appear. The following morning I filmed the interview with Tony and we lunched at the Colombe d'Or in St Paul de Vence. After lunch, I drove down the hill to Cagnes-sur-Mer and had a head-on crash on the coast road. Miraculously, neither I nor the film was damaged, but there was a traffic tailback of almost ten miles between Nice and Cannes.

The car rental firm, very kindly in the circumstances, provided me with another car. I had dinner in Haut de Cagnes after parking my car in one of the narrow one-way streets in that enchanting old fortress village. On emerging from the restaurant, to my horror I found that my exit route was totally blocked. Despairingly I looked into a nearby café and asked the proprietor how I could trace the owner of the offending vehicle. His reply, in very local dialect French, was along the lines of: 'Oh, that is the Citroën of Jacques. He is – how shall I say – visiting his girlfriend. Sometimes this takes one hour, sometimes it is two, sometimes it is three. May I suggest, monsieur, that you make yourself comfortable and I shall serve you a cognac.'

With exhaustion, panic and despair alternating as my dominant emotion, I eventually dropped off. Then the proprietor shook me awake with the words: 'Hey. It is Jacques! He has finished! Now you can go home!' I did, and caught my plane back to London with the crock-of-gold in my canvas carrier bag.

As I crossed the road outside the Terminal Building at Heathrow, the bag slipped on its side and the can of film rolled out, very slowly, on to the road, directly into the path of an oncoming taxi. I stood transfixed and simply could not believe my eyes. I had risked violence, death and incarceration for this can of film and now, with the winning post in sight, it was going to be run over and crushed by a London taxi. As the vehicle drove over the edge of the can I was in shock. How could I contemplate facing the programme editor if the film was unusable? There would be a significant hole in the programme, and my expenses were not negligible.

I used up my monthly allowance of supplication to God and prayed for a miracle. The miracle had happened. The tin was crushed to within an inch of the film, but it was undamaged. My scoop was safe!

I was playing a lot of football at this time, some of it for Denis Waterman's Charity XI, whose regular team included Dave Sexton, Alan Mullery, Bill Dodgin and various other former internationals. The biggest match in the careers of almost all the amateurs who played in it was Norwich City versus the Jockeys' All Star XI at Carrow Road on Monday 26 April 1976. Norwich City paid us the compliment of playing their full team, including Martin Peters, Ted MacDougall, Kevin Keelan, John Bond, Colin Suggett and Phil Boyer. Luckily for us they played out of position – Martin Peters kept goal and Ted MacDougall played right-back, marking our speedy left-winger! (Well, that's my fantasy.) The final score was 12-11.

David Nicholson, in the heart of our defence, had a predictable confrontation with Norwich's so-called 'hard man'. How 'hard' he actually was I don't know, but he went to play football in America and was exposed by a lurid Sunday newspaper as a 'beach boy'. I netted a hat-trick and received a reasonable press in one of the racing newspapers.

The dry wit of the late Roger Mortimer, writing in *The Racehorse*, brought me down to earth. Reviewing the Lingfield Derby Trial, Mortimer wrote: 'Whitstead did make rather heavy weather of vanquishing Son Fils, who is about as likely to play a prominent part in a classic as Julian Wilson is to be signed on by Nottingham Forest; and that is very unlikely indeed!'

Meanwhile, anabolic steroids were rumoured to be in use in the training of racehorses. I filmed a major story with Professor Arnold Bennett, the Olympic analyst, and exposed what threatened to be a major menace in horseracing. I was on the crest of the wave.

But the most important day of the year for me was Wednesday 1 September. Since 1972, I had been breeding thoroughbreds in Ireland under the banner of my company Seymour Bloodstock Ltd, and had boarded my mares with a delightful man called Tony Wingfield (who also boarded the Queen Mother's NH mares in Ireland). I had lunch with Tony at his stud and he broke the news that he was cutting back on his stud farming and would no longer be taking boarders. 'But I know someone who would be very happy to accommodate you,' he said. 'A great friend of mine called Liz Burke. She's not far away – we could go there at teatime.'

So I came to meet the remarkable Elizabeth Burke, the mother of Sir Thomas Pilkington, Sonia Rogers and Moira Hanbury and the mistress of Stackallan Stud. That meeting was the basis of 15 happy and successful years operating from Stackallan. It also led to my buying a racehorse which transformed my life.

## FOURTEEN

# *Four-Legged Friends*

On the September evening in 1976 when Liz Burke showed me round the stables at Stackallan Stud, County Meath, a yearling that really caught my eye was a colt by Tumble Wind. I did not know the stallion; apparently he had been imported to Ireland from America by Liz's son-in-law, Captain Tim Rogers, who owned the world-famous Airlie Stud in County Kildare. He had been a useful racehorse, but was not notably commercial as a stallion in the States. This was his first crop of yearlings in Europe.

The yearling sales at Newmarket were to begin on 11 October, the day after the Grand Criterium at Longchamp. That was a race I hated to miss – it is France's top contest for two-year-olds – and I promised Carolyn that we would spend a few days in Paris afterwards.

So I asked Bruce Hobbs in my absence to look at three yearlings for me, whose pedigrees appealed. One was by Sun Prince, one by Morston, and one by Tumble Wind. He was to bid for any of them that he liked up to 5000 guineas. In the event, Bruce and his house guest, the former amateur jockey and actor Teddy Underdown, found another colt by Tumble Wind – which Teddy, for one, fell in love with. He was a bonny little bay colt by Tumble Wind out of Miss Pinkerton, by Above Suspicion. He was on the small side, but compact and athletic, and had great presence. The first time I saw him he put me immediately in mind of Mill Reef.

I adored him and was thrilled that we had bought him so relatively inexpensively – 4800 guineas. The reason was simple:

no-one knew much about Tumble Wind – 'another failed American stallion' was the consensus of opinion.

Bruce asked me if I would call him Tumbledown, the nickname for Teddy Underdown, but the name was taken. So we did the next best thing and called him Tumbledownwind. This horse was to bring me such joy and excitement – and relative wealth.

The purchaser of a racehorse is expected to settle with the auction house within three weeks of the sale. There was little doubt in my mind that this colt would be 'paid for' by a filly called Welsh Flame, who was running in the Cambridgeshire that Saturday. I had backed her at 33/1 each-way to win a substantial sum. To my amazement the horse, ridden by Compton Rodrigues, ran no sort of race and finished unplaced. Now I had bookmakers, as well as auctioneers, awaiting settlement.

The upshot was that I asked Bruce, with embarrassment, if he could place 50 per cent of our colt with another owner. In the following months Bruce sold a leg each to two charming ladies in Joë Farmer, who lived in Northumberland where her husband Nigel ran a stud, and Norah Hunter-Blair, who had never previously been involved with racehorse ownership and lived in Newmarket. They were to be two very fortunate ladies!

As if to justify my confidence in her, Welsh Flame went on to become one of the great broodmares of the past 20 years, producing a family for her owner Pat O'Kelly which has raised tens of millions of pounds at the sales – including the dual Classic winner Salsabil.

Tumbledownwind, as expected, came to hand early and was Bruce's first two-year-old runner of the season. He was beaten first time out at the Craven meeting, but two weeks later he won the opening race of the Guineas meeting by six lengths. I telephoned Carolyn from Newmarket that evening and tried to contain my excitement. 'I think we might have quite a good horse,' I ventured. His next stop was at Haydock – not a lucky racecourse for me – but he won there fairly comfortably.

Now it was Royal Ascot. We decided to go for the Chesham Stakes over six furlongs, rather than the New Stakes over five.

Unfortunately we ran into a champion filly in Sookera and came off second best. Sookera went on to win the Cheveley Park Stakes in the autumn.

Bruce had really wound the little horse up for Royal Ascot and wanted to give him a rest. Despite that I asked him if he could get the colt ready for the big Goodwood meeting – six weeks after Ascot – because it was always one of my favourite meetings of the year. Bruce had misgivings and was able to give him only a couple of gallops leading up to Goodwood. He ran on the Saturday, in the Rous Memorial Stakes, rather than earlier in the week, to give him a couple of extra days. But Geoff Lewis, the stable jockey, chose to ride at Newmarket, so Geoff Baxter stepped in for the ride. It was Tumbledownwind's best performance yet: he won very comfortably by four lengths, in a course record time.

We were all, including Thomas, staying on the beach at West Wittering and had a wonderful evening at the nearby fair – where we ran into Henry Cecil with his daughter Katie!

Bubbling with excitement I telephoned Bruce, who was in Newmarket. 'Wasn't that marvellous?' I enthused. He was not so ecstatic: 'I don't know what Baxter was doing winning by so far. He looked as if he had a train to catch!' Undaunted I asked: 'Can we go for the Gimcrack?' to which his response was: 'I don't know about that, I've got a better one than yours to run there.' 'Well, run them both,' I suggested, 'we'll be second string and Baxter can ride.' In the event, the 'better one' fell by the wayside and Tumbledownwind faced just four opponents for the historic race at the Knavesmire.

Since 1971 I had been involved in the BBC's radio coverage of the York Ebor meeting (ITV had the television rights). Peter Bromley, the radio racing correspondent, chose to take his holiday during August, which suited me well. York is a wonderful race meeting – the work was challenging but far from arduous, and the radio commentary box was as excellent a place as any to watch the action.

Tumbledownwind certainly seemed to have a favourite's chance in the Gimcrack, although there were whispers for a horse from Ireland, called Octavo, ridden by Lester Piggott for Vincent O'Brien. The jockey/trainer partnership had swept all before them in 1977 and the previous day had won the Great Voltigeur Stakes by a wide margin with Alleged.

My main concern was the weather. Tumbledownwind was a light-actioned colt who seemed to be best suited to fast ground. Since rain was forecast, on the eve of the race I slept apprehensively. I awoke at 5 am to hear the first drops of rain on the windowpane of my hotel bedroom. It was still raining when I breakfasted with my friend John de Moraville, formerly of the *Daily Express*. It was raining when I got to the races and it was raining when racing began. A feeling of gloom set in.

Nevertheless one recollection reassured me. The ground had been soft when Mill Reef ran in the Gimcrack, and his trainer had talked about pulling him out. We all know that Mill Reef splashed through the rain, as nimble as a ballet dancer, winning by ten lengths. I thus encouraged myself with the thought: 'We don't know for sure that our little horse *cannot* go in the soft.'

I made a brief appearance in the paddock to look at the five runners under their rainproofs and to calm the nerves of my two ladies. Norah, in particular, was seriously atwitter. Then it was time to climb to the commentary box and welcome the Radio 2 listeners after the 3 o'clock news. What followed was an unusual experience, but in a way no different from commentating on a race in which you have had a substantial bet. In the end the mechanics of broadcasting take over – and that was certainly a big help on this day of days!

It was an exciting race and I thought that the little horse was beaten when he was briefly headed a furlong and a half out. But he battled back with terrific courage under Geoff Lewis and won by a length and a half from Brian Taylor's mount Aythorpe. I wrapped up the broadcast, stepped out of the commentary box and was suddenly overwhelmed by a tidal wave of excitement and euphoria.

I had won the Gimcrack, one of the greatest races in the calendar and with a first prize of over £26,000! I declined an invitation to be interviewed by ITV, leaving that to our jockey.

After the presentation the York committee invited Bruce, myself and my ladies for a glass of champagne. I was briefly hesitant. 'Come on,' said Bruce, 'for God's sake, you've just won the Gimcrack.' 'That's all very well,' I replied, 'but I've still got to commentate on the Nunthorpe'. Happily, the champagne did no harm and probably the reverse!

I travelled back to London by train with Geoff Lewis. On the journey down he said: 'He's a wonderful little horse and he's very brave, but I don't think he's top-class. Ron Smyth [the trainer] was saying that you should sell him and he could be right.' In London we dined at Pontevecchio on succulent grouse – it *was* 18 August! – washed down with Brunello di Montalcino. During dinner, Geoff's golfing chum Ronnie Corbett rang the restaurant to congratulate him on the big win.

Tumbledownwind's next race was, appropriately, the Mill Reef Stakes at Newbury. Now he carried a Group 2 penalty and was beaten a length and a half into third place by Formidable and Aythorpe to whom he was conceding 4lb. Geoff said afterwards: 'He's run a marvellous race, but I just felt him flinch when I put him under pressure. He just might have had enough for this season.'

The Middle Park Stakes – the two-year-old championship race run at Newmarket – was just 11 days away. I suggested to Bruce that we take Geoff's advice to put the colt away for the remainder of the season. Bruce suggested at first that we wait for a few days, to see how he came out of the race, but then he agreed. The colt was clearly a genuine prospect for the following year's 2000 Guineas.

It was around this time that we received a substantial offer for the little horse. It came from an unlikely source – from my colleague Peter O'Sullevan on behalf of his friend, the Marquesa de Moratalla. It was a doubly attractive offer, because the horse would remain in training with Bruce Hobbs.

Over the past ten years I had learned the folly of turning down generous offers for racehorses, so I was keen to sell. So, too, was Norah Hunter-Blair, whose nerves had been stretched to the limit by the excitement of the last few months. Joë Farmer, however, a wealthy woman in her own right who was having an absolutely wonderful time with this great little horse, was totally opposed to the sale.

To try to resolve the situation I flew to Newcastle races to have lunch with the Farmers. There I explained that I had no inheritance of any consequence, that the BBC paid me an unworthy wage (recalling Eric Morecombe's gag about his BBC suit – small checks!), and that I had a young son who had to be educated. I also believed it to be the correct commercial decision, even though Formidable had gone on to win the Middle Park Stakes. The little horse might not train on and he might not stay a mile.

Joë was absolutely marvellous. Her concern was for me and for my young family and she was totally unselfish. She was heartbroken to part with our little hero, but acceded to my desire to 'cash in'. So Tumbledownwind was sold privately on 8 October. Everyone except Joë was happy: Bruce still had the horse, Geoff Lewis – a personal friend of O'Sullevan – still had the ride, and we had the money!

It was a deal that could so easily have embarrassed and humiliated us, and I shall always believe that Tumbledownwind should have won the 2000 Guineas. But sadly, everything went wrong for him in the spring. The little horse coughed on his way to post for his trial race at the beginning of April and was withdrawn. Now Bruce had a race against time to get him ready for the '2000', but he sparkled in his work during Craven week and I backed him at 50/1.

I stayed with the jockey Brian Taylor for the two nights before 2000 Guineas day and it rained non-stop. I was sharing a room with the Bahraini, Sheikh Essa al Khalifa, and waking at 4 am I thought that Essa was facing Mecca to say his prayers. I was completely wrong: the roof had caved in over Essa's bed and he had moved his mattress to the far corner of the room!

The roads were flooded on the way to Newmarket and no other racecourse would have raced that waterlogged day. But the Rowley Mile, with its remarkable draining properties, remained raceable and racing took place. Geoff Lewis had despaired of Tumbledownwind's chance on the ground and switched horses to Bruce's other runner, Taxiarchos. Geoff Baxter took over.

I experienced an extraordinary sensation during the Guineas. I had backed Tumbledownwind to win £10,000, added to which there was a contingency arrangement with the new owners that would have netted a comparable sum.

As the race unfolded, the favourite, Try My Best, was the first horse beaten and finished tailed off. With 200 yards to go Tumbledownwind was in front, going better than anything. He was going to win! But in that split second I actually felt that I did not want him to win, because despite the bet and the contingency it would break my heart to have *sold* a Classic winner. He did not win: the combination of his interrupted preparation and the soft ground contrived to exhaust him in the last 100 yards and he weakened to finish fourth. The money was lost, but professional pride was intact.

Sadly, the little horse never quite recaptured his two-year-old form, although he never stopped trying his best. He was sold as a stallion to Australia and enjoyed a degree of success.

What a far cry Tumbledownwind was from my ill-fated first Flat racehorse, Whitebridge, whose career constituted a comedy of errors and a catalogue of mismanagement by his 'virgin' owner. He ran just once as a two-year-old, showing a reasonable degree of promise, but his three-year-old career began badly and got worse. The ultimate humiliation came when we tried a pair of blinkers on him at Newmarket on the July Course, and (entirely against my trainer's wishes) I booked Lester Piggott to ride him. Whitebridge carried the great man half way to Cambridge before the start and came back a furlong behind the other runners! I had been introduced to Bing Crosby shortly before the race and the humiliation I felt as we watched this pantomime unfold does not bear description. Whitebridge and Lester were greeted with derision and several catcalls.

I moved Whitebridge away from Newmarket to a West Country trainer and miraculously he won a maiden race for us at Chester. Thereafter, the story became black comedy. He went to the sales, where he failed to reach his reserve. He ran over hurdles, collapsed at the last flight and – for a moment of mixed feelings – looked unlikely to get to his feet, but did. He went to Cagnes-sur-Mer to be trained by Arthur Thomas, where he proved allergic to an injection, came out in huge lumps and never raced. He came back to Warwickshire with Arthur and developed a grotesque knee. I have succeeded in forgetting the remainder of his pitiful story. He was an exceptionally moderate horse, but he provided some extremely valuable lessons. Luckily, I learned some of them.

My first good horse after Whitebridge was called Midnight Cowboy. He was a big, strong , plain chestnut colt by Gratitude, whom he resembled in no way whatever, but Bruce Hobbs bought him for 1200 guineas at the Doncaster October sales and he was a brilliant buy. After a 'sighter' at Newmarket, he was quietly fancied in his next run over seven furlongs at Sandown, but ran into a subsequent Classic winner in Athens Wood. He won comfortably at Newmarket next time out, ridden by Greville Starkey who was the perfect man for him, whereafter I asked Bruce if we could target a nursery at Ayr, another of my favourite meetings. He was withdrawn at Ayr because the going was too soft, but the following week he won a nursery at Ascot, on BBC-TV, and in course record time. He was of the same generation as Mill Reef, My Swallow and Brigadier Gerard and was given 8st 7lb in the Free Handicap, so he was not bad. Then he broke down as a three-year-old and was sold inexpensively as a stallion to Australia.

It was in the 1970s that I started buying and managing horses for people other than myself. Seymour Bloodstock had been launched in 1972 and it operated as a vehicle for breeding and trading. My two principal clients became Clement Freud and the restaurateur, Walter Mariti. It would be hard to find two more contrasting owners – the only common link was that they were both extremely lucky. I think that I bought seven horses for Freud and six of them won. The only 'failure' was a big, good-looking beautifully bred horse called Palace of Medina, who was a shade slow, but whom we sold for profit as a stallion to India.

Freud's requirement was inexpensive horses with high potential. They are not especially easy to find, but we came up with a gem in Escarole, a £1500 reject from Mrs Meg Mullion's string. Escarole won on the flat and over hurdles, and Toby Balding trained him with considerable skill. We found a race for him on the flat at Haydock, on the evening of Oaks day in 1975.

I persuaded Willie Carson to fly to Haydock with me after racing at Epsom to ride Escarole. It was a traumatic journey. As we approached Haydock the pilot informed us that he was not certain whether the landing gear was functioning. There was no-one he could radio at Haydock to ask whether the wheels had descended, so we were obliged to fly on to Manchester Airport. We approached Manchester to see the comforting sight of half a dozen fire engines waiting on the tarmac! It transpired that the pilot's indicator light was at fault, not the undercarriage, and we landed safely. It was a trip that had separated the men from the boys – there were one or two rather pale faces that evening.

We rushed to Haydock and arrived just in time for Willie to weigh out for Escarole, who won by three lengths. The owner had backed him substantially in a double with the Oaks winner, Juliette Marny, so I imagine that Willie received a generous present.

Escarole was also useful over hurdles, so Toby prepared him for a race at Ludlow which he reckoned he should definitely win. Clement asked me to arrange an 'SP job': if he were backed on the course he would probably be 2/1 or less, but if the money was invested off-course he could be 4/1 or better.

I placed the commission with a leading bookmaker, who arranged the 'knockout'. This entails a high-profile bookmaker on the racecourse offering a fraction over the general odds on the horse in question and attracting the bulk of the money available, in the knowledge that he has covered his liabilities, and more, with his SP bet off-course. The more he goes over the odds, the more, inevitably, the other bookmakers follow him and the odds are gradually extended The word goes round that the horse is a 'wrong'un,' and eventually the odds are artificially high.

Everything went like clockwork at Ludlow, until a sudden surge of late money contracted the odds from 5/1 to 100/30. Escarole duly won and we all collected. In the morning I asked my bookmaker associate what had gone wrong at the death. 'It was your friend, the owner,' he complained. 'I'd just knocked him out to 5/1 and in he comes and backs the horse with me, in view of everyone. So now everyone knows he's a buzzer.' I confronted Clement with this claim. 'Well yes,' he admitted, 'he was such a good price that I felt that I should have a bit more on.' Not surprisingly, that bookmaker has not obliged me with an SP job since.

We had a less than satisfactory experience with a horse called Rag Time Band at Taunton. I had bought him cheaply out of Bill Watts' stable for Clement, with a reputation of inconsistency and a bad (hard) mouth. Toby taught him to jump well and gradually he became a better ride. After two educational runs, to develop his confidence and to teach him to settle, Toby reckoned he was ready to win at Taunton. A promising young claiming jockey called Peter Scudamore was booked to ride him.

I travelled down from London with strict instructions from the owner: 'Whatever happens, don't back him on the course and don't let anyone else back him. We'll back him SP.' Rag Time Band won at 33/1. We were ecstatic and expected a eulogy of praise from the owner, but no such luck. According to Clement (now an MP) he had got caught in a debate in the commons, was unable to get away, and did not have a penny on the horse.

The biggest bargain that he ever fell into was a horse called Grunty Fen, named after his constituency in the Isle of Ely. Grunty Fen had been bought for just 500 guineas by Paul Kelleway as a yearling. He was looking for an owner for the tough-looking Prince Tenderfoot horse and I persuaded Clement to buy him.

Grunty Fen ran an extremely encouraging race at Windsor first time out and we targeted him at the two-year-old auction race at Epsom on Oaks day. He was backed from 20/1 to 11/1 and duly won by a neck. I thought that Clement would be over the moon, because to have a winner at Epsom with a horse that cost 500 guineas is something out of the ordinary. Clement was not over the moon and carried out an investigation in every betting shop in Newmarket to discover who had backed his horse. In fact the truth lay rather closer to the racecourse with an associate of the jockey who rode him at Windsor!

Clement Freud's reputation had been built as a journalist, food critic, television performer and star of a popular commercial for dog food. He telephoned me one evening in 1973, stated that he was going to become an MP, and advised me strongly to take the 33/1 available about this eventuality at a by-election. Foolishly, I asked Carolyn to telephone a friend of hers who lived in the constituency, to ask her whether Clement had any chance of winning. 'Good God no,' came the reply, 'they don't really like that sort of person down here. The Conservative is sure to hold on to the seat.' Lesson – never, turn down 33/1 about a genuinely fancied runner. Clement romped in and held on to the seat at five subsequent elections.

For some reason, perhaps not unconnected with politics, Clement was not a particular fan of Margaret Thatcher. On the day her son Mark blessed her with a grandchild, Mrs Thatcher emerged from 10 Downing Street with the immortal quote: 'We are a grandmother!'

Clement was on the phone later that day, saying that he wanted to buy an unnamed filly that was certain to win as a two-year-old that he could call 'Weareagrandmother'. It was a tough order because it was already March and most two-year-olds with any ability had both owners and names. But my friend Gavin Pritchard-Gordon had just the animal. She was a daughter of Prince Tenderfoot – a lucky sire for Clement – and the name and pedigree matched perfectly. I had a good look at her and the business was done.

The miracle happened and Weareagrandmother won a televised

£10,000 nursery at York, in the full glare of publicity. As invariably happened, though, it was an imperfect scenario. Clement was unable to travel to York and stated that we had given him insufficient confidence to have a bet. At the end of the season he moved the filly to another trainer. That really was that.

Walter Mariti, a charming Italian who ran the hugely successful restaurants, Pontevecchio and Ponte Nuovo (formerly Il Girasole), was a horse of a different colour. I had patronized Walter's restaurants since the mid-60s, and in 1981 finally persuaded him to allow me to buy him a yearling. Walter called him Il Pontevecchio and he won as a three-year-old at Windsor on the Monday of Goodwood week. I had tipped him on breakfast television and the celebration at the restaurant that evening was memorable. Friend after friend appeared with bottles of Dom Perignon champagne. I had very mixed feelings – I was presenting the programme at Goodwood the following day, so allowed myself only one glass!

Walter's other notable winners were Scintillo (who won at Glorious Goodwood), Pontevecchio Due (Ebbisham Stakes), Pontevecchio Notte, Pontenuovo (Royal Hunt Cup) and Pontevecchio Moda.

We bought Scintillo cheaply, because he was by an unfashionable sire (Hot Spark) and came from a family with a history of wind problems. After he landed a gamble in the Singleton Handicap at Goodwood – a wonderful day for Walter and very skilful training by Bruce – we ran him the following week at Newmarket. It was my fault. Bruce did not want to run him, preferring to wait for York, but I insisted because he had a small penalty at Newmarket, whereas he would carry 7lb more weight in future handicaps after Goodwood.

Scintillo ran deplorably. Bruce was cross, because he had not wanted to run him and felt that he might be jarred up. Walter and I were bitterly disappointed, although, as usual, Walter did not complain. Some while afterwards I was told that Scintillo was 'got at' that night. I do not know if that is true, but he was a hot favourite and was never the same horse again.

Later in life Scintillo had a very lucky escape. We sold him at the Horses-in-Training sale and he was bought to race in Italy. The following year there was an appalling episode when about two dozen horses were poisoned and died from arsenic in an Italian stable. Scintillo was one of a handful who survived – evidently his stable lad had forgotten, or wasn't present, to feed him that evening.

The October sales of 1986 was the best 'shopping' week of my life. Walter asked me to buy two horses, so we bought Pontevecchio Notte and Pontenuovo, the best that Walter owned.

Pontevecchio Notte was a really lovely colt by Blakeney, bred by Arthur Budgett's Kirtlington Stud. He was not on my list of horses to look at (based on pedigrees), but he caught my eye walking out of his box for another potential vendor and I fell in love with him. We bought him for 16,500 guineas and I took a share in him myself. We sent him to Gavin Pritchard-Gordon.

He won at Lingfield (ridden by Steve Cauthen, a client of Walter's), Ostend and Sandown as a two-year-old and was a really nice horse. Inevitably he was high in the handicap as a three-year-old and it took most of the season before he sank to a realistic mark. Then we backed him in a nine-furlong handicap at York in early September, but he was beaten a short head by a horse of Sheikh Hamdan al Maktoum's called Wabil, which was extremely game and difficult to get past.

We decided to aim Pontevecchio Notte at the Cambridgeshire, and after another good run at Yarmouth (second) he was well backed for the first leg of the 'autumn double', starting favourite at 13/2. In the event he was taken off his feet and ran disappointingly. It was a tactical error to target the Cambridgeshire because he was, in reality, a mile-and-a-half horse.

The following spring we decided to aim Pontevecchio Notte at the Bessborough Stakes at Royal Ascot. He won very stylishly at the Goodwood May meeting and we were very optimistic about Ascot, where he started 4/1 favourite. He was capable of producing an impressive turn of foot off a strong pace, but he had to be settled and switched off. Gavin kept him very fresh for the big day.

Our horse was drawn against the inside rails on the round mile-and-a-half course. The inevitable happened. As George Duffield battled to settle him, he was shuffled back to almost last of the 20 runners. Nearer last than first turning into the straight, George was forced to switch his mount five horses wide. In the final furlong he flew up the outside, but it was too late and he was a narrowly-beaten, fast-finishing fifth. All of Walter's 'friends' told him how unlucky he was and what a mess Duffield had made of it, and it was the only time that Walter ever complained.

I could not blame George, who was the victim of circumstances. The horse was keen and fresh and had to be settled. I made a mental note that, if we ever targeted the Bessborough Stakes or King George V Handicap again, we would need a horse who was capable of lying up in the first six.

Pontevecchio Notte developed an arthritic joint and, in favouring his opposite leg, suffered a tendon sprain. He was sold at the Ascot sales and, miraculously, won over hurdles for his new connections. He stood as a dual-purpose stallion in the West Country, but attracted relatively few thoroughbred mares.

Pontenuovo was a very different kettle of fish. He was a most attractive yearling, and I was exceptionally lucky to buy him for 20,000 guineas. The luck lay in a misunderstanding on the part of the underbidder, Richard Hannon, that he was a rig. The conversation that Richard had overheard related to a different horse that I had looked at earlier!

Unfortunately Pontenuovo developed a slightly malformed off-fore ankle, and so our chosen handler, Ben Hanbury, did not train him seriously as a two-year-old. In April he was turned out at the New England Stud.

We were pretty clear in our minds about his correct distance, but it took us a while to work out how best to ride him. His first race was in the Wood Ditton Stakes, for unraced three-year-olds at the Newmarket Craven meeting, and he astonished us by finishing third to two highly-regarded colts (one of which cost $500,000 and the other $1 million) belonging to the Maktoum family.

We took Pontenuovo to the York spring meeting where the Hanburys and I stayed with Mark and Sue Ronaldshay (now Zetland). We all thought that he was a 'good thing', and I bet accordingly, but he was beaten by a horse called Junayz trained by Barry Hills.

Pontenuovo became progressively sore and intermittently lame on his off-fore. Ben gave him plenty of swimming exercise, but he did not appear to enjoy it. He ran a couple more times but was clearly 'going the wrong way'. After he had been beaten on firm ground at Nottingham we brought him home and almost sold him to Nigel Tinkler. You need to be lucky as well as good in our game!

Pontenuovo spent the next 14 months either in our home paddock or at livery. He thrived physically and his ankle got progressively better. At last, in the autumn of 1989, our vet Nick Wingfield-Digby gave the go-ahead. By now he was a big, robust horse who needed plenty of strong cantering to get him race-fit. We decided to send him to my old friend David Elsworth, whose gallops at Whitsbury offer plenty of hill work, hundreds of acres of fresh grassland, and a perfect remote environment. We ran him twice on the all-weather track at Lingfield, to remove the cobwebs. Both 'Ponte' and I hated the experience: I will never forget the doleful look that he gave me as he returned, covered with oily sand, on that first occasion.

We had a plan, and that was to win the Royal Hunt Cup. It was a dream that we had harboured for 18 months. I do not know how seriously David took our plan, or indeed how highly he regarded 'Ponte' in the spring of 1990. In any case he did not argue when I suggested that we run him in a one-mile claiming race at Ripon. John Williams rode him and David (and Walter) stayed at home.

It was on that day at Ripon that we discovered, by chance, how best to ride him. He was drawn 20 of 20 against the inside rail, so I asked John to be handy and to avoid getting shuffled back on the turn. 'Ponte' jumped well and took charge. He made every yard of the running and increased his lead in the last two furlongs, winning by four lengths at an SP of 8/1! I was terrified that he would be claimed and that we would lose him. There is a wonderful photograph of myself in the unsaddling enclosure looking anxiously at his forelegs, and Mick Easterby – who had backed the runner-up – standing with his hands on hips, with a look that says: 'What the hell did we run into there!' Happily no-one claimed Pontenuovo: it was, after all, his first run on the grass for 21 months and obviously, in principle, his soundness was suspect.

The weights for the Hunt Cup were published and Pontenuovo had 7st 7lb – precisely the bottom carriable weight. There was just one nagging worry: the race had attracted a large entry, with a maximum field of 32 allowed under the safety limits, so would we be high enough in the list of runners to get into the race? I felt that we could afford to pick up a 4lb penalty, to ensure that we were in the final 32, so he travelled to Doncaster on 24 May where we had confidence that he would win.

When we saw 'Ponte' in the paddock we were horrified. He looked as light as a crow and tucked up, and he ran a stinker. What had happened in the previous week? On the same day, David won the Irish 1000 Guineas with the brilliant In The Groove. I was full of despair, but David reported later that he had bounced back to form, so Royal Ascot remained on the agenda – to the relief of Walter's girlfriend Penny Meredith, who had already bought her dress and hat!

There were 41 names above Pontenuovo when the five-day acceptors were published for the Hunt Cup, so we needed no fewer than ten to drop out before the day. It seemed impossible, but exactly ten horses *were* withdrawn at 10.15 on the Tuesday morning. We were in! When my thoughts then turned to the draw, I fancied the stands' side and reckoned that number 4 would be perfect. When Pontenuovo was drawn 4 it started to feel as if fate was on our side.

It was a very, very hot race for the Hunt Cup. There were too many dangers to mention. It rained steadily for much of the afternoon, so the ground was going to favour those on the stands' side, that was for sure. I really believed that Pontenuovo had a major chance, although he was on offer at 100/1. The morning was spent planning how I would introduce the Royal Ascot highlights programme on BBC-TV if he did happen to win. I was that confident.

We stood in the paddock in the rain (luckily Alison had bought me a new raincoat in Henley that morning). David had failed to make it, after something that had happened the previous night. I went over the race again with our jockey, Gary Bardwell. It was straightforward: jump off, let him use his stride, give him a breather after halfway, and go for home from over two furlongs out.

I watched the race, as always, on the television monitor from my presentation position on 'windy corner'. It was going like clockwork. 'Ponte' had been headed after halfway, but was battling back on the stands' rails. He was going to get there! I lifted my arms and gave an almighty shout, with the result that my cameraman jumped backwards thinking that I had gone mad.

'Ponte' had won the Royal Hunt Cup at 50/1 and tears were running down my cheeks. For the only time in my broadcasting career I was too overcome to voice over the action replay. The dream had come true. Penny and I were kissing and crying, while Walter remained remarkably dignified.

The Royal Hunt Cup is a striking and elegantly designed gold trophy. It was my fiftieth birthday on the Saturday of Ascot and Walter allowed me to have the Cup at home for my party. It was a perfect end to an unforgettable week.

Pontenuovo went on to win the LA Studlite Lager Handicap, worth almost £80,000 to the winner, at the Festival of Racing in the autumn. By the end of the season he had won four races worth over £126,000 – a record sum to be won by a handicapper in a single season. When Pontenuovo retired from racing, Walter was kind enough to give him to me. Despite his occasional grumpiness – he was rather liable to give Alison a nip if he felt that he was being overgirthed – he had a happy retirement.

Sadly, he had three serious colics. He was operated on twice, by the excellent Tim Greet who had saved the life of Desert Orchid; but on the third occasion, despite loving care from the staff at the veterinary practice, he failed to respond and we decided against a further operation. On 4 December 1994 he was put down. It was one of the saddest days of my life and I wept unashamedly. His ashes are buried in a wooden cask, overlooking his paddock.

I have been lucky enough to enjoy one further success at Royal Ascot. Tykeyvor, a six-year-old gelding that I had bought partially as a winter companion for Pontenuovo, won the Bessborough Stakes in 1996, in my own colours. He was always handy and won easily. It was a magical day, with Alison – not always a lucky talisman! – and my son Thomas both there.

Tykeyvor is a delightful character with, it must be said, rather better manners than 'Ponte'. He has been trained with consummate skill by Anne Herries and has carried his years exceptionally well. He has a parrot mouth and a rather diminished set of molars, but we all love him to bits. These old geldings provide so much pleasure, while the Classic horses tend to be 'here today, gone tomorrow'.

It was a bit like that with Tumbledownwind. But he, through his success and his sale, was the most important horse in my life. It is ironic that, even as I was delivering my Gimcrack speech to the Anciente Fraternite of York Gimcracks, my first wife Carolyn was already contemplating leaving me.

# FIFTEEN

# *A Period of Adjustment*

The warning signs were probably there but I did not see them. Or if I did, I was too busy to acknowledge them.

Nineteen seventy-seven had been an exceptional year. Apart from the successes of Tumbledownwind, Red Rum had completed his hat-trick of Grand National wins, with Tommy Stack riding. Our friend Susan Crawford painted a wonderful fantasy scene from Aintree for our Christmas card. Surrounding Tommy on Red Rum, and myself with a microphone, were several of our friends, including Chris Collins, Andrew Parker-Bowles, John Oaksey and Sue herself riding a zebra!

I had filmed a definitive story with the great Vincent O'Brien, who had in turn invited me as his special guest to the Stable Lads' Boxing Championships. My Gimcrack speech was controversial and much discussed. It made me some enemies, but heightened my profile. Ironically, Sheikh Mohammed was to adopt a very similar theme 20 years later.

Perhaps I was beginning to think that I was invincible and took Carolyn for granted. I certainly underestimated her antipathy to moving out of London. Having lived in London for the 15 years since I left Manchester, I yearned for fresh air, escape, and the country life. It was my plan to sell the Seymour Walk property, and buy a house in the country and a flat in Hurlingham for Carolyn's use during the week.

Carolyn had never lived in the country, so I arranged a 'dummy run'. I rented a cottage in a village called Herringswell, near Newmarket, for the months of August and September. I was convinced that this would reassure Carolyn of the delights of country life, but I was mistaken. For me it was a delightful interlude. True, I was away quite a lot, at York and Goodwood and the usual racing fixtures, but we did have some kind racing friends in Newmarket – notably Gavin and Coral Pritchard-Gordon – who made Carolyn very welcome.

Carolyn seemed to miss her London friends and the London way of life. It was a disadvantage that the shops in Newmarket were less plentiful and sophisticated than they are now. The final straw came with the violent demise of poor Josh. He was replaced by two brothers, Jim and Joe (named after the Gimcrack and Joe Mercer, the jockey), but neither had the footballing skills of Josh.

The experiment completed, we moved back to London and life seemed to continue as normal. On the night after the Gimcrack dinner we gave a huge celebratory party at Seymour Walk, with disco and dancing. All of the good and the great, and everyone who had ever been involved with Tumbledownwind, were invited and most of them seemed to come. We holidayed in Barbados with the usual gang, and it was frantic and boisterous as always. I flirted with a blonde divorcee from Jersey, but it was totally harmless, a game. A so-called 'friend' was at pains to inform Carolyn what I was up to, but I cannot believe that she took any serious notice.

And then came the bombshell. We arrived home from Barbados on 25 January 1978 and the following day I went into my BBC office. I was back home by early evening and Carolyn said that she wanted to talk to me. She informed me, calmly, that she was planning to leave and would be taking Thomas with her. I was stunned.

She was unhappy, she said, and no longer wanted to live with me. If she enlarged on this reasoning her remarks made no lasting impact. I have little recall of the following few days. Ten days later we had lunch and I begged her to change her mind, if only for the sake of Thomas. But Carolyn was implacable and was clearly receiving advice from others. Her parents were horrified, but her mind was made up. I threw myself into my work and tried to plan for the future.

The first practical necessity was to put 58 Seymour Walk on the market. The house belonged 75 per cent to Carolyn, so it was she who arranged the business with estate agents and she chose a friend called George Pope. The house was priced at £115,000. The first person who came to view, the former amateur jockey Edward Cazalet (whose father, Peter, had trained for the Queen Mother), bought it on the spot.

I started to look at houses in the country and flats in London, but the flats were exceptionally expensive and none was quite what I wanted. An agent suggested that I look at a house across the road from a small, two-bedroomed flat in Old Church Street, Chelsea, which was roughly the same price. I loved the house and bought it – it has been my principal residence ever since.

But I was still looking for a cottage in the country, either in Berkshire where I had enjoyed my adolescence, or near Newmarket where my racehorses were trained. Dick Turner, who had left Ireland and moved to Suffolk when he retired as Turf Club handicapper, came up with just the place, in the village of Burrough Green, five miles from Newmarket. My share of Seymour Walk paid for the cottage, Tumbledownwind paid for the London house. Capital remained in short supply.

Inevitably I was missing my four-year-old son, so in July I rented a house in West Wittering for a couple of weeks so that we could spend some time together. I employed a pleasant girl called Carole Ridehalgh, whose father John owned horses with Jeremy Hindley, to cook, clean and generally look after Thomas. We had a delightful fortnight of shrimping and sandcastles. Other friends and relations came and went. It was different from Scotland, but the weather was warmer.

Meanwhile, as my career continued to flourish, 1978 also saw the breakthrough in Desmond Lynam's career in television – and it happened in unexpected circumstances.

I had known and admired Des as a radio performer for several years through my regular work on the 'Today' programme and BBC sports radio. He was an excellent boxing commentator and had obvious personality. Des was offered a trial on television, but the presenters and performers were defending their corner and no-one was clear what Des was going to do. Eventually, some bright spark suggested that he should introduce Sunday cricket. Now, Des had a wide knowledge of many sports, but as a man whose family hail from the south-west of Ireland, cricket was not amongst them.

Des floundered like a goldfish on grass, and those who felt threatened by his imminent switch to television chorused: 'We told you so. He's a radio man. He can't do television!' Des's television career was therefore put on the back-burner.

Then in the spring of 1978, as I was returning from a 'recce' at Aintree with the BBC's head of sport, Alan Hart, the subject came up as to who should present the first two days of the Grand National meeting. Since there being still no such thing as a mobile videotape unit, all our preprepared items had to be edited and dubbed at Lime Grove, or Television Centre, in London. In consequence I would travel to Aintree and back on the Thursday, voice over the stories on Friday afternoon, and return to Liverpool on Friday night.

For years the first two days of the meeting were presented – like 'Grandstand' – by David Coleman. But David was no longer used as a presenter on outside broadcasts. Frank Bough had taken over on 'Grandstand' but had no desire to present midweek horseracing programmes. So we needed a presenter for the first two days. I suggested Des.

Alan was equivocal. 'The boys say he can't do television,' he replied. My riposte was: 'I don't agree. He hasn't had a chance. He's got presence. You'll see.' So Alan agreed to let Des do the job. Whether Des was grateful, I rather doubt. His number-two least favourite sport was racing. But we sat down together on the Tuesday of National week, went through it with a toothcomb and Des was fine. The rest, as they say, is history.

I was amused by a newspaper feature headed: 'One million

pounds for Desmond's smile?' The story suggested that after Des's triumph during the 1996 European football championships, Sky-TV were prepared to offer him £1 million to lure him away from the BBC. As with a high-class stallion, I should have bought a share in him. However, it seems that his long-time girlfriend, the lovely Rose Diamond, owns 100 per cent.

Des has several burdens in life, not least that – having started his career with BBC Radio Brighton in 1969 – he is a Brighton & Hove Albion supporter. I invited Des to Swindon for Swindon against Brighton in April 1990 but it was not a very successful evening: one of the players broke a leg and Brighton won 2-1!

After Des's debut at Aintree, Frank Bough took over on Saturday for the big day. It was a thrilling Grand National and a marvellous result. Lucius, the winner, was owned by a delightful hunting and racing enthusiast in Fiona Whittaker, while the jockey was one of my best friends, Bob Davies.

The Cheltenham Festival, however, came up with a surprise. On Gold Cup day we awoke to find the hills and the roads covered with snow. The race was postponed until April, when John Francome gained a hugely popular win for Fred Winter on Midnight Court. This was the race that completed the 'set' for the incomparable Fred. He had won the Grand National and Champion Hurdle both as a jockey and trainer, but until now the Gold Cup and eluded him as a trainer.

For John Francome the celebrations were muted. On the morning of Gold Cup day it was revealed that he and bookmaker John Banks were to face a Jockey Club inquiry into allegations of bribery and corruption. If found guilty, he faced a ban for life. There was a suggestion that Francome had been 'stopping' horses in collaboration with Banks – notably, ironically, a horse called Stopped in the Imperial Cup at Sandown.

In the event, an association between the two men was proven. John Banks, with whom I had always enjoyed a good professional relationship, revealed to me the races that were involved in the inquiry, so that I was able to show recordings in a 'Sportsnight' story on the day after the inquiry. Both men were found guilty of a breach of the rule which relates to causing 'serious damage to the interests of horseracing,' while Banks was also found in breach of the rule relating to obtaining information from a jockey. Banks was 'warned off' for three years, while Francome had his riding licence suspended for six weeks and was fined £750.

I moved into my cottage in Newmarket on 24 May. My friends could hardly have been more helpful and supportive, especially Coral Pritchard-Gordon who helped me with curtains, flooring and decorations. I had central heating installed – the cottage had previously depended on night storage heating. My carpenter worked around the clock, television was installed, and I was recommended to approach a villager called Doris Jaggard to help me out with the house.

Doris, a statuesque evacuee from the East End of London, grudgingly agreed to 'give me a trial'. She and her husband Ron, the 'estate' factotum, are still with me after 20 years, so I presume that I have come through the 'trial' successfully.

On the following Tuesday my new secretary arrived. She was Alison Ramsay whom I had met her through my former jumping trainer Neville Dent, to whom she was related by marriage. She had three or four local clients, for whom she worked on one day a week. She managed to find me a slot in her schedule.

Alison arrived looking rather superior, in a pair of dark glasses. We did a morning's work and I invited her to a pub lunch at the King's Head at Dullingham. Sir Mark Prescott, also lunching there, gave her a big 'hello'. She seemed reasonably competent, so we made a regular arrangement. Three years and 23 days later, I married her.

In the week following my move to Burrough Green I moved into my London house. This was somewhat less complicated because I bought the curtains, carpets and fittings virtually *en bloc* from the previous owner and the house needed very little adjustment. My furniture – notably my antique bookcase – fitted in comfortably. Betty Ditch, who had been with me as housekeeper since 1971, was happy to transfer to the new premises, so we were up and running. Remarkably, she has stuck it out for another 20 years, despite the fact that I completely overlooked our silver anniversary in 1996!

I have always been happy in Old Church Street. Alison does not spend a great deal of time in London, so I enjoy having guests staying in the house.

The first to become a permanent resident was Isla St Clair. She arrived in London in November 1978 and moved into my spare bedroom 'for a few weeks'. I cannot remember how long she stayed, but it was certainly for more than one series of 'The Generation Game' and I was genuinely sorry when she moved out. We would sit in bed, in adjacent bedrooms, Isla learning her lines for her weekly spat with Larry Grayson, and I learning my 'links' for racing at Ascot the following day. Otherwise, our taste in politics, music and friends were entirely diverse. Our common bond was Nigel Angus – Thomas's godfather – whom we both adored. It was a great shame when the two of them, separated by 400 miles, grew apart. Nigel, on his rare visits, found it hard to cope with being a celebrity's walker with all that entailed.

My next 'lodger' was Angie Greenslade, the older sister of Penny who was a friend in the 1960s. Our relationship was entirely platonic and eventually Angie married a sports promotion executive, Mike Storey, who made his name in Peter West's company, West-Nally. Mike and Angie are great friends and have owned a leg in more than one of my syndicated horses.

My longest 'lodger' was Bill Shand-Kydd, an old friend whom I ran into while dining in London in the spring of 1985. Bill and I had a brandy after dinner and he confided that his relationship with his wife Christina was going through a difficult phase. Could he possible stay in my house for a couple of weeks for a 'cooling-off' period? Bill and Christina had been married for over 20 years and were both exceptional people and very good friends. I told Bill he was welcome. He moved in – and stayed for six years.

In London, I arranged a double-date, matching Bill with an old friend of mine from the period between my marriages, Sally

Ramsay-Patrick. Sally, who had Guinness relations in Ireland, was an attractive, volatile blonde, keen on skiing, riding and racing. Despite their short fuses, she was perfect for Bill and they became an item for 12 years. For the last six of those Sally was living in Bill's Buckinghamshire house, Horton Hall. It was only the riding accident on 22 October 1995, which left Bill paralysed from the neck down, that finally drove them apart.

Bill spent over a year at the National Spinal Injuries Centre at Stoke Mandeville, near Aylesbury. He had broken the highest and second highest vertebrae of the spine, an injury even worse than the high-profile paralysis of 'Superman' Christopher Reeve. Typically Bill faced it head on, incredibly brave as always. With the aid of a tracheotomy and fitted ventilator, he learned to speak by alternately breathing in and then breathing out. Now he is able to steer a wheelchair with the use of his chin and to write letters and articles on a voice-activated computer which translates his dictation into the written word. He entertains friends with a glass of champagne and an excellent lunch, both of which he is able to enjoy.

But Bill's convalescence was emotionally as well as physically traumatic. In the morning Sally would visit him from the relatively nearby Horton Hall. Christina, who still lived in their London house at Parson's Green, would visit after mid-day. Their children, Caspar and Lucinda, had never accepted Sally.

Despite their 11-year separation Christina was anxious to move back to Horton Hall to supervise the obligatory conversions to the house and to support Bill through his convalescence. Sally, however, had the same agenda, and for the time being remained mistress of Horton Hall. That was a decision for Bill, which I had no desire – as a friend of them all – to be any part of.

One morning I visited Bill at Stoke Mandeville before Sally arrived. He had made up his mind: the family wanted him back and, somehow, this was a family affair. They had always remained close in a crisis. When Bill's brother-in-law, Lord Lucan, disappeared – Lucan was married to Christina's sister Veronica – it was Bill and

Christina who had helped to bring up the three children, George (Lord Bingham), Frances and Camilla. Now it was time to close ranks again.

Bill was anxious to avoid a scene with Sally at Stoke Mandeville. 'Could you take Sally out to lunch and explain it to her?' he asked. There was no need for further words: I knew what Bill meant and what he was feeling. Words were easier for me. Needless to say, there were no words that could lessen the pain of Bill's decision for Sally. It took almost 18 months for Sally to accept that there was only one decision that Bill could have made. She had listened to my words, but she had been unable to hear. Eventually, she left Horton Hall and began to build a new life in Gloucestershire.

Bill celebrated his sixtieth birthday in May 1997, with a terrific party at Glaisters in London, organized superbly by Christina. It was like old times. Bill is without doubt one of the bravest men I have ever met.

During our six years together in Old Church Street we rarely discussed the events of that awful night when Sandra Rivett was murdered and 'Lucky' Lucan disappeared. But it appears very clear to me what actually occurred.

The lead-up to the horrific murder has been well-chronicled – there is no doubt that 'Lucky' had been driven to distraction by concern for his children and his obsession that Veronica was an unsuitable mother. From my knowledge of 'Lucky' – he had a few racehorses, trained by Arthur Freeman and Tom Jones, including a useful jumper called Le Merveilleux – he was personally incapable of murdering a woman. At the time, 'hitmen' were readily available for hire in the East End of London to do 'a job', and I believe that 'Lucky' enlisted such a person to murder his wife while he was establishing an alibi for himself in Mayfair.

What nobody knew was that the nanny, Sandra, had altered her day off, and when Sandra came downstairs the hit man had no means of distinguishing her from Veronica Lucan who was supposed to be the only woman in the house. Lucan let himself into the house to 'find the body', only to discover that the wrong woman had been murdered. It is easy to imagine his torment as he drove out of town to the home of his friend Ian Maxwell-Scott in Sussex.

Ian, like himself, was an erratic and obsessive gambler who liked to play long-shots. I would often exchange opinions with him in the betting shop in Draycott Avenue in the 1960s. 'Lucky' sat down with a whisky and wrote his two famous letters to Bill Shand-Kydd. He had made up his mind to fall on his sword and needed the cooperation of one of his friends to help him to do so. Who that friend was has never been made known.

'Lucky' is no more alive than Shergar. His son George is now 30 and I hope that he will forgive my returning to this unhappy page of the family history. The foregoing account is, I repeat, only my personal interpretation of the events of that night, but it is a version that fits the character-profiles of those involved.

Bill's tenure of Old Church Street was, in 1979, still some years ahead. At that time Isla continued to prosper in showbiz and earned the distinction of appearing on 'Blankety Blank'. By August 1981 she was starting her fourth series of the 'Generation Game'. Ironically, in the light of subsequent events, she was hugely supportive of racing's major initiative to help Stoke Mandeville Hospital.

It was Jimmy Savile who launched the Stoke Mandeville Appeal in 1980, to rebuild the ceilings of five of the spinal wards, which had collapsed the previous year. The target was £10 million. The racing industry staged several events, large and small, largely driven by the tireless John Dunlop. I was asked by Bruce Hobbs's wife Betty to stage an event, and we decided on a charity football match, at the Newmarket town ground, during the Guineas meeting. Thanks to almost universal support from my friends, it was a huge success.

The match was billed as Mick Mills' XI versus the Jockeys' XI. Mick, captain of Ipswich Town and a key member of the England team, led a strong team of professionals, including Lou Macari, Paul Mariner, Bobby Robson, Laurie Madden and five of my friends from Swindon Town FC. The Jockeys' XI, captained by John Francome (who did not show), included Willie Carson, George Duffield, Brough Scott, Steve Smith-Eccles, Walter Swinburn, Brian Taylor and a 'ringer' in QPR's Don Shanks. They did exceptionally well, considering that Bobby Robson, the Ipswich manager, insisted that all of his players played flat out!

There were two mishaps during the evening. The first was that Dennis Waterman arrived too late to play, claiming that his 'roadie', the BBC producer Chris Lewis, had misinformed him of the kick-off time. The other, far more amusing, mishap was that Bobby Robson fined two of his senior players for drinking alcohol after the match – it was Thursday evening, so the '48-hour rule' applied!

Isla St Clair drew the Raffle and Lucky Programme number at half-time, and there is no doubt that her presence put several hundred on the gate. In fact we greatly underestimated the appeal of the match, to the extent that there was a queue well over 50 yards long down the road at kick-off time.

Jimmy Savile more than deserved his ennoblement for his wonderful work for Stoke Mandeville. For myself, it was nice to have done something, indirectly, which helped my friend Bill.

# SIXTEEN

# *Wembley! Wembley!*

My 25-year love affair with Swindon Town FC developed into a high-profile relationship in 1978. Until then I had been a fan on the terraces or, more recently, in the stands. Now I was invited by the editor of 'Grandstand' to film an item on the club for 'Football Focus'.

I made the necessary arrangements with the club, met the producer and crew for a liquid lunch at the Crown at Faringdon, and drove to the County Ground. The match, Swindon versus Chesterfield, was pretty dreary, but Swindon won 1-0. Afterwards I interviewed Bob Smith, the manager, and several of the players.

The item was transmitted a week later, and the following Saturday BBC cameras covered Swindon versus Watford for 'Match of the Day'. That was a thrilling game, which Swindon won 2-0. Afterwards, Barry Davies interviewed Bobby Smith and the young Watford manager, Graham Taylor. As both sides were still contenders for promotion, Barry asked the two managers: 'Will you be happy to settle for promotion, or do you mean to go up as champions?' 'Champions!' snapped back Taylor, and he was to have his wish: Watford won the division and Swindon missed out narrowly on promotion.

That was ten years after the greatest day in Swindon's history. In the spring of 1969, Swindon had battled their way through to the League Cup Final at Wembley, after a thrilling semi-final duel with Burnley, which went to extra time in the third encounter at a neutral ground (The Hawthorns). Now they faced Arsenal at Wembley. I was miserable that because of my duties for 'Grandstand' – I was due to race-commentate at Bangor-on-Dee – I was unable to go to the game. But the Lord, in his mercy, threw down so much rain that the Bangor meeting was abandoned.

Sam Leitch, the head of sport, managed to get me a ticket (amongst the Arsenal supporters!), and I spent a sleepless night of excitement on the eve of the match. On the Saturday I first went into the 'Grandstand' studio to present a Cheltenham preview – completely messing up one of my 'links' – and then raced by taxi to the Twin Towers.

The heavy rain had turned Wembley into a quagmire, which was not going to help the Arsenal players, several of whom had been suffering from 'flu. Swindon went ahead with a scrappy goal and fought hard to defend their lead. With seven minutes left, Bobby Gould – how I hated that man! – equalized for Arsenal. In the first period of extra time Don Rogers scored for Swindon. Were Arsenal weakening? Could we do it? The sweetest moment was yet to come. Rogers ran 60 yards from his own half, on the break, leaving full-back Ian Ure floundering in the mud, then neatly rounded Bob Wilson and slammed the ball into the back of the net. They think it's all over! Of course we were ecstatic.

We stood and cheered ourselves hoarse as Stan Harland lifted the trophy. The Third Division no-hopers had humbled the giants from Highbury. Donald Rogers became a legend in the town, and to cap a wonderful year, Swindon went on to win promotion. That, however, is another story. The laws of libel prevent me from discussing Dave Mackay's period of management.

In the 1979-80 season, Swindon were a high-class side, capable of holding their own against the very best. After my 'Football Focus' item several of the players were now my friends, notably Kenny Stroud, a former schoolboy international, Chris Kamara, Chic Bates and Brian Williams. Eleven years on from Wembley and Swindon were having a sensational run in the League Cup. The fifth-round tie against Arsenal was a thriller.

At Highbury we equalized to 1-1 with five minutes to go, by means of a bullet header from our centre-half Billy Tucker. Back at the County Ground the following Tuesday, we won another very exciting game. We had been leading 3-1, but the brilliance of Liam Brady pulled the score back to 3-3. Extra time again was needed. I had a severe cold and had all but lost my voice. When Andy Rowlands stabbed in the winner, I could only croak. It was a heroic game and afterwards I joined the players and Bobby Smith for a champagne celebration. I could only drink and make approving noises.

The first leg of the semi-final was at home, against Wolves. We were in Barbados at the time and so missed the game. Swindon won 2-1. Swindon were just 90 minutes away from Wembley, and somehow it meant so much more to me now that the players and their wives were our friends. The second leg was at Molyneux on 12 February. I took Alison to the historic match and we booked into a good hotel at Tettenhall. Dinner was arranged in the five-star restaurant for after the match.

We lost 3-1. There were a few general recriminations, but we had fallen at the last fence and were out of the League Cup.

I was speechless with disappointment. Alison and I travelled in silence to the hotel, stopping only for fish and chips and two cans of Fanta orange on the way. 'What about my dinner?' complained Alison. 'This is it,' I replied. That was about the extent of our dialogue throughout the evening. Ever since then, Alison has never volunteered to visit a high-profile football match, nor is she likely to take her holidays in Wolverhampton!

It was a heart-breaking month for the Town. Two weeks earlier we had lost a fourth-round FA Cup replay against Spurs at White Hart Lane, after leading 1-0 with seven minutes to go; while the previous Saturday we had lost against Sheffield Wednesday to a last-minute goal from Terry Curran, which effectively ended our chances in the League.

The home FA Cup tie against Spurs almost landed me in trouble. I had been commentating at Cheltenham and, as I signed off after the 2.45 race, Frank Bough wished us well and informed the nation that I would be driving flat out to Swindon for the second half of the Cup tie. Who should be waiting for me in a layby in Cirencester, but the local constabulary. Talk about semaphoring a punch!

The previous autumn I had persuaded three of the team, Kenny, Chic and Brian, to buy a quarter share each in a racehorse. This was a filly by Roi Soleil, trained by Gavin Pritchard-Gordon, which we called Sea Aura (Kenny's choice of name). She had reasonable talent. The filly ran an encouraging race first time out at Newmarket, and then we took her to Lingfield with expectations of her running a big race.

Brian Taylor was riding the favourite called Hot Ember and gave me every encouragement to believe that Sea Aura might beat her. I booked Lester Piggott to ride our horse. The boys were almost mesmerized in the paddock, but Lester was quite talkative. Sea Aura won very cosily at 3/1, and a great deal of champagne was drunk in the owners' and trainers' bar that evening.

The following season Sea Aura finished fourth in a listed race at Goodwood. When we came to sell the filly, it was hard for the boys to understand that, although they had had plenty of fun, they had not made a profit out of the transaction. Those, sadly, are the facts of life about racing in Great Britain. It would be laughable were it not so depressing for the future of the industry.

Later that autumn, a brilliant 16-year-old talent appeared on the scene for Swindon FC. His name was Paul Rideout, whose family were local and connected with the football club. Paul made his first appearance for the club on 29 November, against Hull City. It was a date to be remembered, for two reasons.

In the spring of that year I had bought a big chestnut mare at the Doncaster sales. She was called Charming Thought (by Stage Door Johnny) and was in foal to the 1978 St Leger winner, Julio Mariner. She produced a reasonably attractive chestnut colt foal which I entered in the Newmarket December sale. He was in the catalogue on 29 November, and I privately valued the foal at £4500. On the eve of the sale I was offered £5000 by my neighbour Cormac McCormac. Now, Cormac is a good judge and undoubtedly knows how many beans make five. Since he is always ahead of the game at the sales I reckoned that he knew something! So, with reservations, I turned down his offer.

On 29 November I was racing at Chepstow. I left the course immediately after the last televised race and quickly devoured the 50 miles to Swindon. The foal had been sold early in the afternoon, but in those days car phones did not exist. The priority was Swindon versus Hull. In the event, Paul Rideout 'scored' a quite stunning goal from about 30 yards, but it was disallowed for off-side. Later he scored a second, less spectacular goal. He had a 'blinder', and Swindon won 3-1.

I rang Alison at Newmarket from the Rendezvous Club at Swindon Town FC. The conversation went something like this: 'Hello darling. Three one. Brilliant. The boy Rideout was a bit special.' 'Do you want to know about your foal?' 'In a minute, let me tell you about this goal.' And so I went on. Eventually I paused for breath. 'What did the foal make?' I asked as an afterthought, expecting the answer to be around 5000-5500 guineas. '16,500 guineas.' There was a long pause. 'Um, did you say 6500 guineas?' 'No, 16,500 guineas,' replied Alison.

I was flabbergasted. The buyer was Julio Mariner's owner, Captain Marcos Lemos, and he was to be trained eventually by Clive Brittain. The Captain was a good judge – the colt, called Mitilini, grew into a big fine horse and was good enough to run in the Derby.

Paul Rideout, of course, enjoyed a hugely successful career with Swindon, Aston Villa, Bari and Everton, amongst others. But he will rarely have scored a better goal than his disallowed effort against Hull City.

Sad to report, in the next two years Swindon Town went into decline. We had poor players and indifferent management. In 1982 I drove all the way from Goodwood to see the final match of the season against Newport County, which we had to win to stay in division three. We did not win. There followed another long, quiet evening, and then the long drive back to Goodwood the next morning.

In the summer of 1984, I learned that Lowndes Lambert, the insurers who had offices in the area, were prepared to put up £50,000 sponsorship for the wages of a top-class player-manager for the Swindon club. It occurred to me that I might have the answer. Through racing I had become friendly with the Scottish international Lou Macari, and was aware that his playing days at Manchester United were coming to an end. Lou and I spoke on the telephone one Sunday morning, after which I contacted the Swindon chairman, Maurice Earle.

The outcome was that Lou Macari was appointed player-manager, and this was the start of the ten most successful and exciting years in the 100-year history of the football club. Inevitably, Lou was unable to achieve overnight success – the club had sunk too deep into mediocrity for that. There was an embarrassing defeat by Dagenham in the FA Cup, and Lou got off to a false start in his choice of assistant manager. Harry Gregg and Lou found that they were unable to work together. There was an unhappy episode when Lou was sacked and then reinstated, over the Harry Gregg affair. Eventually I introduced my friend Chic Bates to Lou and the two of them made a brilliant management team.

Meanwhile, Lou was working on a two-year plan, gradually building a new team of underrated, inexpensive players. He would buy them, make them fitter than they had ever been, and pay them no more than £400 a week. The club's entire weekly wage bill at that time was no more than £3500. A few years later, under the subsequent management, it rose to £50,000 a week.

By the spring of 1985 the revival was starting to take shape, and by the autumn we were a difficult team to beat. In 1986 we had clinched promotion to division three with four matches still to play. We had beaten Chester at the County Ground and we sang and cheered for long after the game: 'Going up . . . Going up . . .'

The following season Swindon did not gain automatic promotion to division two. We were involved in the playoff competition, first against Wigan, and finally against Gillingham. My trip to Wigan was relatively painless because Pontevecchio Notte had run at

York the previous day, so it was simply a question of crossing the Pennines. I drove south the following morning to do television at Newbury. We had the tie won after the first leg at Wigan.

The trip to Gillingham around the M25 on a Friday evening in May was less straightforward. I was seriously late for the kick-off and listened to the early part of the match on Radio Medway. The team left Gillingham that evening a goal down, and mid-way through the second leg we were two goals behind. Dramatically, we drew level and the tie went to a deciding playoff at Selhurst Park four days later. There, Steve White scored an early goal and we never looked in danger of defeat. It ended 2-0, so we were back in division two! There were wild celebrations in the dressing room, and Lou – who was no longer playing – may have been pushed into the bath. I later drove Lou to London and we had a celebratory dinner at the Ritz Casino Club. It was magic.

Interviewed on 'Grandstand' from Lingfield Park the following day about Swindon's triumph, I obviously sounded like an assistant manager because I was subjected to considerable ribbing afterwards.

Could Swindon go straight through to division one? Lou was cautious to say the least, because he simply did not have the resources to build a promotion side. He had bought some ordinary players and turned them into good division three players, but now he needed more money to spend. That money, despite careful housekeeping, did not exist. It was against this background that the seeds were sown for the so-called 'Swindon Scandal'.

There were two factors, above all, which led to the chairman, Brian Hillier, and Lou appearing in the law courts. The first was some creative accountancy, which was widespread – indeed normal practice with several football clubs – at the time. The second factor was the determination of a hostile group to gain control of the football club. They employed questionable tactics, including enlisting the help of a key employee, who ultimately betrayed the club and its principals. This, in turn, led to the 'exposure' of the club in a lurid and unpleasant Sunday newspaper article and an investigation by the Inland Revenue and Customs & Excise. When the case eventually came to court, the so-called 'fraud' involved no more than £80,000 over a five-year period.

Lou had a habit of providing the players with *ex gratia* bonuses to supplement their meagre wage packets. Knowing that good housekeeping was never a footballer's strongest suit – especially with the availability of a betting shop at the football ground – he liked to keep them hungry and short of cash. If, however, a necessity arose – like a wedding reception or a mortgage repayment that had to be met – Lou would provide the player in question with a cash 'bonus'. It was grey accountancy, which when the balloon went up did not meet with the approval of the Inland Revenue. Brian Hillier was convicted of an offence and sent to jail; Lou was acquitted.

The FA held an enquiry into the so-called 'illegal payments', and the decision of their tribunal on 7 June 1990 was that Swindon Town FC – who had just won promotion to division one (now the Premier League) for the first time in their history – should be relegated by *two* divisions, back to division three. This was reduced, on appeal, to one division, but the club has never, nor ever will, recover from that judgement.

Compare that with the case of Tottenham Hotspur FC. Irving Scholar was rather more fortunate when considerably more spectacular irregularities were discovered in the club's finances during his period of tenure as chairman. The club was fined £1½ million for 'irregular payments', share dealings in the company were suspended, and an Inland Revenue investigation invoked. But were Tottenham Hotspur relegated? No. Was Irving Scholar called a villain? No. Were Arsenal relegated following the George Graham scandal? No. One law for the rich and one for the poor, or what?

Meanwhile, the so-called Swindon Town 'betting scandal' was not only a farce, but also grotesquely misrepresented. The true story was as follows.

Swindon were drawn away to Newcastle United in the fourth round of the FA Cup. It was the biggest match for the club since Lou had taken over. There was terrific excitement in the Town, and

I was commissioned to do a 'Football Focus' profile on our centre forward, Dave Bamber. It was so important an occasion for the club that the BBC kindly gave me a day off work – we were racing at Cheltenham – to travel to Newcastle.

Lou's normal method of preparing the squad for an important match was to take them away to an army camp for 48 hours before the event. It was good for camaraderie, he could keep an eye on them, he would usually take a few quid off them playing cards, and it cost the club virtually nothing. On this occasion, however, Lou decided to treat his players with the respect they deserved. He booked the entire squad into Newcastle's Gosforth Park Hotel, and on the eve of the match took them out to an Italian restaurant to eat the prescribed, energy-giving pasta, instead of fish and chips. After all, they were about to play one of the most famous sides in Europe, with an international line-up, including the 'boy wonder' Paul Gascoigne.

On the eve of the match, Brian Hillier approached Lou and asked: 'By the way, how are we going to pay for all this?' 'Well,' said Lou, 'if we win we're in the fifth round of the FA Cup. If we draw we'll have a sellout for the replay at the County Ground. So, all you need to do is to take out insurance against our being beaten'. 'How do we do that?' said Brian. 'It's quite simple. The bookmakers are betting only 8/11 Newcastle to win, but they should be about 2/5. If we bet £5500 Newcastle and they beat us, at least we have £4000 to pay the hotel bill.' So that precise bet was struck by a third party, at Cheltenham racecourse to avoid paying off-course betting tax.

In the event it was a miserable day. The pitch was heavy and the boys played their heart out, but Newcastle scored midway through the first half and then added a second 'killer' goal just before half-time. In the end we were beaten 5-0, which was probably a fair reflection of the gulf in class between the two sides. The players were gutted and we supporters returned south deflated, despite a certain exhilaration over the excitement of the occasion. When you're used to travelling to Walsall, Darlington, Aldershot and Carlisle, a trip to St James' Park is a day to talk about for years to come.

It *was* talked about, but for the wrong reasons. There is no question that the bet struck was an infringement of FA rules. It was improper, but it was not immoral. Robert Sangster, for example, sometimes uses a similar ploy when he has an important runner in a prestigious race. Obviously he hopes to win the race, but if there are, say, two big dangers to his runner he will back those two horses, as insurance. It is a straightforward business practice. In racing it is legal and acceptable to do that. In football, it is a breach of the rules.

But is it a scandal? No way. Yet a disreputable Sunday newspaper wrote an article suggesting that Swindon's management had contrived to 'throw' the game for a bet. Using the time-honoured technique of putting words into someone's mouth, Colin Calderwood was quoted as saying that the 'preparation' for the game was very different from usual and, no, they had never been served pasta previously before a match. If it were not so wicked, it would be hilarious.

Swindon did not make the playoffs that season (1987-88), but they did the following spring. The semi-final, second leg, was at Selhurst Park on the Wednesday night of the Goodwood May meeting: Pontevecchio Notte had won that afternoon and I was obliged to play truant from a formal dinner party with the Earl of March (now Duke of Richmond), claiming ill-health. It was probably the wickedest thing that I ever did at the BBC.

It turned out to be a miserable evening. Chris Wright, now the QPR supremo, had offered to arrange tickets, but they were bang in the middle of a howling menagerie of Crystal Palace supporters. Swindon were never really in it and lost 2-0. Division one was thus postponed for another year. Once again we were deeply deflated.

That summer, Lou Macari decided that he had gone as far as he could with Swindon Town FC. He had taken them to the frontier of the first division, but reckoned, quite rightly, that they did not possess the framework, resources, or tradition to become a successful club at the highest level. The storm clouds were brewing in the 'illegal payments' affair, and Lou decided it was time to leave. He moved to West Ham, until the roof fell in and he was obliged to take 'time off' from soccer.

Ossie Ardiles was appointed as the new player-manager. I had nothing to do with the appointment and had grave reservations. In a way they were justified as, in my opinion, Ossie needed a top-class assistant manager to be thoroughly effective. At Swindon, he inherited Chic Bates and the partnership worked.

Ossie had also inherited Lou's brilliantly bought players, who reacted positively to his creative and adventurous management and responded to the opportunity to express themselves in ways that Lou had not encouraged. There was talk of 'samba' football, but it was great to watch and the spring of 1990 was a memorable period. I followed the team to Newcastle and Stoke, and then to Blackburn for the first leg of the semi-final playoff. We stood behind the goal at the old Away Supporters' end, and the roar bouncing off the old cantilever roof when Steve Foley bulged the net with a thunderbolt volley at our end left my ears ringing for days!

The playoff final against Sunderland resulted in my second-ever visit to Wembley, and we parked our cars and had a pub lunch at Harrow-on-the-Hill. There is something ethereal about the atmosphere at the stadium. Our supporters 'team' was Frank Crocker, Jonathan Powell, and my son Thomas. Thomas was vital: he never had – and never has! – seen Swindon Town lose a match.

The only goal of the match was struck by Alan McLoughlin into the goal on our right. We had a perfect direct view of Alan's shot taking a deflection into the right-hand corner of the net. The last 20 minutes were endless, but eventually the referee blew the long-awaited whistle, and we were there! Frank and I had dreamed about this moment for almost 40 years. We were in division one!

The official celebration was held at the Blunsdon House Hotel in Swindon that evening. There was red and white bunting hanging on all the motorway bridges as we got closer to Swindon. The match had been shown live on ITV and the whole community were drowning in Wembley fever. Ossie was regaled as a super-hero and we truly believed that we had a team that would hold its own in division one. I still believe that, but it was before the era of the Premier League, with its non-stop importation of foreign players and salaries of £2 million a year.

The euphoria lasted for just ten days. On the evening of 7 June came the news that we dreaded, but could not believe would actually happen. The 'three wise men' of the Football League decreed that we should be sent back to where we belonged – division three. A few weeks later we were reinstated to the second division, which was better than nothing, but it took most of us several weeks to revive an appetite for football.

Ossie was ambitious and Chic Bates guessed correctly that he would not remain at Swindon indefinitely. Chic asked the board if they would consider appointing him manager when Ossie left, but they refused. So Chic left Swindon Town and rejoined Lou at his new club, Birmingham City. Ossie then appointed Tony Galvin, his former team-mate at Spurs, to replace Chic. At the end of March we were dangerously near the relegation zone when Ossie announced, shortly after a home fixture against Newcastle, that he and Galvin were leaving Swindon Town to take over at – Newcastle! The love affair with Ossie was over. His record at Newcastle, and then Spurs, did not sustain the achievement of that first season at Swindon.

When Glenn Hoddle was appointed to succeed Ossie the excitement was tangible. Glenn was still playing and we were to enjoy a brand of football at a higher level of skill than even Ossie had created at the County Ground. We narrowly avoided relegation that first spring, in 1991, and the following season it took a while for the players to adjust to Glenn's extraordinary football vision and tactical demands. We played with overlapping full-backs and built methodically from the back. It was a very far cry from Lou's successful variation of Route One.

The colossal wage bill inherited from Ossie's regime imposed a block on spending, so Glenn set about turning good players into better players. He succeeded, and in the 1992-93 season we again won our way to the playoffs and again (via Tranmere) to Wembley. This time our opponents were Leicester City. As supporters, our pre-match routine was the same, with John de Moraville added to our team. I checked daily on Thomas's availability and he duly appeared.

If ever there was a roller-coaster of a match, this was it. Swindon played some superb football and went 3-0 up. The Leicester fought back, and with ten minutes to go it was 3-3. We were numb with shock: the ultimate prize seemed to have slipped from our grasp. But centre-forward Steve White never stopped running, and with five minutes remaining referee David Ellery (Harrow) made the finest decision of his career, when Steve was brought down in the box. Penalty!

Paul Bodin stepped up to take the kick. Thousands of Swindon supporters were unable to watch. There were prayers, supplications, and deals made with the Almighty. I swallowed and my eyes misted over. 'Ye-e-e-e-s!' We hadn't doubted you, Paul! Thank you God, thank you Ellery. That's got to be it!

It was, and we won 4-3. For the next 48 hours we were all on cloud-nine, as we had been three years earlier. Once again, though, the cloud had a jagged lining.

As we had expected, Glenn Hoddle resigned and announced that he was going to Chelsea. What we did not expect was that his assistant, John Gorman – whose only managerial experience was with Leyton Orient Reserves – would be appointed in his place. To say that the following season was disappointing would be an understatement of grotesque proportions. We had a team that was totally inadequate for the needs of the Premier League and, although the football was attractive, we lost consistently.

The season that we had all looked forward to for most of our lives was the ultimate anticlimax. I went to very few games. In the end, the only moment of pleasure that I recall was drawing 2-2 at home with Manchester United and seeing Eric Cantona sent off for stamping on a Swindon player. That was fun!

The final straw was seeing an unfit, overweight player on loan from Celtic – who had once provoked the Stratton Bank end – pulling on a Swindon jersey. We had lost our pride as well as our common-sense. I had given Swindon Town Football Club 40 years of my life and I had nothing more to give.

At last, the love affair was over, and I have only seen two home games since 1994.

# SEVENTEEN

# *A Shattered Dream*

Brough Scott telephoned. We had been good friends, and latterly rivals, since BBC-TV launched his television career ten years earlier. 'Andrew and I would like to come and see you,' he said.

'Andrew' was Andrew Franklin, now the executive producer of Channel 4 Racing. At this stage, in 1981, ITV Sport continued to be responsible for all racing output on the independent channel.

Andrew Franklin was determined to streamline ITV's coverage of racing and to hire a high-profile race commentator. At the time the ITV commentaries were shared between John Penney and Raleigh Gilbert, two experienced racecourse commentators. Andrew offered me the position of 'senior race commentator', covering all the Classics and the other big-race days. I was also invited to coordinate ITV Racing's editorial strategy.

It was a terrific offer and entailed a considerable increase in salary. I asked for time to think it over, but in the end, with mixed feelings, turned them down. There were two separate reasons.

First, I had waited for 16 years for Peter O'Sullevan to retire and, from our conversation on the train from Warrington some years earlier, reckoned that there were just a further two years to wait. He was now 63 and had stated quite clearly that he would retire at 65.

The other reason was my fanatical support for Swindon Town FC. I was able to watch at least 17 or 18 games a season, thanks to the format of our racing coverage in 'Grandstand'. The BBC liked to be finished with racing – described once memorably by the producer as 'a breather for the studio' – at 2.30 pm, or even earlier in the event of a Rugby Union international. This meant that if we were racing at

Newbury (25 minutes from the Swindon ground), Cheltenham (50 minutes) or Chepstow (50 minutes), I could see the majority of a game after we had come off the air. If, however, I switched to ITV, there would be no more Saturday football for me as their coverage lasted well into the afternoon.

The right decision had been made, I felt, but I made one major mistake. I told no-one outside of my immediate circle about the approach. Nowadays, the regular procedure is to knock immediately on the head of department's door and ask for a substantial increase in salary! Nor did I tell Peter O'Sullevan because he was still active in Fleet Street and I respected the confidentially of the approach from Andrew and Brough.

It is hard to recall my precise feelings when I approached Peter in the press room at Newbury a couple of years later. 'So this will be your last year?' I ventured. 'What do you mean?' he replied. 'Well, you told me that you were going to retire at 65, which is this year.' 'Retire from *Fleet Street*, yes,' said Peter, 'but I'm not going to retire from *this*.' 'Well, when are you going to stop?' I replied aghast. 'Oh, like that Australian caller, I should think – when I just dry up.'

I was quite shattered, but the ITV job had gone. They had appointed the excellent Graham Goode in 1981.

It was soon after O'Sullevan's bombshell that Channel 4 Racing was launched, on 22 March 1984. ITV continued to cover racing in 'World of Sport,' until the programme ended in September 1985. Thereafter, all racing coverage was transferred to Channel 4.

It cannot be denied that the misunderstanding between us affected my relationship with O'Sullevan. I felt betrayed. What rubbed salt in the wound were comments attributed latterly to O'Sullevan when Jim McGrath was finally announced as his successor. He was quoted as follows: 'Jim is the best around. I heard him first in Hong Kong, where he was working at the time, and was very impressed. . . . When someone at the BBC asked me what they would do when I retired, I told them without hesitation to get this fellow over from Hong Kong . . .' Every time I read those words, I find it difficult to repel a feeling of bitterness.

I had one further opportunity to move into high-profile race-calling, when Satellite Information Services (SIS) was launched in 1987. Mike Murphy was coordinating a streamlined élite of racecourse commentators and invited me to join the team. I accepted, on the basis that I could select my days, which would include the Classic races. Mike agreed to that and a story appeared in the *Racing Post* headlined 'New job for TV's Wilson'. It read: 'Julian Wilson is to become the voice of the betting shop. He is joining the Racecourse Technical Services team as a course commentator on a freelance basis. . . . Wilson is joining RTS to add further authority to their commentaries.'

Unhappily, Mike was unable to 'deliver'. Commentators Robin Gray and Raleigh Gilbert were horrified that they were going to lose their plum days and encouraged the RTS mafia to defy Mike Murphy. After weeks of political in-fighting, I was advised that my first day's commentary at Newmarket on 7 July would be shared with Robin Gray on a fifty-fifty basis. That meant that I would commentate on some races from down the course. I said: 'Thank you, but no thank you.' A replacement had to be found at the last moment, and the deal fell through.

There was an ironic sub-plot to this affair. The Jockeys Association, in their wisdom, had decided that they were entitled to a cut of the huge sums now sloshing about in racing, following the deal to transmit a dozen races a day – and eventually up to three dozen – in Britain's betting shops. They were demanding a contribution of one-tenth of a penny for every horse in races covered by SIS, to be paid to the Jockeys' pension fund. I was in disagreement with this concept, on the basis that jockeys were performing for, and being paid by, owners – as opposed to by television.

The jockeys embarked on a sorry programme of civil disobedience to delay the start of races, refusing to come out of the weighing room. Their action came to a head when they arranged a 'TV strike' at Royal Ascot. The ringleaders decided, before racing, that no jockey was to be interviewed on television. The problem was that no-one knew.

It was a complete fiasco. Michael Kinane won the first race of the meeting and immediately came up to my balcony to be interviewed. No-one had told him that they were 'on strike'. By the end of the day it was obvious to me that something was up, so that evening I telephoned Steve Cauthen, a friend, who admitted rather sheepishly that they had decided to withdraw their cooperation. I was very angry and remonstrated with him: 'Steve, what the hell's it got to do with us? Your argument is with SIS and the bookmakers. Why take it out on the BBC?'

The following day I saw the Jockeys Association president, Paul Cook. 'What the hell's going on?' I asked him. 'Well,' said Paul, 'I read that you're going to work for SIS so you're obviously on their side.' So we continued with our coverage of Royal Ascot without a single interview with a jockey. We talked instead to owners, trainers and breeders, and at the end of the week not a single viewer, or newspaper man, knew that the jockeys had been 'on strike'!

While I was turning down ITV in 1981, I was hoping that Alison Ramsay was not planning to change her mind and turn down my proposal of marriage. According to her, it was voiced in the following terms: 'The idea of spending the rest of my life with you is not entirely unattractive.' A bottle of Dom Ruinart had been placed in the refrigerator in the hope of a similarly positive reply.

Her only possible competitor as the second (and last) Mrs Wilson had been eliminated by British Airways in October 1979. Her name was Julia Murray, and for three years she had been on our team in Barbados with Nigel Angus. Nigel had diverted his interests to Isla St Clair, but Julia and I remained friends. It was a friendship that I felt could possibly have been translated into romance.

That possibility was killed off by the 'weekend-that-wasn't', arranged for the last weekend in October 1979. Julia had arranged a house party and a big dinner party on the Saturday night. The family lived in Northumberland, where Julia's father was a popular local landowner. I had been racing at Newbury and was booked on a flight to Newcastle from Heathrow. It was a flight that checked in at the departure gate, and when I presented myself to board the plane I was advised that the aircraft had been changed from a Trident 1E to a Trident 2, with reduced capacity of 19 passengers. Because I had sheltered in a quiet corner so as to check in inconspicuously, at the last moment, there were now no further seats on the plane. I felt like Victor Meldrew: I could not *believe* it!

The trip aborted, I then drove back to Newmarket. Julia, I believe, was more angry than disappointed and has probably never forgiven me.

I took my complaint to the highest level and wrote a stinging letter of frustrated rage to BA's chief executive, Roy Watts. His reply was acceptable on a technical level – 'compelled for operational reasons to substitute a different type of aircraft in order to avoid more serious disruptions to the schedules' – but it did not compensate for a ruined weekend.

This was, however, the last of a series of travel disruptions caused by the airline. One beneficial outcome was that I became, at last, a complimentary member of BA's Executive Club – whereupon they changed the system and made everyone pay for the privilege! It is only fair to add that a large number of the airline's on-flight personnel have been extremely kind and helpful over the years.

Nonetheless, the other 'BA experience' that sticks in the mind was an episode about 20 years ago on a flight to Paris. It was a raging hot day and the baggage-loaders were on strike. Passengers were invited to assist with the loading and I volunteered. We worked flat-out for about 20 minutes. When we finally took off, those who had assisted were offered a complimentary drink, and I asked for a glass of champagne. Came the reply: 'I'm sorry, sir, but I'm afraid I can't serve you champagne – only beer or soft drinks.'

Alison was now my pretty regular companion – she even claimed to have been to 14 different football grounds – and she joined the winter team to Barbados in 1980. We spent our summer holiday that year with my friend Chris Collins and his wife Suzanne in Chris's lovely hillside house, St Benedict, between Magagnosq and Grasse in the south of France. The previous year I had spent much of the trip in long and animated conversations about handicapping with Jack

Ramsden, while Linda Ramsden and the remainder of the party were trying to read or sleep. On this occasion the Ramsdens and Wilsons were invited in different weeks!

It was an idyllic location. For breakfast we ate baguettes with locally made honey, and drank delicious coffee. Lunch on the terrace was light, with salads, local cheeses and rosé wine. In the later afternoon we would go for long and challenging walks in the Gorge du Loup, walking at times through the river at about waist height. In the evening there was the choice of a dozen or so top-class restaurants within a range of 20 kilometres. On some days we visited Tahiti Beach at St Tropez, and on others we lunched in the courtyard, with the doves, at the Colombe d'Or. But it was designed as a switching-off holiday, in the warm sun and by the welcoming pool.

The following January, Alison and I decided to take a break from Barbados. We travelled to Kenya, visiting Kilifi, the Island of Lamu, and Malindi. It was an expedition of mixed fortunes and mixed emotions.

On our first day on the beach at Kilifi, I heard a familiar voice behind me. I thought that I was dreaming or hallucinating. It was Raleigh Gilbert, whose job as an ITV commentator I was about to be offered! Raleigh was in charge of two apprentice jockeys who had won the prize of a working holiday in Kenya in a series for apprentices, sponsored by Crown Paints.

'Good God, fancy seeing you, old boy!' exclaimed Raleigh, before I could hide in the sand. Bwana Raleigh, who always looked like a tea-planter, had been invited on board a yacht in the creek. 'What a bit of luck,' he continued, 'I wonder if you'd mind looking after the boys while I hop on board this yacht for a while. Bit of a party, y'know.' 'The boys' were Kevin Darley and Shaun Payne, who remained with us the entire day. We gave them drinks, some lunch, and took them water-skiing. They were delightful company, but by sundown Alison was finding the experience a shade tiring.

Finally, Raleigh reappeared after his day on the yacht. 'Thanks so much, old boy. Delightful chaps, aren't they? I'll do the same for you one day.' And off they went. Raleigh was always in his element in Kenya, and he had recently returned from Africa when he was found dead in his London flat early in 1998.

The following day we went water-skiing in the creek and enjoyed good sport. We had been told that sharks rarely, if ever, swam into the creek, but when Alison was skiing I was certain that I saw a fin breaking the surface about 50 yards behind her. Laughing, I pointed back over her shoulder and made a gesture like jaws snapping. Alison ignored me and looked straight ahead. The following day there was a story in the local English-language newspaper that a boy had been killed by a shark in the creek the previous day, very close to where Alison had been skiing.

At Lamu – where the skiing was hopeless – a more serious development came about. Alison suffered an acute attack of diarrhoea, which left a legacy of irritable bowel syndrome from which she suffers to this day. At Malindi we stayed at the Indian Ocean Lodge, where the food was quite excellent. Our best friend was a remarkable Australian cattle dog called Digger, who would chase low-flying birds along the rocky seashore, without ever once stumbling and impervious of the hard surface. Oh, to own a racehorse with legs like him!

We did not return to Kenya. In particular I was distressed by the long queues of people waiting for food. I felt that perhaps we had arrived 50 years too late.

It was in the spring of 1981 that the Prince of Wales, for several years an accomplished international polo player, decided to have a stab at riding under National Hunt rules. He acquired a horse called Good Prospect, which Nick Gaselee trained for him, with the objective of winning the Grand Military Gold Cup. Unhappily, on the big day, the heir to the throne was unseated when Good Prospect was travelling well on the final circuit.

The following week Prince Charles decided to ride the same horse in the Kim Muir Memorial Chase at the Cheltenham Festival. Unfortunately, it was not a race covered live by BBC-TV – children's programmes were sacrosanct – but we recorded the event for our evening highlights programme. On this occasion Prince Charles's fiancée, Lady Diana Spencer, had accompanied the royal party to the races. The Kim Muir was the fifth race and Good Prospect fell at the tenth fence. Evidently, Lady Diana's reaction could be paraphrased as follows: 'Oh dear, Charles has fallen off again, I suppose that means we'll be late home.' I feared for the relationship – especially when their magnificent wedding took place bang in the middle of Glorious Goodwood!

Prince Charles enjoyed his race-riding greatly, and was quoted as saying: 'I wish people could only understand the real thrill, the challenge of steeplechasing. It's part of the great British way of life and none of the sports that I've done bears any comparison.' Under pressure from those concerned for his safety – especially with his marriage imminent – Prince Charles gave up race-riding at the end of the season.

A month earlier, at the age of 40, I had made an equally distressing but inevitable decision – that I could not continue to play football. I had been invited to play for a Jockeys' XI against Swindon Town FC and my name actually appeared on the Match Day programme. But I had to decline because it was on the Tuesday of Grand National week and I just did not have the time to get fit and to play.

So my swansong was booked for the annual Press versus Jockeys match in aid of the Injured Jockeys' Fund at Hayes FC on 26 April. I reckoned that 45 minutes would be the limit of my endurance, so for the first half I commentated on the match. I ran on to the pitch for the second half to a reception of overwhelming indifference. Alison, who might have applauded me, had joined the queue for the ladies' loo. We were trailing to a penalty converted by the stable lad, Tudor Jenkins. But within 45 seconds of the restart we were level, a cross from the right converted with inch-perfect precision by the substitute. I raised my arms and looked round for the bank of photographers – she was still in the loo! In the end we lost 3-1, but it was a good way to finish.

The day before that historic game of football, something of even greater significance happened at Sandown Park. A colt belonging to the Aga Khan – called Shergar – won the Sandown Classic Trial by ten lengths. A week earlier, after an impressive gallop on the Waterhall at Newmarket, I had backed him to win the Derby at 33/1. He duly won his next race, the Chester Vase, with an equally impressive performance – and yet was still on offer at 4/1 to win the Derby. I remember confirming to the professional backer, Alec Bird, who lived in Cheshire, that this must be the value bet of a lifetime.

The big hitters went to work on Shergar, and he was sent off at 11/10 on Derby Day. The result was never in doubt – he was clear at Tattenham Corner and galloped on to win unchallenged by ten lengths.

I presented Alison with an emerald, sapphire and diamond engagement ring, which had been paid for by Shergar. The story of our engagement – celebrated at Pontevecchio on the evening of the Derby – appeared in Compton Miller's diary in the *Evening Standard* two days later.

We were married at the Chelsea Register Office on the Monday after Royal Ascot. It was a quiet, informal affair, followed by a wedding party at Old Church Street for family and close friends. My father was unable to attend because it clashed with the first day of Wimbledon. We gave a big party, with dancing, in a marquee in the garden of our cottage in Burrough Green, in the autumn.

Alison and I enjoyed our wedding immensely. We spent our wedding night in a huge suite at the Dorchester Hotel, and the following day flew off to the south of France for the first week of our honeymoon with Chris and Suzanne Collins and several other friends. We were spoiled, and a chilled bottle of champagne was awaiting under our pillow.

The second week was spent at the Waterville Lake Hotel, in the Ring of Kerry, owned by the multimillionaire racehorse owner, Jack Mulcahy. Jack's horses were trained by Vincent O'Brien and there was a great bond between the two families. Alison seemed to spend much of the week dancing with Vincent's brother Phonsie, who was playing golf nearby.

For a period there was a threat of disruption to the honeymoon, when Vincent was reported to be helicoptering to Waterville with a videotape of the interview I had conducted with Robert Sangster at Royal Ascot two weeks earlier. The interview concerned the controversial outcome of the Irish 2000 Guineas won by King's Lake, owned by Robert and trained by Vincent, from To-Agori-Mou, trained by Guy Harwood. King's Lake had been disqualified for interference, but then reinstated on appeal after blown-up photographic evidence was presented by Jacqueline O'Brien. Opinions were strongly divided. Many felt that To-Agori-Mou's connections had been 'robbed'. The 'decider' between the two horses took place at Royal Ascot shortly after my interview with Robert, and To-Agori-Mou won by a neck.

Vincent felt that the interview had been unsatisfactory, but his secretary Derna Dwyer – Coral Pritchard-Gordon's sister – forbade him to interrupt our honeymoon. In the event, Vincent did travel down to play golf and we spent a very pleasant evening fishing on the river.

Shergar was now being trained for the King George VI and Queen Elizabeth Diamond Stakes. I filmed the great horse on the Wednesday of the race and unearthed an amazing story. A short while previously, Shergar had whipped round at the top of the Limekilns gallop and unseated his rider. He galloped a mile in the opposite direction to Newmarket, to the Boy's Grave, galloped across a fast-moving main road on to the road to Moulton, and turned right in Moulton to gallop back down the road the four or five miles to Newmarket. He had apparently sought refuge in Henry Cecil's stable at the top of Warren Hill and waited to be collected. When he arrived at Warren Place no-one took too much notice of him – loose horses are not uncommon in Newmarket – but eventually a bright spark piped up: 'You know, that loose horse looks a bit like Shergar.' A call was made to Michael Stoute's stable: 'I don't suppose you're missing a dark bay horse with a white face?' Amazingly, Shergar was none the worse for his adventure and duly won the 'King George', although not as easily as some expected.

Alison was only to meet my father once, when he and Sally came to stay at Burrough Green in July 1980. It was a typical Wilson evening: Alison and Sally retired at 3 am and my father and I at 5 am. I served the Warre 1970.

My father died 15 months later at the age of 68. To pay tribute to his life, I could not conceivably – with the use of every word in my vocabulary – improve on the generous and brilliantly-penned tribute by that leviathan of Fleet Street, Ian Wooldridge. He wrote in the *Daily Mail* as follows:

> *A great era in our business of sportswriting died in the early hours of yesterday with Peter Wilson, for 36 years the* Daily Mirror*'s Man They Couldn't Gag.*
>
> *It was typical of the man that it took cancer ten years to kill him. It was equally typical that five days before his death at 68, he had just completed another series on the great boxers of his time. His knowledge of boxing and tennis was unrivalled.*
>
> *He joined the* Mirror *just before the 1936 Berlin Olympics and went into semi-retirement during the 1972 Munich Olympics.*
>
> *Apart from five years fighting Hitler in between, he devoted most of that span to delivering himself and his newspaper of strident conviction, much rage, massive common-sense, uncompromising campaigns against the corrupt and ill-mannered and inventing a style of writing that brilliantly managed to incorporate staccato slang phrases with the most elegant similes.*
>
> *An entire generation of sports reporters tried, at some time, to imitate him. None succeeded.*
>
> *Peter Wilson developed his style in the days before television made everyone an expert. The advent of the box never changed him. He had a massive ego, brooked no contradiction, dressed better than any of his subjects, terrified fools and was immensely generous to beginners and old friends who had fallen on hard times.*

> *If one knows a man by his enemies, Peter Wilson's enemies were ill-behaved sports stars, apartheid, Avery Brundage of Olympic hypocrisy fame, bullfighting, boxing's mafia, pompous Establishment administrators and a one-time sports editor of the* Daily Express *for whom he worked briefly indeed.*
>
> *He wore a Homburg, carried a cane, spoke like the Old Harrovian he was proud to be and enhanced the status of British sportswriters all over the world by his sheer presence and style.*
>
> *When it came to the crunch with cancer almost ten years ago he faced it with the courage he expected of a big heavyweight paralysingly hit in the 12th round.*
>
> *Supported by Sally, the American wife he loved to distraction, he fought out the last three rounds, returned to Wimbledon this summer to say goodbye to his friends and then died at his home in Majorca.*
>
> *Peter Wilson was not the sort of man you mourn. He was a man whose life and influence on our game you celebrate after his own uncompromising fashion.*

Those words made me immensely proud. I wish I had written them.

## EIGHTEEN

# *Fury and Frustration*

Early in December 1982 the BBC transmitted what I considered to be a disgraceful, dishonest programme in its '40 Minutes' series, and as a direct result of that transmission I tendered my resignation. I had given myself a five-day cooling-off period, but the anger was still boiling inside.

The programme, called 'The Lads' Night Out', focused on the stable lads' boxing championships, which over the years have raised millions of pounds for the Stable Lads' Welfare Trust. I had heard a whisper that this programme, which operated under the 'current affairs' banner, was up to some mischief, so I asked specifically to view the item before it was transmitted.

After some ducking and diving by the production team and straightforward evasion by the series editor, I attended the official press preview at the Run Run Shaw Theatre, at BAFTA, on the afternoon prior to transmission. There I watched appalled at the monstrous collation of distortions, misrepresentations and downright lies. The editing was selective and dishonest. Through the editing, decent men were represented as insensitive charlatans, while others, enjoying relaxation, were depicted as buffoons.

During the closing stages of the preview I considered long and hard the conflict between my moral and contractual duty. My instinct was to stand up at the end and address the audience unequivocally. I wanted to say something like:

> *My name is Julian Wilson and I am the BBC's television racing correspondent. I was not consulted in any way over*

> *this film and I regard it as a disgrace. It is untruthful and dishonest and if it is transmitted in its present form I shall offer my resignation.*

In the end, to my shame, I decided to play it by the book. On returning straight to the BBC's offices, I confronted my immediate superiors – Cliff Morgan and Jonathan Martin – and advised them that if the programme was not 'pulled' I would resign.

The theme of the programme, made by an opportunistic, independent producer, was the contrast between the wealth and opulence displayed at the fund-raising evening in London and the unhappy plight of three former stable lads, now disabled and, in the words of the programme, 'cast on the scrap heap'.

I had personal knowledge of one of the so-called victims, 'Taffy' Williams, the brother of the successful jockey Colin Williams. 'Taffy' had been head lad to my friend Gavin Pritchard-Gordon and had been treated with every possible consideration and kindness once he was unable to work. The owners in the stable contributed a large sum of money to his retirement fund, whilst Gavin arranged comfortable and custom-built housing for him to accommodate the restrictions imposed by his disability. 'Taffy', no doubt overawed by the film-makers, had had words put in his mouth and afterwards was deeply ashamed that he had appeared to betray those who had been so loyal to him. The programme also carried a similar story about a former employee of the Lambourn trainer, Peter Walwyn.

I explained all this to Cliff Morgan, the head of outside broadcasts, who was profoundly uncomfortable. He undertook to talk to the head of the current affairs department. Nothing happened – the programme was transmitted and the racing world was embarrassed and outraged.

Peter O'Sullevan, like myself, was horrified. Peter has given countless hours of his time to support the Trust, through after-dinner speaking and auctioneering. It was the weekend of the annual BBC-TV Sports Review of the Year, but Peter and I boycotted the show – a gesture that was reported in the *Sunday Times*.

On the morning of Tuesday 14 December I went to see Cliff Morgan and confirmed that I no longer wished to work for BBC-TV. Cliff pointed out that I had a further year to run on my contract and that I would be in breach if I walked away. He begged me to reconsider. I also went to see Mike Murphy, editor of 'Grandstand', and told him that it was my intention to resign. 'Don't do that,' said Mike.

I drove home to Newmarket, reflecting on the fact that there was on the table an offer of the job of stud manager at Stetchworth Park Stud, one of the half dozen top thoroughbred studs in England. My friend Bill Gredley was in the process of buying the operation from Colonel Douglas Gray. My company, Seymour Bloodstock, had acted as consultants to Mr Gredley, and our first initiative was to prove very successful. We had suggested a mating between Derby winner Troy and Gredley's foundation mare, Docklands. The resultant yearling filly, Port Helene, made 400,000 guineas at the sales. It was a business in which I was anxious to broaden my involvement.

In the end, though, I was talked out of my resignation from the BBC. On the one hand, Cliff reiterated that he was not prepared to accept it; and on the other it was pointed out that the damage had been done and that it was better to fight from within than from without.

A postscript to the unhappy episode was that I went to see Aubrey Singer, Managing Director of BBC-TV, to ask him to apologize personally to those who had been injured by the monstrous allegations in the programme. Despite the fact that the Broadcasting Complaints Commission upheld every complaint made against the programme, Aubrey Singer took no personal action. As a result Peter Walwyn has not allowed BBC-TV to film his horses and has not given an interview to BBC-TV since 1982.

It was around this time that I sat for the first and only time on a BBC 'board' to appoint my next secretary, whom I would share with the other occupant of my office. We interviewed four or five girls, of whom one had outstanding qualifications – an honours degree from Leeds University and a CV that made impressive reading. She wanted the job and for obvious reasons I favoured her over the other applicants. My colleagues turned her down on the grounds that she was 'over-qualified'! Instead I was delivered a girl who, although less qualified, was an extremely talented exponent of netball.

I shared an office with various other commentators during my 32 years, notably Frank Bough, Nigel Starmer-Smith and Bob Wilson. Frank was always a very companionable fellow, whose greeting was invariably: 'How are *you*?' I found him to be deep on the surface, but a shade shallow underneath. He made a bold move when he switched to news and current affairs on 'Nationwide' and 'Breakfast Time'. I felt considerable sympathy for Frank when he was paired with the divine Selina Scott on 'Breakfast Time'. Frank was always a conscientious, reliable and well-rehearsed operator, whereas Selina found some of the extemporary aspects of the job difficult. But, of course, Selina attracted the headlines and the media attention. One year we asked Selina to act as fashion commentator for the Royal Ascot coverage, but her agent turned the offer down.

Nigel Starmer-Smith has been one of the most successful sportsmen-become-commentator. He was an affable stablemate, although I did not get to know Nigel as well as my old friend Ian Robertson. Ian has always been the recipient of reliable racing information, firstly through coaching at school the grandson of the legendary trainer Harry Wragg, and latterly through his friendship with another top-class rugby player, Ian Balding. Robertson part-owned a 200 guineas bargain two-year-old called Rugby Special (by Murrayfield), who won several races, trained by another rugby enthusiast in the late Ryan Jarvis.

My relationship with Bob Wilson was always a shade uneasy, because every time he looked at me he saw Donald Rogers waltzing round him at Wembley in 1969. Or if he didn't, I soon reminded him! Bob was much smarter than me when ITV came in for him. Instead of keeping the approach quiet, his agent made it known that there were huge sums of money on the table. In the end Bob 'defected' and collected almost double his salary at the BBC.

My final office-mate at Kensington House was an ambitious young assistant editor from Liverpool called Brian Barwick. Brian was to rise through the ranks to be editor of 'Match of the Day', editor of 'Sportsnight', and finally head of sport. It was his elevation to the final status that indirectly led me to leave the BBC. Ironically, within a month of my giving notice of my departure, Brian himself left BBC-TV to become head of sport at ITV!

My office was, for the sake of convenience, adjacent to the 'Grandstand' office, and I lived through seven editors of that programme with varying degrees of pleasure and job satisfaction.

The first was Laurie Higgins, an old-fashioned, no-nonsense, former newspaper man, who got the job done and had a good team around him. He was followed by Alan Hart, a tall, willowy Watford supporter, with talent, *joie de vivre*, a sense of humour and a delightful wife called Celia. Alan became a good friend and accompanied me to Paris on one or two working weekends. I introduced him to my favourite Paris bistro, Chez André, in the Rue Marboeuf, where I have dined regularly since the mid-60s. He loved it and was an excellent companion. Alan progressed to head of sport and eventually to Controller of BBC-1, where he was responsible for the launch of 'EastEnders'.

My association with Alan's successor, Paul Lang, came to an abrupt and unforgettable end. I had an idea for a pool bet, linked to the races transmitted on BBC-TV, to compete with the highly successful 'ITV Seven' bet. I arranged a lunch at Tote House with the Tote chairman, Woodrow Wyatt, and took Paul along with me. Throughout the lunch I enthused about my exciting idea and how it could generate carry-over pools to compete ultimately with the absurd sums available to be won on the ITV Seven. Paul sat listening calmly and then excused himself, stating that he had an important meeting at 2.45 pm. The extent of the importance was conveyed to me later: his meeting was with the head of department, whom he informed that he was leaving the BBC to join ITV! His desk was cleared that evening. Paul was actually an extremely likeable guy, whose life was cut tragically short by a fatal illness.

Harold Anderson joined the BBC from New Zealand. He was solid, serious and companionable, and had extremely high principles. In 1979 the management at Crayford greyhound track staged a charity evening in aid of the Injured Jockeys Fund, the highlight of which was to be a handicap relay race between teams from BBC and ITV. We were still extremely competitive and I was determined that the BBC should win. Our team was Harold Anderson, Ian Robertson and myself, matched against Brough Scott, John Oaksey and John Penney.

Not a lot was known about Harold at the time and he was given a 'start' of several yards. Ian Robertson, as a former Scottish fly-half, was inevitably off scratch. What I knew was that Harold was a New Zealand rugby trialist! We won by a mile.

There was no betting on the race, but the public could buy tickets, choosing either team. At the end of the race all the tickets bought by those supporting the successful team were put in a hat, the owner of the first ticket drawn winning £200. Harold, as the successful team captain, made the draw, but the ticket he picked was, incredibly, his own! Harold put it back in the hat and drew a different ticket, whereupon his wife gave him a very old-fashioned look.

Mike Murphy took over from Harold in 1980. Mike was a terrific editor. If the story was strong enough, Mike would say 'Let's do it!' and to hell with the expense. He was a pleasure to work with and of all my seven editors he was the only one who took a direct interest in horseracing and would, for instance, have a bet.

He joined Alison and me in Paris one racing weekend, just for the crack. We had a memorable evening, dining at Louis XIV in the Boulevard St Denis and ending up in a nightclub, where Mike sent more and more money to encourage the pianist to stop playing. Unhappily, owing to a breakdown in communications, the pianist was convinced that Mike wished him to continue!

One weekend we had a hilarious trip to the Deauville races, accompanied by Mike's friend, the late Bobby Keetch (the former Fulham footballer), and Gavin Pritchard-Gordon who had a runner at the meeting. We lunched at Ferme St Simeon at Honfleur, went to the races during the afternoon, and had early evening cocktails at the Hotel du Golf. Actually, for 'cocktails' read an extremely expensive bottle of champagne bought by Bobby, while I was recording my story on the day's racing for BBC Radio. We then dined at St Gatien airport from two of the largest *plats de fruit de mer* ever assembled, overflowing with oysters, grey shrimps, prawns, langoustines, oursins, mussels, cockles and tiny winkles. Our pilot became increasingly agitated over the arrival deadline at Stansted airport, but we needed one more bottle of Cidre Normande to see us through the trip. When we finally boarded we played spoof all the way home, while Gavin took over the pilot's intercom. We laughed all the way to Stansted. It was a magical day.

In November 1983 Mike decided to leave the BBC and branch out on his own. He created a company called TSL (Television Sport & Leisure), which does contract work in several sports for a number of clients. He has provided masterful coverage of the Tour de France, and when racing at Goodwood was put out to contract by the BBC under the Thatcher guidelines, Mike's company serviced that. It was good to work with him again.

We decided to give him a big send-off from the BBC. He was tricked into appearing at the BBC offices at 7.30 am where we had arranged for a coach to drive us to Dover, board the cross-channel hovercraft, and deliver us to Boulogne. His passport had been smuggled to us, the coach had been loaded with a case of champagne and a video camera, and we were on our way.

I had arranged a special lunch at a quality restaurant just outside Boulogne. Because it was a Monday it was officially closed, so we had the restaurant entirely to ourselves. There were numerous speeches of varying length and quality and a quite exceptional amount of calvados was drunk. I cannot recall any illness on the way home, which speaks volumes for the constitution of members of the outside broadcast department. We stopped in south London for fish and chips and got home at about 9.30 pm after 14 hours non-stop liquid enjoyment. It was a proper 'Goodbye' and Mike loved it.

Mike's successor was John Philips, an iconoclastic Scotsman with a massive talent, but seemingly an inner torment. He was whimsical and off-the-wall. He possessed an exfoliating personality, which never quite showed its true self. His attitude towards horseracing, if not already developed, was moulded conclusively in June 1970, when he was a junior assistant producer.

He was sent to accompany me filming at Ian Balding's stables at Kingsclere on the eve of Royal Ascot. We had gone primarily to film the Queen's horse Magna Carta, but we also filmed the emerging two-year-old superstar Mill Reef.

We were invited to report to the main yard at 6.45 am. This was not John Philips' time of day, unless he was going to bed. He stood in the centre of the yard looking rather vacuous, like a man who had landed by mistake on the moon. A large lurcher walked up to him, looked him up and down and cocked his leg against John's jeans. John stood as if transfixed. The dog finished his business and walked away. I may be completely wrong, but I always thought that incident coloured John's attitude to horseracing and the people involved with it!

John was anxious to animate our pre-race build-up, but also to shorten it. He reduced the time allocated to five minutes, whereas in the 1960s and 70s it had been ten minutes. He was creative and inventive and a pioneer of the sports-music culture. But he was also anarchic and often infuriated the head of sport. In the end it was a row over coverage of the Irish Derby that led to his resignation. I was sorry to have been indirectly responsible and wrote to him asking him to reconsider. But he had had enough.

David Gordon, an assistant producer who had crossed from BBC Radio and who had originally been employed selling shirts in Carnaby Street, took over the reins. We had worked together when he was allocated the job of editing the highlights of the Cheltenham Festival.

We got off to a bad start. David wanted to drop coverage of the Lingfield Derby Trial meeting because it clashed with Cup Final day. I said: 'Over my dead body'. We had always covered the big

12.30 and 1.00 races from Lingfield in the early part of Cup Final 'Grandstand'. There was still a further two hours to the kick-off. We were hardly likely to lose viewers at that stage – in fact quite the reverse.

I appealed to Jonathan Martin, the head of sport, and got my way. It would be an exaggeration to say that David took it with good grace. He was, in many ways, an excellent editor, but without the flair of Philips and the flamboyance of Murphy. I would not go so far as to say that he was over-cautious, but you felt that if he were managing the England football team, he would play four defenders, two sweepers and three defensive midfield players.

Of course, our programme-making opportunities were always inhibited by the escalating lack of resources and finance, but it did seem that whatever was offered by our racing contributors the answer was invariably 'no'. We felt frustrated and undervalued. On occasions horseracing would be the only live outside broadcast in 'Grandstand', and yet prerecorded coverage of minority sports would occupy so much time between races that we were unable to do ourselves, and our sport, justice.

'Grandstand' had always been a happy office, with plenty of verbal rough and tumble and give and take. Perhaps I was insensitive to the changing balance between the sexes – there were an increasing number of talented female assistant producers – but I paid them the compliment of not withholding friendly abuse and colourful terminology. So I was quite stunned when David Gordon called me into his office in the spring of 1995 and said: 'I must ask you to be careful about what you say in front of the girls in the office. I mean, blokeish behaviour is all very well, but some of your remarks are likely to offend.' I was quite speechless. This may have been the beginning of the end.

But all this was some way in the future from that first 'resignation' at the end of 1982. Although I felt disillusioned by the affair over the programme about the stable lads, after a winter break in Jamaica I returned hungry for work. It was not long before a monster story broke.

Shergar, the brilliant Derby winner of 1981 – the horse that paid for Alison's engagement ring – had been kidnapped from the Aga Khan's Ballymany Stud at the Curragh, County Kildare, on the night of Tuesday 8 February. It was his second season at stud and he was valued at £10 million. It soon became clear that the unthinkable had happened: Shergar had been taken by Irish republican terrorists.

That evening I was interviewed on 'Sportsnight' about the crime and explained that the ownership of the horse was complicated. He was now the property of a 40-share syndicate.

The Irish republicans who had unilaterally perpetrated the crime had not, until then, understood this factor. They believed that the Aga Khan still had overall ownership, and it was with him and his stud manager, Ghislain Drion, that they began to negotiate, demanding £2 million for the return of the horse. The Aga Khan stalled and explained that it would be necessary to contact every member of the syndicate before a decision could be taken, which could take days.

The criminals began to realize that they had made a major mistake, in several respects. The animal could not be secreted for a lengthy period, even within the region of Crossmaglen. On the Saturday morning they cut their losses and killed it.

The following August, I met two entertaining girls, Ruth Caleb and Cherry Hughes, who were researching a documentary on the extraordinary and tragic story. Their programme, which appeared on BBC-TV, came as close to the truth in this octopus-like saga as any analysis has achieved. There have been plots, sub-plots and fairytales entailing stunning imagination and creativity. Some individuals have been made to look extremely gullible and foolish. The bottom line is that the horse was dead within four days.

That autumn Alison and I explored fresh ground in Europe. Walter Mariti, whose Scintillo had won at Goodwood, invited us to stay in his beautiful apartment in Puerto Romano, near Marbella. We swam, played tennis and ate plenty of seafood – too much in once instance.

I have never come to terms with metric weights, so when told that the lobster I had ordered weighed two kilograms it did not mean a great deal. The waiter presented me with the largest crustacean I have ever seen, for which I was charged £80 – and it did not even taste especially good! That was a hard way to learn that 500 grams is quite sufficient for any one diner.

That autumn I filmed 'The History of Newmarket' with producer Paul Fabricius. In the opening sequence I was to canter Bruce Hobbs's hack, Summons – who went on to win several races under NH rules – up Newmarket's Warren Hill. The script demanded that I should pull up at the top of the hill, face the camera and voice an introduction along the lines of: 'It was here, 300 years ago, that King Charles II would sit astride his faithful hack, Old Rowley . . .' The payoff to the soliloquy was: 'Very little here has changed since then.'

On the first 'take' I delivered this speech with perfect timing from, thanks to Summons, exactly the agreed spot. Whereupon, just as I was mouthing the final sentence, an immense and very noisy Harley Davidson motorbike came roaring up the Moulton Road, almost drowning my words. I paused briefly, before adding: ' . . . except for f---ing motorbikes.' It became my most notorious 'out-take'.

Thanks to the compliant and extremely patient Summons, we were able to complete the job on the second take. By a miracle, we arrived on the same spot and I remembered my lines. Although my riding style did not attract universal acclaim, I was offered a day's hunting with the Galway Blazers on the back of it. The Irish have a wonderful, if sometimes reckless, sense of humour!

The following year a terrific piece of good fortune came my way. Brough Scott was asked to write an illustrated book about Lester Piggott, who was widely believed to be retiring at the end of the season. Brough, as usual, was hugely over-committed and – repaying once and for all the good turn that I had once done him – suggested to the publishers that I should do the book in his place.

I had asked Lester many years before whether he would approve of my writing his biography, but as early as 1970 he had arranged with Dick Francis that, when the day came, Dick should write the book.

I was slightly embarrassed by this new scenario, but I explained to Lester that if I didn't write the book, someone else would. He took the view 'the devil you know . . .' By incredible good fortune, the publication of our book, with magnificent photographs, coincided with Lester's retirement at Nottingham on 29 October 1985. It enjoyed a period of nine weeks in the bestseller list. Now I was seriously indebted to Brough!

At the same time I was investigated for the first time ever by the Inland Revenue. This made me both bemused and angry, particularly because I had always employed top-class (that is, expensive!) accountants and our books were kept fastidiously accurate. The tax inspector questioned how I could afford my lifestyle on my BBC salary. I explained that I won up to £30,000 per annum backing horses and that this, where appropriate, was taxed at source.

I was asked to produce my betting books and accounts for the past three years, which appeared to satisfy the inspector. Following a further trimming of my allowed expenditure as a self-employed person, the episode was ended. It was only much later that it struck me that the interview might have contained a hidden agenda. During the course of our discussion I was asked about payments by the BBC to Lester Piggott. I thought nothing of it at the time, but in retrospect I can see that my interview was just one small piece of a very large jigsaw puzzle. Whilst I tried to be helpful to the inspectorate, I do not feel that I confided anything that led directly to Lester's incarceration!

It was the following year that saw Michael Grade's cutbacks across the board in the BBC. The loss of race meetings like Chester was deeply depressing.

In contrast, one addition to our portfolio was coverage of the Ulster Derby meeting at Down Royal on 14 July. The senior sports producer in Belfast, Rupert Millar, persuaded me (without much difficulty) to fly over to commentate on the two-day meeting, which was fronted by the excellent Jim Neilly. As part of the deal I asked Rupert to arrange some fishing for me, as normally I would be in Scotland at this time. He came up trumps with a couple of days at Ballynahinch Castle, in County Galway, in the south-west of Ireland.

It was terrific crack, although not many fish were caught. I fished from the famous Ranji's rock but without success. The evening was, in true Irish fashion, such fun, when the hospitality was almost overwhelming. You would be finishing a glass with a man who hunted a pack of hounds when the local priest would appear and declare: 'Ah now. I heard you were here. May I have the honour of buying you a drink?' After Waterville Lake, though, I was beginning to think that there were more monsters in Loch Ness than fish in Ireland. But then, on my second day, I caught a couple of nice fish in the loch, so went home happy.

In the spring of 1988, I paid my second visit to Dubai. I had made a brief, exploratory visit two year earlier, during which I had been generously entertained by Sheikh Hamdan al Maktoum and by my friend Colonel Abdullah Abulhoul, the former chief of police. I bought Colonel Abulhoul a couple of racehorses in England, the second of which, Luna Shamal-gal, won at Warwick as a two-year-old.

On this second visit I was invited to reconnoitre for a BBC-TV documentary on the burgeoning Emirate. My hosts gave every possible cooperation, including the use of a helicopter to gain an aerial view of the ever-growing city and surrounds. I had a meeting with Sheikh Mohammed on my first evening, and doors were opened to the most powerful individuals in the administration of the Emirate. By the end of my visit I had composed the synopsis for a major documentary.

On returning to England at the end of January, I arranged a meeting with Jonathan Martin, who had taken over from Cliff Morgan as head of outside broadcasts. Jonathan was guardedly enthusiastic and allocated me a producer for the project, Bob Abrahams. I had explained that we would receive cooperation as well as logistical assistance from our subject.

I was bursting to make the film. The Arab influence had not yet overwhelmed British racing, but was about to do so. There was so much beautiful scenery, so many exciting projects in Dubai, so many other unexplored sports – like falconing and camel racing – that would make magnificent television.

What happened in the following months is a mystery, but whenever I attempted to progress the project I ran into a brick wall. There was a suggestion that this was too important a project for the sports department, that the budget would be too high, that if it were done perhaps it should be allocated to current affairs department.

But nothing happened, so the project went stagnant. Finally, Bob Abrahams left the BBC in April the following year and the story was officially dead. That may have been the starting starting point of my disillusionment with BBC-TV.

Nineteen eighty-eight was certainly a bleak and negative year. On the racing front, Pontenuovo was lame, and Pontevecchio Notte had a disappointing year. The year ended with the introduction of the abominable five-day entry system, which has cost owners so much money.

Nineteen eighty-nine was another less-than-perfect year, with Swindon Town beaten in the playoffs, Pontevecchio Notte beaten in the 'Bessborough', and the introduction of another abomination – racing on so-called all-weather tracks.

Furthermore, in October of that year I became aware of a disability that has inhibited me ever since – the hearing disorder, tinnitus. The affliction brings a ringing in the ears that is with you for all your waking hours and, in certain circumstances, impairs your hearing. Tinnitus is incurable and is certainly not an ideal condition for a broadcaster. At times that autumn I felt at a low ebb.

But luckily, during the summer months, I had developed a new obsession to take my mind off my professional frustrations. I was now playing cricket for the Lord's Taverners, with some of my great sporting heroes. In the next few years I was to learn more about the game of cricket than I had in the previous 40 years. And 1990, in several respects, was going to prove one of the best years of my life.

# NINETEEN

# *Fantasy Cricket*

It was Derek Ufton, chairman of the Lord's Taverners cricket committee and former Kent wicket-keeper and England soccer international, who invited me to play as a 'celebrity guest' at Fenners, Cambridge, in August 1988. I knew him through his excellent work for the Sportsman's Club and Ritz Casino Club – latterly London Clubs – in promoting the hugely successful Ritz Club Charity Trophy at major race meetings. Now Derek, in introducing me to the Taverners, opened the door to a sporting eldorado.

The cricketing backbone of the Taverners XI in the late 1980s were John Price (Middlesex), 'Butch' White (Hampshire), Mike Denness (Kent), David Bairstow (Yorkshire), David Steele (Northants), John Snow (Sussex) and Farokh Engineer (Lancashire) – all of them, except Farokh of course, former England players.

The Taverners are, however, a mix of cricketers and entertainers, in roughly equal measure. For those of us cricketing wannabees, it is a wonderful way to live out our fantasies. The Taverners play between 15 and 20 fixtures a season, the length and breadth of the country. The team raises well over £l million a year, which is channelled towards the central concept of giving disabled and underprivileged children a sporting chance. Former Test cricketers are wonderfully supportive. At Fenners one year, Ian Chappell answered my invitation to coach some local kids during the teabreak, while in 1997 at Bury St Edmunds I managed to persuade the great Michael Holding ('Whispering Death') to come out of retirement and bowl a few overs.

Before long, I was elected Lord's Taverner no. 2419. I have made some wonderful friends and met some remarkable people, through the fellowship of the Taverners.

As a schoolboy and young man I had bowled left arm, medium pace, round the wicket. In my forties, I conceded that what little pace and penetration I still possessed was now ebbing away, so I switched to bowling slow left arm. To begin with, I mimicked the action of Tony Lock, the supreme left-arm leg-break bowler of my schoolboy generation. But there seemed to be an unnecessary amount of arm-flapping, so I modified the action to what could be best described as Philip Tufnell without the hop.

The technical benefit – not to mention sheer enjoyment – of playing with the Taverners, has been immense. To play with, and against, spin bowlers with the virtuosity of Dilip Doshi, John Emburey, Graham Johnson and Don Wilson, to name but four, has been an education beyond value.

It has been generous of these masters of the art to play charity cricket at all. Even world-class spin bowlers are liable to get clattered by robust young men with their eye well in. Some have their sense of humour stretched to the limit. Being hit for a six is, in my opinion, even more painful and irritating than being stood up by a girl. Nothing consoles, except for capturing the wicket of the offending batsman!

Surprisingly, it was the legendary John Price – whose run-up at Lord's would start close to the sight-screens and which, according to Ian Chappell, contained four changes of gear – who gave me the most vital piece of advice. He pointed out that my grip was incorrect for a finger-spinner. I made the recommended adjustment and found that I was able to turn the ball considerably further.

During the first seven years that I spent my weekends at Burrough Green, I played only a handful of games. The one regular fixture was an annual charity match against the village on the first Sunday of September, for the Lester Piggott Trophy. It was launched in 1981, with the help of Cormac McCormac, an associate of the Piggotts, who at the time was managing the Hall Stud in Burrough

Green. After 18 years, the event, preceded by a large open-air lunch, is still going strong.

It was in 1986 that I won a regular place in the Newmarket Trainers' XI, an occasional side with about half a dozen fixtures a year, the most abrasive of which is against the arch-rivals Lambourn. This needle match was video-recorded in 1997 by the Racing Channel and turned into 40 minutes of television. It is not unfair to say that Newmarket, not for the first time, let themselves down badly, although the conduct of Lambourn in playing two minor counties players from Shropshire was open to question.

In the spring of 1987, Newmarket embarked on a three-match tour of Barbados. It was arranged substantially by our no. 4 batsman, Michael Stoute, who had won the Derby the previous year with Shahrastani and had ended the season as champion trainer. Our fixtures secretary (and wicket-keeper) was Jeremy Richardson, a solicitor who was shortly to embark upon the highest-profile case of his career, following the arrest of his client Lester Piggott for alleged tax evasion.

Other notable stalwarts on tour were William Haggas, who had once played for the Yorkshire Second XI and was to train the 1996 Derby winner, Shaamit; Guy Harwood, who trained in Sussex but somehow slipped into the side; Nick Wingfield-Digby, the well-known vet; Tony Jakobson, the *Sporting Life*'s Newmarket correspondent and a former 'Blue'; and Walter Swinburn, at the time Michael Stoute's stable jockey.

The Barbados tour got off to an uncomfortable start. On the first Sunday we were invited by Peter Short, president of the Barbados Cricket Association, to a day of rum punches, lunch and beach cricket, at Tony Cozier's house on the south coast. Some of our squad were unaware of the destructive potential of sun and rum punch. One player, who shall remain nameless, fell out of his mini-moke on the way home and was untouchable with sunburn for several days. (There is worse, but detail is best left unspoken!)

Our first fixture was against Peter Lashley's XI at the Kensington

Oval the following Sunday. This was the match of the tour. The opposition included Sir Garfield Sobers (stepping from the new pavilion named after him for the first time) Wes Hall, Charlie Griffiths, Seymour Nurse and Lashley himself. We were focused and apprehensive. The match was well publicized and a reasonable crowd was expected.

On the eve of the match, Robert Sangster gave a big party at Jane's Harbour. Both teams were invited and it was a spectacular evening. I was determined to be in bed at a sensible hour on the eve of my first match on a Test match ground, so Wally and Doreen Swinburn – Walter's parents – drove Alison and me back to our hotel before midnight. I slept well and was in good shape on Sunday morning.

The wheels fell off when, after breakfast, I embarked on some loosening up exercises. I felt a spasm of pain in my left shoulder-blade, which immediately began to ache. I had pulled a minor muscle, and nothing that Alison could do with her massaging skills would alleviate the discomfort. I already knew the worst.

For some reason I asked Walter Swinburn to drive me to the ground. He accelerated over every 'silent policeman', which jarred the shoulder and increased the discomfort. When we arrived we had a net at the edge of the ground, but every time I lifted my shoulder it was agony. Half an hour before the match that we had been talking about for weeks and months, I was declared unfit. It was the second biggest disappointment of my cricketing life. Wally Swinburn senior took my place in the side and I was invited, callously, to score.

It was, however, a marvellous 'fun' match, after which the veteran West Indians must have creaked for several days. Guy Harwood had the temerity to hit the great Sir Garfield for a six into the popular stand, which pleased neither the bowler nor the West Indian spectators in that area. To my horror, Man of the Match was awarded to my old adversary Swinburn junior, who took four wickets for just 25 runs, including those of Sobers, Nurse and Lashley.

All the while my agony grew worse and worse as I sat in discomfort in the blazing sun. Even a regular injection of rum punches proved an inadequate anaesthetic. To add insult to injury, there were those who claimed that I invented the whole disability, having 'lost my bottle' at the prospect of facing Hall and Griffiths (not very likely for a no. 10 batsman!).

The sun has wonderful healing properties and I was fit for the second match of the tour against Barbados Wanderers at Christ Church. This was a far more competitive affair. Wanderers are historically the number-one club side on the island, with a great tradition for producing Test cricketers.

We batted first and made the reasonable score of 190-8 in 40 overs, which the home side then knocked off with considerable ease. Their opening batsman Armstrong (a Barbados trialist) and his partner Newsome dealt severely with our opening attack, scoring over 60 runs in the first six overs. When it was my turn to confront Armstrong, the ball was returned regularly over my head at considerable speed to hit the pavilion wall with a heavy 'thunk'. I can still hear that humiliating sound, and recall the considerable damage to the ball!

Our third fixture was two days later, against Denis Atkinson's XI at the Windward Club. Denis and Eric Atkinson had played in the great West Indies sides of the 1950s and both brothers are great racing enthusiasts. Denis picked a side to ensure a well-balanced match, and so it proved. We batted first again and scored 138 all out. The opposition's innings see-sawed, but in the end we won by 12 runs. It was my turn to take four wickets and, to Swinburn's annoyance, I was awarded Man of the Match.

The ensuing party, around Michael Stoute's swimming pool, was rowdy and wet. The tour had been a colossal success. We returned to England the following night and have never toured again. We could never recapture the magic of that wonderful week, with its unforgettable hospitality from so many kind people.

By 1990 I was fully integrated into the Lord's Taverners' XI. From playing only a handful of games, I was now playing, either for Newmarket or the Taverners, on almost every Sunday of the summer.

In September 1990, I suffered a major humiliation. The Taverners were playing at Gateshead, in the north-east, and the opposition team included two England lady cricketers. When the Taverners came to bat we lost three quick wickets. Farokh Engineer and Eddie ('The Eagle') Edwards were the next men in, but nowhere to be found, so I was asked to get my pads on post-haste and to enter the fray. I *hate* being rushed out to the wicket. I walked out totally unfocused and was bowled second ball off an inside edge, by Jill Smith of Middlesex and England. All evening I was ribbed unmercifully.

It did not stop there. During dinner, I mentioned that I was playing cricket in Oxfordshire on the following day. Jane White, the wonderful, warm and mischievous late wife of 'Butch', played me like a brown trout. 'Where exactly are you playing?' asked Jane. I explained. 'Oh good, that's handy. I'll drop in on my way home from Heathrow. And where will you be having lunch?' I identified the Boar's Head at Ardington, near Wantage. 'I'll do my best to get there,' enthused Jane. Of course she had not the slightest intention of driving to Ardington. When I duly arrived at the pub at mid-day there was a huge banner over the bar which read:

*ASK JULIAN HOW HE GOT OUT YESTERDAY*

I retrieved the situation minimally with an innings of 64 runs – my first 'fifty' since my schooldays!

In June 1991, Newmarket played a match which was billed officially as Walter Swinburn's XI versus Canterbury. It was played at Tonbridge Wells and was part of Mark Benson's testimonial year. Swinburn's side consisted mostly of jockeys and trainers, while the Canterbury side included most of the Kent XI. This match produced another exemplary lesson of the chasm between 'occasional' cricketers and the first-class game. The pace of the professional game, the speed with which the ball travels, and the fielding and catching ability of county players, are all on a different level to that of part-time cricketers. I suffered severely at the hands of Mark Benson and Trevor Ward, in particular. But friendships were made that day which I value greatly, notably with Graham Cowdrey, Mark Benson and Matthew Fleming.

Three summers later, the Newmarket gang clubbed together to buy me a day with the team during Kent versus Australia at Canterbury. It was a sacred occasion on the ground where my grandfather had played his county cricket in 1905. There was a magic about sitting on the balcony with the official Kent twelfth man, while the Australians awaited their turn to bat on the adjacent balcony. I was close enough to Shane Warne to see him flex his wrist!

My worst piece of bowling for the Taverners, which was rightly rewarded by the biggest hammering, was against the village of Collingham, near Wetherby, in Yorkshire. The opposition contained several robust young graduates of Leeds Grammar School and the local cricket college. They don't stand on ceremony in Yorkshire. There are no concessions for soft southerners, or feelings of 'let's make a game of it'. They are there at the crease to hit the ball as far as it will travel, regardless of whether the bowler is a revered veteran or a harmless entertainer. They took one look at me and licked their lips.

I blame our captain for acceding to my request to bowl with a strong following wind. As a result, I was overpitching the ball, which was coming invitingly on to the bat. I wrote at the time:

*I was bowling to two lusty, well-covered specimens of Yorkshire manhood, who combined the power of Ian Botham with the physique of Colin Milburn. By the end of my first over, my out-fielder, Ralph Middlebrook, had struck up a pleasant acquaintanceship with the attractive, blonde owner of the house and garden beyond the deep mid-wicket boundary. 'By the end of the second over, they were on first-name terms; and by the end of the third over, Ralph had been invited for hot high-tea.*

I was also out first ball, so had reservations about returning to Yorkshire. However I was lured back in August 1992, to play against Brian Close's XI at Bradford Park Avenue.

The last time I had seen Brian was when we appeared on a 'pilot' production of a show to be called 'A Question of Sport', back in 1976. Despite an extremely indifferent performance by the two of us – caused largely by pre-programme hospitality – the show got off the ground and has prospered in a way no-one could ever have anticipated, despite the occasional accusations of question-rigging and pre-supplied answers.

Brian, a man who hates to be beaten – an attitude that served England so well – had got together a formidable team, including Don Wilson, Bob Taylor, Barry Wood and Roger Knight, but more important, some thrusting young Yorkshire teenagers in Ian Houseman, Paul Grayson and Michael Vaughan.

Michael Vaughan faced the first over from John Price and dispatched it for 22 runs. John was not amused. 'Closey' came in at no. 6 and it was my turn to bowl. In the first over it was honours-even, but in the second over Brian looked like opening up. I took the precaution of positioning John Jeffrey, the giant Scottish rugby union international and British Lion, on the boundary at long-on. Brian duly opened his shoulders and was caught over his head in John's immense hands. I have never seen such hands: catching a cricket ball for John must be like a normal person catching a moth ball.

Another mis-hit gave me the wicket of the celebrated Bob Taylor – caught at mid-on by the racehorse trainer, Richard Whittaker – so it was a good day for important scalps. 'Closey' was not amused, and we paid for it when we were batting. Needless to say, the Taverners suffered a rare defeat!

It is extraordinary how some cricket fixtures can acquire a character of their own, and develop into meticulously-planned sporting warfare between two opposing teams. In August 1994 I accepted an invitation to play at Fenners for a side called the Pimpernels, managed by the veteran Suffolk youth coach Rod Blackmore, against the Cambridgeshire Police. What I did not know was that there was a recent history of hostility and ill-will between the two sides. I found myself bowling at a left-handed batsman who neither looked like a policeman nor batted like one. Fairly soon, he hit me for a six just forward of square-leg. I moved a fielder to close the gap, thinking that perhaps it was his speciality shot, and bowled him the same ball. This one he hit for four in exactly the spot from which I had moved the fielder. Now we knew what we were up against!

That player turned out to be Ivan Pistorius, the wicket-keeper and no. 8 batsman for Northern Transvaal. He was spending the summer as guest-player for March CC, and had been co-opted as a 'ringer' in what turned out to be a fiercely contested needle-match. He scored 150 runs.

My Sunday cricket was being threatened by the increasing number of race-days that we were covering from France and Ireland in 1995. In June I had already accepted an invitation from Mike Denness to play for the Lord's Taverners against the Wine Trade Benevolent Fund XI, at Chiswick, when David Gordon asked me to come into the 'Sunday Grandstand' studio to present the French Oaks at 3.45 pm. I did the only thing possible. Having asked Mike Denness if I could bowl first change, I left the field soon after 3.00 pm, changed my shirt and drove into the studio still wearing flannels and cricket shoes. I was back in Chiswick in time for tea – and a heroic innings!

But throughout that summer I had been playing through almost intolerable pain, ironically the result of a cricketing mishap. In June 1990, the Taverners had a fixture against Gestetner at Stocks, in Buckinghamshire. The match was played on an artificial, felt wicket, but no-one had warned me. I foolishly wore my boots with studs and during the match twisted my left thigh round brutally. Suddenly, in the bar afterwards, my leg seized up completely. When it was time to go home I had to lift up my leg manually to get it into my car. It seized up again later that evening as I tried to walk upstairs to bed.

For the next five years I walked with a slight limp and with varying degrees of pain. I had endless physiotherapy and tried to persuade myself that the problem was a sprained adductor tendon. But the reality was that I had a degenerating arthritic hip. Painkillers were necessary both morning and night. Indeed, I found it impossible to sleep without Volterol and alcohol.

Sooner or later the need would come to succumb to the surgeon's knife. It seemed to me inevitable that an operation would bring an end to my last pleasurable sporting pursuit, so I put it off until the last possible moment. Finally, on 26 October 1995, I presented myself for hip replacement surgery to the eminent Richard Villar at the Cambridge Lea Hospital.

It was not until the eve of the operation that I really came to terms with what the operation entailed. Because of the roller-coaster of work (and cricket!), I had put off reading the relevant literature. When the realization struck me that, according to the booklet, my life would never be the same again, I was horrified. My first reaction was to cancel the operation; my second was that Alison – who organized, activated and stage-managed the build-up to the 'event' – would never forgive me if I did so.

The booklet talked about how the patient must avoid lifting anything of substance, and avoid pulling open drawers below a certain height. It even described procedures for how to sit on a sofa and the most fundamental day-to-day activities. This was most distressing, but I only knew the half of it.

Towards bedtime an anaesthetist came in, asked if I had undergone a major operation previously (no), and offered me something to help me sleep – which I declined, having no concern about not sleeping. I still had no idea what I was in for.

The operation took place at 8 am the following morning. When I came round from the general anaesthetic there followed an excruciatingly painful and traumatic 48 hours. When my hourly feed of morphine was withdrawn, the pain was almost unsustainable. I could only sleep, or doze, for a couple of hours at a time. For the next three months I was obliged to sleep on my back without turning, although I have always slept on my side. My diet included a mix of painkillers and sleeping pills. The pain eventually became bearable, but the discomfort was ever-present.

I remained in the Cambridge Lea hospital for nine days after the operation. The staff had been wonderful. When Alison collected me and drove me home, I found that the entire house and garden had been realigned and adjusted for my convenience. Railings and supports had been erected, chairs and sofas reshaped, and a shower and other conveniences installed in the bathroom. I was to remain on crutches for three months – the first six weeks 'non-weight-bearing' on my operated leg, and the second six weeks partially weight-bearing.

The BBC, and especially Jonathan Martin, had been exceptionally generous. They had offered me three months' sick-leave and I shall always be grateful for that. After eight weeks' convalescence at home, Alison and I flew to South Africa for the last period of recuperation in the sunshine. We stayed for six weeks and returned to England on St Valentine's day.

I saw Richard Villar the following Monday and he expressed himself delighted with the X-rays and my general recovery. I shall always be indebted to Mr Villar for the remarkable skill of his operation. I played my first game of cricket post-operation on 7 July 1996, and by the end of the season I had taken 24 wickets.

Every game played since the operation has been a bonus. Several occasions have been memorable, notably a 15-over spell at Linton Park, Kent, in September 1996 and a magical day on the County Ground at Cheltenham in August 1997, for the Lord's Taverners versus Lord Vestey's XI. In one instance the scorebook read: ' . . . caught Walsh b Wilson'. Courtney was not a bad fielder to have at second slip.

What sustains us cricket wannabees is not just the occasional dismissal of a super-hero – through a combination of pitch defect, extraordinary luck, or the desire by a batsman to surrender his wicket – but the kindness and encouragement given by senior players who have earned our respect in the past.

There is no kinder man in this regard than Colin (now Lord) Cowdrey. Colin was unquestionably one of our finest postwar batsmen, but he has spent most of the past few years giving to others and sustaining others. He was a magnificent president of the Lord's Taverners for three years, working tirelessly despite suffering ill-health, and he has worked energetically to progress cricket in schools. But he has never neglected the grassroots. In 1995 he devoted a day of his life to the opening of the new pavilion at Burrough Green CC and presided over Sir Colin Cowdrey's XI versus Burrough Green All-Stars. Everyone who met Colin that day had their life enriched.

That is why I shall always regard Farokh Engineer as one of the finest cricketers and finest men ever to represent India. In a postscript to a letter in August 1994, Farokh wrote to me:

> *You were the best SLA* [slow left arm] *I kept to for a while – the previous, of course, being a turbaned guy answering to the name of Bishen Bedi!!!*

Of course, there was not a word of truth in it, but it gave me immense pleasure faxing Farokh's letter to all of my friends. They were livid!

## TWENTY

# *Winning Ways*

There is a story that Cyril Stein, former chairman of Ladbrokes the bookmakers, once arranged a special lunch for all of his winning clients. He booked a small private box at Ascot, with one small table.

That story may be apocryphal, but it has become increasingly difficult over the years to beat the bookmaker. The first major setback for punters was the imposition of a tax on betting in 1966. With built-in further deductions from winnings to accommodate payments to the Betting Levy, bookmakers have charged a 'tax' of up to 10 per cent in recent years.

It has been said that the bookmakers' information network compares favourably with that of MI5. Exaggeration or not, several leading bookmakers have their 'card marked' about fancied runners from many of the leading stables. There has also been a mushrooming cancer of telephone 'information services'. The well-informed services act as a benefit to bookmakers, as well as to punters, and odds about well-tipped horses contract absurdly. So, more and more, it becomes difficult for punters to find 'value'. Very few old-fashioned professional punters still exist.

Betting as a professional, or semi-professional, on horses is totally different from gambling. The classic gambler has a Dostoyevskian streak which feeds a hidden desire to lose. There are others who are said to enjoy gambling as a sex substitute. For the professional, betting is entirely asexual.

I must qualify that last observation in one respect. One June afternoon, after a bottle of Dom Perignon and lunch, I took a girlfriend back to my house and we made love on the sofa. I had a decent-sized ante-post bet on the Coronation Cup at Epsom, covered by ITV. As my horse passed the post, so did we! It was the best experience of its kind that I have ever enjoyed.

But normally, winning and losing is too important to be shared with frivolous social activity. I, for one, hate losing – which is why Alison built me a 'sulk house' at the bottom of the garden in Burrough Green to accommodate me after a losing Saturday and when it mattered to me that Swindon Town FC had lost.

The essence of winning money through backing horses is a knowledge of mathematics. It is that factor – the ability to judge 'value' – that separates the winners from the losers.

For instance, imagine there is a hypothetical series of races between two horses, A and B, of exactly equal ability and over a consistent terrain and the identical distance. Provided the horses are both at their best, under these circumstances each horse represents exactly an even-money chance to win in every race. If a punter bets 5/4 *on* horse A in every race between the two (as a legacy of paying 10 per cent tax on returns) he is certain to lose in the long run. If, however, he manages to bet 5/4 *against* horse A in every race, he is equally certain to win in the long run. If the two horses raced against each other 20 times and, as would be likely, each won on 10 occasions, the first punter would lose £20 to a £10 level stake, whereas the second punter would win £25. That, in a nutshell, is the difference between winning and losing at betting.

It helps, of course, to have an intricate knowledge of horses, breeding and the formbook. It is also obligatory to spend hours a day evaluating form. Occasionally, inspired 'information' relating to reliable and authentic gallops can be an advantage.

Perhaps the best betting opportunity that I was ever offered was on 4 May 1991. My friend Bill Gredley telephoned me mid-morning to ask whether I would place an ante-post commission for him. I said 'fine', thinking that his bet would be a maximum of £500. Bill said: 'I want £5000 each way on User Friendly in the Oaks.' The filly was a 33/1 shot.

I gulped silently. Although I had eight different bookmakers' accounts, there would be logistical difficulties in getting this sum on, especially at 33/1. It would create a major stir. It would be seen as the biggest bet of my life, and there was a question of credibility involved. Privately, I could not see User Friendly winning the Oaks. She appeared to be filly who needed soft ground to be seen at her best, and such going on Oaks day is about as likely as Swindon Town FC winning six games in a row.

I called around discreetly to confirm the price and then 'bottled out'. 'Bill, I can't do it. It's just too big. Why don't you try --?' What I did not know was that Bill had watched User Friendly that morning in a sensational gallop with the Classic winner Mystiko and another high-class older horse. She had murdered them! Bill was eventually accommodated with some of his commission, but I did not get involved.

All At Sea, owned by Prince Khalid Abdullah, went to Epsom a hot favourite for the Oaks, but the rain pelted down on the day of the race and the going became 'soft'. User Friendly won at 5/1. She was a wonderful filly, who went on to win the Irish and Yorkshire Oaks and the St Leger. I was delighted for Bill, but felt ever so slightly foolish!

For anyone who backs horses, it is the ones that 'get away' that you recall as vividly as the ones that win. One such was a horse called Habus, owned by Bill Gredley. When my company became consultants to Stetchworth Park Stud, I was anxious to modify Bill's training arrangements for certain horses that seemed to be under-achieving. Because of his understandable loyalty to his friend and senior trainer, Clive Brittain, this was difficult to implement. But I did manage to arrange for Habus, who had a back problem and appeared jaded, to be transferred to the stable of Peter Easterby in Yorkshire. I felt that he needed, above all, a change of scenery. He had been trained at Newmarket for a long time.

Habus arrived at Habton Grange, near Malton, in May. Peter Easterby was not over-enthusiastic and there followed a depressing series of communiqués from Yorkshire: 'Not a great mover, is he?' he ventured. And then: 'I don't know what to make of his back.

Sometimes it's all right; sometimes it's not.' And: 'He's not showing me a lot.' Eventually came the message: 'The 'oss seems well – might as well give him a run.'

The run he arranged was at Ripon on 22 June. It was my wedding anniversary and I was fishing at Achiltibuie, in Sutherland. Bill Gredley was disinclined to travel – York and Doncaster are his only favoured locations in Yorkshire.

I was convinced that the change of routine and location would have benefited Habus, but Peter was unwilling to commit himself to any degree of encouragement. Thus Habus was unbacked by the owner and manager. He won by a short head at 33/1. Bill was livid and the manager was discredited. To add insult to injury, it transpired that Tim Easterby, Peter's son, *had* backed Habus, because 'he moved so well on t'way to post – better than I'd seen 'im move'.

There followed an evening of restrained anniversary celebrations at Achiltibuie. To put it another way, it was a sulk. It is imperative – if only for one's piece of mind – to have at least a small bet on a genuine contender at 25/1 or 33/1. Clement Freud at Ely, User Friendly in the Oaks and Habus at Beverley were three such missed opportunities.

Another occurred in my first year at Newmarket in 1961. It was while I was consorting with the former apprentice jockey Ken Thompson, who was working for Norman Bertie's stable. In fact, Norman Bertie, the nominee, was the head lad. The stable belonged to a gentleman trainer, Jack Clayton. In those days it was regarded as socially eye-raising for a gentleman to hold a trainer's licence. A gentleman chose to, and a lady trainer was obliged to, hold a licence in their head lad's name.

Jack Clayton ran two horses in the Elveden Maiden Stakes at the Newmarket Craven meeting. One was called Crosspatch, owned by Lady Porchester. Ken told me that he had ridden her in work and that she moved really well. 'Kipper' Lynch was to ride her and Ken told 'Kipper' that she would win. I was convinced that the filly would be given an 'educational' run and declined to back her. Whatever Kipper's orders were, he rode like a man inspired and Crosspatch won at 25/1. On the Tote, she paid 85/1.

Invariably, it is more acceptable to a serious punter for a horse, or a bet, to be desperately unlucky than to miss backing a winner. I suppose that not placing that bet on Crosspatch suggests human error, whereas bad luck is beyond anyone's control.

Nonetheless, unlucky losers can be desperately painful. I have already told the story of Qalibashi, and the quadpool near-miss in 1965. But the unluckiest loser that I ever backed was a horse called Fainne Lea, at Wye in 1965. It was at a time when cash-flow was a major problem. I raised all of the available cash at my disposal – credit had become an on-going problem – and took the train from London to the friendly country racecourse in a remote corner of Kent.

Wye, now defunct, was a tight circuit, no more than a mile round. The straight was short and narrow. It was a left-handed course, so the final fence was to the left of the grandstand, and the first fence to the right. Somewhere in between was the gate that led from the paddock to the course.

Fainne Lea was a lovely bay horse from Ireland, trained by the McInnes Skinner family in Norfolk. He had caught my eye running over hurdles and I was convinced that he would make a decent steeplechaser. This was his first race over fences and the opposition was modest. He was certain to be a 'value' price because the stable was unfashionable. I got 5/1 to my money – my last £50 in the world.

What happened that afternoon will forever remain etched in my mind. A horse fell at the last fence on the first circuit, but got up quickly and started to pursue the other runners. However, he declined to jump the next fence (the fence to the right of the stands) and ran back, looking for the paddock exit. No-one let him out, so he ran up and down the course. Meanwhile, Fainne Lea was jumping like a bird, and Michael Scudamore, his jockey, eased him into the lead on the final turn. Fainne Lea came to jump the last fence three lengths clear. As he did so, and I dreamed of £250, the obscene nightmare unfolded. The loose horse was running directly towards Fainne Lea. Too late, Michael Scudamore saw the danger and attempted to take avoiding action. The loose horse ran straight into Fainne Lea, giving Michael no chance of staying in the saddle.

No words can describe a man's feelings at a moment like that. They are a mixture of stunned incredulity, self-pity, and finally a conviction of divine conspiracy. Why, oh God, why? I stood for several minutes, in silent disbelief. Luckily, I had taken the precaution of acquiring a day return train ticket. It was a procedure that I had adopted since an early indoctrination into the uncertainties of racing in 1958.

What is now known as 'Whitbread Day', but was then known as 'Esher Cup Day', has always been one of the best and most enjoyable racing days of the year. It blends the last big race of the National Hunt season with an exciting early season programme on the Flat.

The last race of the day was a one-mile maiden race called the Marcus Beresford Stakes, for which the favourite was a colt called Parma, trained by Marcus Marsh. Parma had finished second in the Greenham Stakes at Newbury – a significant Classic trial – a week earlier, so I considered him to be a certainty. He was ridden by a great jockey in the twilight of his career, Charlie Smirke.

Parma opened odds-on at 4/7 and I had a bet of £3 10s 0d – I had been having a decent day and had backed Lynch Law, the winner of the Esher Cup. To my amazement, Parma drifted rapidly to 'even money', so I had a further even £2. But still Parma continued to be opposed, until he reached 7/4 against. Convinced of the solidity of my judgement, I struck a further bet of £2 at the new odds. I now had collectively an even £7 10s 0d – a huge bet for a schoolboy (I was on the threshold of my final term).

Parma was always travelling well in the race, but in the straight made his run on the far rail. His passage was clearly blocked, but Smirke sat and waited. Finally, about 150 yards from the finish, Smirke extricated his horse, switched to the wide outside, and with a clear run at last started to cut down the leaders. It was too late – he was beaten by half a length.

It was an important, albeit painful, lesson. The last £2 staked had included my train fare home. I had to walk over five miles towards London before I reached a station from which I could afford the fare back to Waterloo. For the record, the long-standing association between Marcus Marsh and Charlie Smirke was terminated soon afterwards.

The most heartbreaking near-miss of a major win came at Newmarket in July 1991. There was a fairly substantial jackpot carry-over on the first day of a two-day meeting on the July course. I thought that the 'pot looked very winnable, for an outlay of £160. During the morning I spoke to Moira Hanbury, the wife of the Newmarket trainer, and daughter of my mentor, Elizabeth Burke. We discussed the card and Moira agreed to take a quarter share of my combination bet.

There was one race that I was worried about. It was a four-horse race, for maiden three-year-olds over a mile and a half. There were two exposed runners with reasonable form, trained by Henry Cecil and Barry Hills. They looked obvious contenders. But there was a 'dark' horse, trained by Geoff Wragg, which had run only twice and was tipped by one of the Newmarket correspondents. I was uneasy about leaving him out, but to include him would have increased our investment by 50 per cent to £240. I consulted Moira again. 'Oh let's leave him out,' said Moira, 'he'll probably need another race.' I was inclined to agree.

We found five out of six winners, and the one that we missed was – of course – the one that we left out in the four-horse race. He was a horse called Arcadian Heights, who three years later won the Ascot Gold Cup. The jackpot paid £113,000.

I have rarely attempted the Jackpot since then, but there was a substantial carry-over on the Monday after the Cheltenham Festival in March 1995. I spent most of the Sunday afternoon handicapping the designated Jackpot card at Uttoxeter on the Monday. To my horror, I discovered in the morning that the Tote's chairman Lord Wyatt, in his wisdom, had switched the Jackpot overnight from Uttoxeter to the all-weather flat programme at Southwell. I was livid, after wasting almost four hours' work. Worse was to come – I would have won the Jackpot if it had taken place at Uttoxeter. No-one else was able to win it at the execrable all-weather meeting.

Lord Wyatt tried this trick again during the summer, when he switched the pool from the big day of the week at Glorious Goodwood to an evening meeting of quite exceptional mediocrity at Epsom. It was an outrageous decision, spoiling the enjoyment of thousands of racegoers at Goodwood, not to mention the million and a half viewers watching on television.

I challenged Lord Wyatt to defend the decision on television. He claimed that it was the correct decision because Epsom was the meeting where the Jackpot was least likely to be won. Our dialogue continued:

| | |
|---|---|
| *WILSON* | *You've had a 16/1 winner of the first race here, everyone knows the horses running at Goodwood: I defy you to name three horses that are running at Epsom.* |
| *WYATT* | *That's exactly why it is very unlikely to be won.* |
| *WILSON* | *But you can't, can you?* |
| *WYATT* | *Why should I? And as a matter of fact, I can't name any horses running here, either!'* |

What an ass! This was the day of the Sussex Stakes, one of the top one-mile races in Europe.

Sadly, Lord Wyatt died suddenly in 1997. I was very fond of him as an individual, and he was a most entertaining speaker and journalist. The Tote Luncheon, in March, was one of the most prized invitations of the year. But I do feel that the Tote should have progressed more rapidly under his tenure. Racing's best chance of financial stability was to launch a 'Superbet' that would attract hundreds of thousands of pounds from a television audience each Saturday. Unfortunately, the National Lottery hit the jackpot first, and there is no second prize.

Against all the bad luck that any punter suffers in horseracing must be balanced the good luck. Almost all of the biggest wins of my life have resulted from being in the right place at the right time.

I was parking my car on the playing fields of Harrow for Speech Day, on 27 May 1987, when my car-phone rang with news of an exceptional gallop by a filly called Unite, who was being prepared for the Oaks. She was a 33/1 shot. I placed a substantial each-way bet, just minutes before the news circulated and the price came tumbling down. Unite started at 11/1 and won easily. It was the biggest win of my life.

In March 1992, William Haggas had been my guest at a Lord's Taverners evening at Chilford Hall, near Newmarket, on a Friday night. He excused himself early on the grounds that he would be galloping a horse called High Low, in preparation for the Lincoln Handicap, at dawn the following morning. I rang him at breakfast time and he was delighted with the gallop. I backed High Low at 33/1 and watched him win the Lincoln the following Saturday from the betting shop at Swindon Town FC.

Back in 1970, my friend Nigel Angus rang from Scotland and told me in passing that a disappointing horse that he trained, called Arco Star, was exceptionally well and should run a big race at Hamilton the following day. He would be wearing blinkers for the first time. Arco Star was another 33/1 shot, so I dual-forecasted him with the field. He finished second to a 5/1 shot, and the forecast, amazingly, paid £94 14s 0d to a four-shilling stake!

I am an avid collector of ante-post vouchers because – freak forecasts and jackpots apart – it is bets struck early that yield the biggest wins. They are also occasions to reminisce during the bad times.

Among my happiest keepsakes are ancient documents revealing bets on Royal Palace (10/1), Sir Ivor (4/1) and Nijinsky (5/2) to win the Derby; Altesse Royale (7/1) to win the Oaks; Aldaniti (33/1) to win the Grand National; Salmon Spray (100/8) to win the Champion Hurdle; Alignment (25/1) and Bonne Noel (20/1) to win the Ebor; Prince de Galles (25/1) and Siliciana (25/1) to win the Cambridgeshire; and Jacinth (100/6) to win the Cheveley Park

Stakes. All of these animals won at considerably shorter prices – that is what is meant by 'value' betting.

Of course, there are also plenty that do not win. For almost 11 months I was sitting on a voucher struck at 16/1 against Mill Reef winning the 2000 Guineas. By sheer bad luck he was born in the same year as Brigadier Gerard and My Swallow!

My favourite races to bet on are the Derby and the Ebor Handicap. Staying horses are easier to handicap than milers and sprinters, and both those races are usually won by the best horse on the day.

Handicapping – and hard work – have been the basis of my good fortune in backing horses. But occasionally information is received that only a lunatic or a dogmatist would ignore. One evening in May 1985, dining with Steve Cauthen in Pontevecchio, Steve bet me £50 that, if the going was 'firm', Slip Anchor would win the Derby by five lengths. Five lengths! That was how confident the man was. In the event, the going was good and Slip Anchor won by seven lengths.

Another occasion on which a friend advised me to get rich was before the Bradford & Bingley Handicap at York on 22 August 1991. Our horse 'Ponte' had been severely handicapped after his great season in 1990, but David Elsworth now felt that he was especially well. The ground had become soft at York, which was no problem for him. What it did was to improve the chance of a front-runner, like 'Ponte'. It is exceptionally difficult for a horse to make up ground when the going becomes holding at York. The best ground was on the inside rail, so all 'Ponte' had to do was jump off (he was drawn low), take his position on the rail and dictate the race.

Willie Carson was unavailable, so I booked Pat Eddery, with his beautiful hands, to ride. David and I watched 'Ponte' and Eddery canter to post – it was poetry in motion. David turned to me and said: 'However much you've had on this, you can double it.' I did not like to tell him that I had already had my maximum each-way bet at 10/1!

It went like clockwork. 'Ponte' jumped off, made every yard of the running and won in a canter. It does not often happen like that, but when it does it makes up for an awful lot of disappointments.

## TWENTY-ONE

# *A Brave New World?*

It was in the early 1990s that I finally despaired of the politics of racing. During the 1970s I had tried to play my part, through airing the important issues on television, by interviewing certain individuals that it was no pleasure to confront – notably Lord Wigg – and at a personal level.

The 'personal' stage was highlighted when Tumbledownwind won the Gimcrack Stakes and I was accorded the privilege of making the traditional speech at the Gimcrack dinner. I decided not to shirk my responsibility for the sake of retention of popularity, and delivered a hard-hitting speech, decrying the lack of finance in British racing and suggesting various remedies to make the accountancy more viable.

These proposals included withdrawing support from a large number of racecourses and creating a two-tired structure of racing. There was nowhere near enough money to go round, but I emphasized the importance of maintaining the value and prestige of our great races – what are now known as Group One races. I made suggestions about autonomous Totes, and the modification of travel allowances.

Sir Desmond Plummer (now Lord Plummer), the new chairman of the Horserace Betting Levy Board, claimed to be impressed by my ideology of élitism. Lord Plummer had succeeded the former Gaming Board boss Sir Stanley Raymond – the man who had the misfortune, at his inaugural press conference, to call the champion jockey *Lionel* Piggott!

After my speech very little happened. Admittedly, Lord Plummer did shore up the Group One races. He also completely abolished the travel allowances, which was not what I had in mind! My proposal was to curb the abuses and to disqualify horses from claiming the allowance once they had run a certain number of times without attaining a certain standard.

The overall effect of the changes was what it has always been – a process of moving the pieces around the draughts board, ignoring the fact that there are not enough pieces to play the game. British racing has been under-financed ever since it became a high-profile international business, yielding almost £5 billion in annual betting turnover, and earning £200 million in exports.

The level of prize money was not a significant factor while racing remained a parochial sport, largely the province of the aristocracy and the landed gentry. In those days it was sport, pure and simple. That was the case until the 1960s. But when it became a multimillion pound business, providing extensive employment at many levels, and earning the government hundreds of millions of pounds a year through betting tax and other direct taxation, it was a different ballgame.

Or it should have been. Successive governments have, despite occasional concessions, turned their back on racing's fundamental need, which is increased financial support. To put it another way, it would be helpful if they returned to the business a rather greater proportion of the money they take out of it.

To put the argument in its most simple terms, horseracing receives just over £50 million from the Betting Levy. It needs about £100 million.

For almost 40 years, since off-course betting offices were legalized in 1961, these arguments have been ebbing to and fro. Every now and then there is an acceleration of effort by the industry to impress upon government its deepening financial crisis and the pitiful comparison between money from betting returned to our industry and that provided elsewhere in the world. But the story is always the same – too little too late, and a series of missed opportunities.

In 1993, British racing took a major step forward. At least, that was the concept. A new body called the British Horseracing Board (BHB) was created. It was designed to take over the organizational responsibilities of the Jockey Club, to give streamlined administration, to improve marketing, and to drive racing forcefully into the twenty-first century. It was also conceived as a vehicle to achieve meaningful dialogue with government, which was considered to have little regard for the undemocratic status of the previous rulers of racing, the Jockey Club.

It was the Marquis of Hartington, in his role as senior steward of the Jockey Club, who masterminded and implemented the transfer of power from the Old Rulers to the new. The Jockey Club, an autocratic self-electing body, would continue to have responsibility for licensing and discipline. Otherwise, the BHB would take control of the industry. Several personnel overlapped on the two regulatory bodies, but by and large the BHB presented a fresh façade.

It was here that a great opportunity was missed. The two contenders for the chairmanship-apparent in the BHB were two former parliamentarians, Lord Wakeham and Brian Walden.

I was fervently in favour of the appointment of Walden, the former Labour MP. He is a man with a brilliant brain, a photographic memory, and a determination to succeed in whatever he takes on. He was the very first lobbyist for the bookmaking industry in the House of Commons – there are now 60 – and he knows the business of betting and parliamentary procedure inside-out. With his extraordinary memory he can absorb statistics and swathe through documents in double-quick time.

His opponent for the position, John Wakeham, is a likeable man, but with the traditional gentlemanly instincts of playing by the rules, not rocking the boat, and living by precedent. He lacked, I felt, the cutting edge of Walden. It was Lord Wakeham who was elected, thanks largely to the support of various influential members of the Jockey club, notably the late Lord Swaythling.

Lord Wakeham's appointment was a mistake. His period of office was not a success and he resigned in January 1998. After three years in the role, at the Annual Industry Committee Forum his message was: 'Well, *you* tell *me* what to do!'

The root cause of the industry's failure to activate a financial improvement is its inability to march behind the same flag. There is also the conflict between the racing industry and the betting industry. One is financially unviable, and the other is 'doing-very-nicely, thank you'. The BHB under Lord Wakeham tried to walk hand in hand with the bookmakers. It didn't work – for racing.

The way ahead, as I see it, is leadership from a man with no compunction about treading on toes, no personal bonds that will cause embarrassment or betrayal, and no fear of disrupting traditional procedures and establishments. Such a man is Peter Savill, former chairman of the Racehorse Owners Association, who has an outstanding business pedigree and a considerable grasp of mathematics, and is a tireless researcher. I am pleased that Peter was elected to the post in mid-May 1998, after considerable debate by the members of the Board. He is capable, in my view, of uniting – and ultimately rescuing – the ailing racing industry.

I had several friends in the brand new BHB in 1993, but also at least one enemy. The cause of the antagonism was my outspoken opposition to the concept of horseracing on Sunday in Great Britain. This was to be the flagship of the BHB. Indeed, when I interviewed Tristram Ricketts, the chief executive, at the end of 1996, he claimed that the introduction of Sunday racing was the BHB's foremost achievement in its three years of office.

I was violently opposed to Sunday racing. When the Jockey Club staged two experimental days in 1992, without betting, I was contractually obliged to present the television coverage from Cheltenham on Sunday 15 November. I found it possible to live with, as I was able to go to church in the morning and there was no betting on-course. When I renewed my BBC contract in 1993, it was with the stipulation that I was not compelled to cover Sunday racing in Great Britain.

There were several reasons for my antipathy, not least the damage that it would inflict on the industry. It drove me mad that no-one could appreciate that the betting shops would be empty. They are the refuge of office, factory and building-site workers during the week, notably at lunchtime. On Saturdays they are filled with shoppers and those with the dying embers of a pay packet. On Sundays, even the inveterate gambler has a different agenda, while the average working man is in his garden, in the pub, or enjoying television and Sunday lunch.

But it wasn't just the bookmakers who were going to lose money – which they did. Owners would face increased training fees because trainers would now be obliged to work seven days a week; jockeys would face complications with their arrangements abroad; and stable lads would, in some cases, be working for 29 days a month.

Stable lads were supposed to receive a special Sunday bonus of £29, for taking a horse to the races. In many cases the payment was 'overlooked'. The lads in horseboxes stuck in the Sunday night traffic would return home towards midnight, and be on call at 6 am the following morning. In the meanwhile, they had missed a day with their family.

The partner of a lad working in racing is *obliged* to find a job, owing to the paucity of a stable lad's basic wage, and a Sunday is normally the only day they can spend together. No more.

No-one was going to make money out of this brave new concept, except for one body in racing – the racecourses. Sundays were marketed as Fundays, and parents and children were welcomed through the turnstiles with offers of bouncy castles, sky-diving displays, and acres of grassland for picnics. Oh yes! – and there would be horseracing as well.

Some racecourses have prospered beyond their wildest dreams. Chester races have attracted crowds of over 30,000 on Sundays. Of course, there has been the down-side of drunkenness, fighting, endless traffic jams, and inconvenience to the few regular racegoers – but these, we were told, were the 'new racegoers', the 'racegoers of the future'.

A stark problem of British racegoing is that is so incredibly expensive. A badge into the Members' Enclosure on a British racecourse is liable to cost £20, against a similar facility in South Africa costing £1.25. A ticket to the Members', with lunch in a restaurant overlooking the racecourse, would come to about £50; in South Africa it costs £8 a head.

For this reason few can afford to go racing on a Saturday *and* Sunday in Great Britain; it has to be either/or. Saturday is our traditional sporting day, and the traditional racing high point of the week. Almost all our big races are run on a Saturday, whereas the great races in France, Ireland, Germany and Italy are almost without exception run on a Sunday. It is terrifyingly dangerous to jeopardize the sporting sanctity of our Saturdays, especially as Saturday delivers the largest television audience.

These were all views – combined with a personal view of the need to keep Sunday as a special day – that I put forward before the introduction of Sunday racing. They were especially unpopular with the Racecourse Association. Jonathan Martin, my head of department, was advised, confidentially: 'Julian Wilson has his own agenda. It's not the way forward.' Jonathan was told that I had 'many enemies in racing', and that it was wrong for me to 'use the BBC as a platform for my views'.

But the accusation was wide of the mark. I gave interviews to the *Daily Telegraph* and the *Independent on Sunday*, and was then told that I must no longer discuss the matter in public. I obeyed that instruction – with a minor blemish on the 'Michael Parkinson Show'! In short, there was a conspiracy to discredit me. Happily, my superiors took little notice and were entirely supportive.

But it was a depressing period, and it has to be said that 1992 had been an unhappy year from the outset. To start with I had lost a good friend in Tony Murray.

Tony had moved away from Newmarket on the breakdown of the marriage to Jane Jarvis, sister of our friend the Newmarket trainer William Jarvis. He had acquired a management job with the wealthy Midlands-based owner, Tony Budge, on his retirement from race-riding. This seemed an ideal appointment, with several useful horses to supervise in a number of different stables. But the legacy of so many years of fighting a constant battle against the scales had taken its toll. Tony had always lived life to the full and punished himself with excruciating sessions in the sauna to counteract the eating and drinking excesses of the weekend. His weight, and with it moods, had yo-yoed, and his sleep cycle was one of several mechanisms to suffer.

In 1985 he had been determined to ride Kayudee for his friend, the Malton trainer Jimmy Fitzgerald, in the Cesarewitch. Tony's minimum weight was 8st 4lb, but Kayudee was handicapped to carry only 7st 11lb. Tony begged to be allowed to ride the horse. Jimmy Fitzgerald had considerable misgivings, but finally acceded.

Tony boiled himself down to 8st 1lb and Kayudee battled on bravely to land a substantial gamble. For once, Tony was almost too weak and dehydrated to celebrate. That weekend took a terrific toll on his health.

Jane is a charming and extremely intelligent girl, who for several years has been the backbone of the International Racing Bureau in Newmarket. The marriage with Tony would have seemed perfect, were it not for our knowledge of how difficult his former fiancée Margaret O'Toole had earlier found it to live with Tony. He would awake at 2 am and be unable to return to sleep. Even in retirement his sleep cycle, and with it his state of mind, was erratic. Jane tried to hold the marriage together, but it was like trying to contain water in a sieve.

Now Tony had been found dead in his cottage in Wiltshire. Alcohol and sleeping pills were found in the house. There was a huge turnout of friends at his memorial service at St Paul's, Wilton Place, on 20 February. I think many of us there felt that we could, and should, have done more to help Tony through his difficulties.

The Cheltenham Festival in 1992 promised to be a superlative week, as it invariably is, but on the Thursday evening I drove away from Prestbury angry and depressed.

Carvill's Hill, the favourite for the Gold Cup, had put up some staggering performances the previous autumn, including a 20-length win in the Welsh Grand National. The margin of his wins, combined with the weights he had carried, evoked comparisons with the great Arkle. He was a favourite of mine, because I had drawn attention to his ability and filmed him in Ireland at the start of his career, when he was trained by Jim Dreaper. Carvill's Hill started at even money in the Gold Cup, despite a small question mark about the reliability of his jumping.

Jenny Pitman ran two horses in the race – Toby Tobias, ridden by her son Mark, and Golden Freeze, ridden by her brother-in-law-to-be, Michael Bowlby. Golden Freeze was a complete outsider at 150/1.

Carvill's Hill was a big horse with a terrific stride, who was happiest bowling along in front. It was very rare for an opponent to contest the lead with him. He would just gallop them into the ground. When the field jumped off, Peter Scudamore on the favourite took him straight away into the lead, but even before the first fence he had been joined by Golden Freeze, who jumped upsides of him and forced Carvill's Hill into a fairly serious mistake. At the second fence, Carvill's Hill was again uncomfortable with Golden Freeze upsides, but going to the third fence Scudamore reined him back so that Golden Freeze would jump the fence ahead of him. As he did so, Michael Bowlby reined back Golden Freeze, so that again he was catching the eye of Carvill's Hill.

And so it went on. If Scudamore kicked on, Bowlby went with him. If he took a pull, Bowlby did the same. At the seventh fence, Bowlby looked over to Scudamore and said: 'Look. I didn't want to do this. I hope you win.' Golden Freeze tired soon after halfway and was pulled up, and by the second last fence Carvill's Hill was also out on his feet. He came up the hill at a walk, was found to be chronically lame, and never raced again. He had, quite simply, been destroyed.

It was a widely held view that Golden Freeze had been run in the race as a 'stalking horse', whose only purpose was to prevent Carvill's Hill from winning. In my broadcast I made it clear that those were my feelings, and added that I felt it was a sad day for National Hunt racing.

The Jockey Club held an inquiry into the running of the race and found that there had been no breach of the rules of racing. Michael Bowlby denied that he had spoken to Peter Scudamore during the race. Michael, an extremely pleasant and personable young man, and a very competent jockey, retired from race-riding not long after.

During the summer, Jenny Pitman took legal advice and threatened to sue me and the BBC for the comments that I had made during the broadcast. The action did not progress.

I was filled with sadness as much as anger. To see the end of a potentially great horse is always heartbreaking, but the loss was greater than that. The true loss was the spirit of Cheltenham, where the best are matched against the best and the racing enthusiast hopes that the very best racehorse will win – whether he or she be English, Irish, Scottish, Welsh or from further afield. In the evening all over the Cotswolds the toast is 'The Winner!', and just as important, 'The Sport of Steeplechasing!'

Jenny Pitman is a woman with remarkable training skills and exceptional determination. Her achievements as a trainer can only be admired. But I wish that she had not run Golden Freeze in the 1992 Gold Cup.

It was during this summer that Jonathan Martin made it clear that he saw my future as a presenter, rather than as a race commentator, and that Jim McGrath was his choice (on the advice of others) to take over from Peter O'Sullevan when the time came. I had reached the same conclusion myself, but had looked forward to commentating on my twenty-fifth Grand National the following spring. Jonathan stated that he wanted McGrath to take over my role at Bechers.

There was a further sadness in the summer when my old friend Dick Turner died. It was Dick who had helped me launch Seymour Bloodstock in the Kildare Street Club, Dublin, back in 1972 and had always been a director of the company. He was a good judge of a horse, a good shot and a good friend.

Despite some memorable days of cricket – notably playing with Colin Cowdrey for the Duke of Edinburgh's XI at Windsor Hall

– it was a year that I was pleased to see come to an end.

I signed a new five-year contract with the BBC, knowing in my heart of hearts that it would be my last.

## TWENTY-TWO

# *Close of Play*

My Aunt Diana, my mother's older sister, died in the spring of 1993. I was deeply fond of her. She had attracted many suitors before the war, but the man she loved was killed during the hostilities and she never married. In 1966 she owned a share in my first National Hunt horse, Partlet, who won the Lord Mildmay Memorial Trophy at Newton Abbot. I still treasure a photograph of Diana grappling with the huge silver cup!

She spent her later years living in or around Rye, in Sussex, ultimately with my Aunt Sylvia in Peasmarsh. She fought a brave battle against cancer, which she finally inevitably lost.

My aunt was kind enough to leave me a significant legacy, which we decided to invest in a holiday house in South Africa. After exploring some possibilities in 1994, we finally bought an old Cape Dutch house in Tokai in the southern suburbs of Cape Town in January 1995. I intended to call it 'Diana Lodge' as a memorial to my aunt, but decided against it – for the time being at least – in case anyone should misconstrue the motivation for the naming.

Meanwhile, 1994 was another roller-coaster year. It was to prove the last year that BBC-TV covered racing at Cheltenham. Michael Grade, now the supremo of Channel 4, was determined to reward his production team for their outstanding efforts in competing with the BBC's coverage. He offered almost ten times what the BBC was paying for the rights to cover Cheltenham. The BBC narrowed the gap between the two offers, but to have bid any further would have established a new benchmark for horseracing contracts. There were also other elements in the negotiations, including the desire for editorial input on the part of the racecourse, which we fiercely resisted, but in the end the superior bid won. Channel 4 Racing would be covering the Cheltenham Festival from 1995 onwards.

When the news broke, it was flattering to receive letters – many from Ireland – which suggested that Cheltenham's decision was the end of civilization as we knew it. We had been there for a long time – almost 40 years.

From a selfish point of view, I had mixed feelings. It was almost 30 years since I had seen a race at Cheltenham (other than the last race on the last day) from the grandstand, with the naked eye! The extraordinary and unique sensation of watching the leaders jump the last fence and battle bravely up the hill, lifted by the explosive crescendo of sound from the lawn and the grandstand is one of the great experiences in sport. Now I could enjoy this from the private box shared by Michael Buckley and Bill Shand-Kydd, whilst enjoying the additional hospitality of other friends and box-holders. It was certainly a compensation.

But the parsimony of the BBC was becoming an unbearable irritation. During almost 30 years with BBC-TV, I had never once been sent on a subsidized broadcasting mission beyond France or Ireland. I had 'offered' original documentaries on Hong Kong, Dubai and Japan – all with unconditional local subsidies – all of which had been turned down. For years, during the 1970s and 80s, I had flown to Paris and Deauville regularly at my own expense, returning with video recordings of major French races for transmission on BBC at no cost. My only 'income' from these trips was a small fee – around £30 – for my BBC Radio report.

In 1994, I was invited by the Victoria Racing Club to fly to Australia to cover the world-famous Melbourne Cup for BBC-TV. The Melbourne Cup is truly a horserace that stops the nation. Cup Day is a public holiday, and everything comes to a standstill while the race is run. The crowd at Flemington is upwards of 90,000 and they start to arrive at early breakfast time. The traditional start to the day is chicken and champagne at 6.30 am, then off to the races!

It is a pageant of fashion and fancy dress and there is nothing quite like it anywhere in the world.

In 1993, the Irish trainer Dermot Weld had pulled off one of the great training feats in the history of racing by travelling the stayer Vintage Crop from the northern hemisphere to win the Cup. It entailed two periods of quarantine – one in Ireland and one in Australia – a change of climate, and a time difference of 11 hours. Now in 1994 Vintage Crop was travelling again, together with an English-trained horse called Quick Ransom. Of course, it was unthinkable that the BBC would cover the race live at 4.20 am British time, but I offered David Gordon a 10-12 minute recorded package of Cup day, to be shown in 'Grandstand' on the following Saturday. With the British and Irish interest and the remarkable colour of the occasion, as yet unexplored on the network, I felt that it would make irresistible television.

David Gordon's response was that if I paid my own fare, 'Grandstand' would pay my hotel bill ('within reason') and that I could use a BBC camera crew from Sydney. Enthusiastic, or what? I accepted the deal because I wanted badly to do the story.

My friend Angela-Belle McSweeney, who had made a notable and, I thought, outstanding contribution to our fashion commentary at Royal Ascot that year, arranged for the VRC to send me airline tickets. I understood that they would be first class, but unhappily they were tourist class.

I arranged special-rate accommodation at the Melbourne Hilton and liaised with the VRC's remarkable and inexhaustible chief executive, Les Benton, over access and facilities. The crew would fly from Sydney on the morning of the race – not ideal, but I would already have planned what I wanted to do. I was to be researcher, producer, director and presenter!

It was the best, and worst, working week of my life – but mostly the worst! The flight was a nightmare. We travelled via Bangkok, where a small but fairly vocal Chinese infant was positioned next to me. The journey seemed interminable. When we arrived at Melbourne at 11 pm local time, the following day, my backside was numb to the point of paralysis, while I had no wish to eat an aircraft meal ever again.

On the Friday I was invited to the Carbine Lunch, but my host had not arrived from the outback so my ticket was not available. I cut my losses, returned to my hotel and ordered a Bloody Mary, which seemed to include half a pint of tobasco (two drops is the correct quantity).

In the evening I was the guest of Elizabeth Armstrong – the sister of my schoolfriend Jimmy – at the Eve of Derby Ball. (The Victoria Derby is run on the Saturday, three days before Cup Day.) This was a magnificent occasion and Elizabeth had a terrific party, including the Freedman brothers – Lee Freedman is the top trainer in Australia – and Simon O'Donnell, the former Australian cricketer. It was a battle to converse against the band and, thanks to my Bloody Mary at lunchtime, I lost my voice.

Elizabeth drove me to Flemington the following day. We picnicked in the Reserved Car Park and talked through the card. The previous evening, the Freedman's vet had marked my card for the day. A glance at the Tote board revealed that his selection for the first race was a 50/1 shot! I made my way towards the Tote, but was waylaid by Les Benton. Les invited me to his office to collect accreditation, so by the time I emerged the race was 'off'. To my stunned horror, the vet's selection made almost every yard of the running to win at 51/1.

On the Sunday morning my new colleague, Jim McGrath, a native Australian, drove us to Sandown at 5.30 am to watch Vintage Crop work. His preparation had suffered an interruption, but he looked in good shape.

I lunched with the top Australian jockey Brent Thomson, who had been race-riding in England and was now to ride the English horse, Quick Ransom, on Tuesday. Another fatal mistake – I ordered a Bloody Mary! This one was as lethal – if not more so – than the Hilton version. At 5 pm my voice had gone again, so I went home.

The evening before the big day was spent swimming and working out in the gym at the Hilton. I was terrified about my voice – it was a long way to come to produce a tape with no words on it! On awaking at 6 am on Cup day, I spent the first two hours of the day treating my throat. We left for the races at 9.15 am and the crew arrived mid-morning.

We spent the next six hours working flat out, without food or drink. It rained persistently and I was soaked to the skin. We filmed horses, people, races, trains and more people. We even filmed Clive James. We spoke to trainers and jockeys and winners and losers. We worked our butt off. The crew were magnificent. At one stage I was interviewed live on Channel-10 television, but while I was on air some local lightfinger 'lifted' my extremely valuable raceglasses! I never saw them again.

Vintage Crop was disappointing, while Quick Ransom finished twenty-second of 24. However, the winner, Jeune, had previously raced in Britain, and his jockey, Wayne Harris, had spent a season in Ireland and been almost killed in a racing accident. In the end, I was delighted with what we had shot.

The following day, Angela-Belle McSweeney arranged a special lunch for me at a restaurant called Lynch's in South Yarra, Melbourne. It was a place designed for me: there was an area of the dining room that excluded all children. I have always been a disciple of W. C. Fields on children: 'Mr Fields, how do you like children?' – 'Boiled'.

Angela's guests included Jack Ingham, the 'chicken man', whose company is said to gross £3 million per week from the sale of chickens. Jack, who had recently bought Lord Derby's stud in Australia, was on-and-off his mobile phone throughout lunch, following the fortunes of his runners at meetings across Australia. 'They tell me this one's got a bit of a chance,' he confided at one stage, 'I'd better have $10,000 on just in case!'

Inevitably, by Thursday morning I was beset by a cold. I had been looking forward to watching cricket at the Melbourne Cricket Ground, but it was still raining. There was worse to come. My flight was delayed by four hours because of a fuel-worker's strike in Sydney. No-one would admit me to the Qantas Lounge – I was, after all, travelling 'tourist'. By the time we left Singapore we were six hours late – and my eardrums were vibrating from the screams of an Asian child in the row behind.

I finally returned to London mid-morning on Friday. Thanks to the editing skills of Gerry Morrison, we produced a programme that evoked favourable comment. I was drained and exhausted, but rather proud.

Meanwhile, racing on Sundays was drawing irresistibly closer. I was in despair. In August, Colin Cowdrey invited me to his box for the Oval Test match against the South Africans. After lunch, I sat next to the Archbishop of Canterbury and unburdened my concerns, both for the racing industry and for society in general, if racing and betting were allowed on the Sabbath. I urged him strongly to speak out against it in the House of Lord's debate. I fear that the Archbishop was unimpressed by my arguments as he made no significant contribution to the debate. Our Lord said: 'The Sabbath was made for man and not man for the Sabbath', but we clearly had different interpretations of that statement.

Some of my colleagues at the BBC found my attitude to racing in France on a Sunday ambivalent. But there is no contradiction. France, Italy and Ireland are Roman Catholic countries, whose principal day of recreation and sport is Sunday. It is wrong to interfere with the beliefs of others. When in Rome we do as the Romans. As a journalist I am accustomed to working on a Sunday. But I do believe strongly in the concept of a day of rest in everyone's life. The Sabbath, I believe, should be special. I try not to bet on Sundays.

In 1995, we recovered the rights to televise the racing in France. We should never have lost them. For years we had taken the Eurovision pictures of the Prix de l'Arc de Triomphe and embellished them with our own build-up and Peter O'Sullevan's commentary. That was not entirely satisfactory because Eurovision would often stay with cycling until the last moment before switching to their cameras at Longchamp, so we were obliged to 'fill' from the studio in London. But it was inexpensive.

Back in 1986, a BBC executive (who shall be nameless) advised M. Louis Romanet of the Société d'Encouragement – the French Jockey Club – that the BBC could not guarantee to cover the 'Arc' that autumn. The UK coverage was, however, vital because Romanet had obtained a new commercial sponsor with a high profile in Britain. So Romanet arranged for an independent production of the day's racing, eliminating Eurovision and thus the BBC. The company chosen was Sunset & Vine, who sold the UK rights to Channel 4. That year Dancing Brave won the best race for the 'Arc' since Sea Bird II's victory in 1965.

When Andrew Franklin of Channel 4 Racing and Colin Frewin of Sunset & Vine fell out, the French racing package was up for grabs. We bid for it and got it – in truth there was no other competitor. Andrew Franklin wished us well. As Cliff Mitchelmore said to me when Lord Wigg moved from politics to racing: 'You're welcome to him.' That was the message from Andrew.

It was terrific to be back working live from Longchamp, but the honeymoon did not last for long. Soon, instead of being in the paddock at Longchamp I was back spending Sunday in the studio in London. As always, the money had run out. But we did give the Prix de l'Arc de Triomphe the full treatment and it was a great day. Lammtarra became the first unbeaten winner of the Derby, King George VI and Queen Elizabeth Diamond Stakes and Prix de l'Arc de Triomphe, and Frankie Dettori, his jockey, did us proud.

It was three and a half weeks after the 'Arc' that I entered hospital for my hip replacement operation. The next three months were painful, tiring and tedious, with the many hours spent lying awake at night, aching and waiting for dawn. There was one dream that sustained me all through those long hours of darkness – the thought of Tykeyvor winning the Bessborough Stakes at Royal Ascot. I had asked Anne Herries the previous October if she would train the old horse specifically with this race in mind.

I ran the plan, the occasion, and the race through my mind a thousand times. It shortened the nights and created an objective. It was only an 'impossible dream', but George Duffield, my jockey, was pleased with the horse in the spring. He felt that he was stronger than in the previous year.

'Tyke' ran well on his reappearance and then finished a good third at the York spring meeting. We chose the Watt Memorial Stakes at Beverley as his final pre-Ascot race. George was unavailable to ride him, so Kevin Darley took over. He won comfortably, which was exciting because Anne had left something to work on. Inevitably, the handicapper raised him 4lb in the weights, which would make his task relatively harder at Ascot. So, with misgivings about leaving out George, I booked the 5lb claiming apprentice, Fergal Lynch, to ride him. I had been watching Fergal throughout the spring and reckoned that his apprentice allowance was a 'steal'. He was riding as well as most senior jockeys.

The Bessborough Stakes, like most Ascot handicaps, is invariably exceptionally difficult to win. But I had a quiet feeling that we might have hit a 'soft' Bessborough. There was no outstanding contender and no substantially backed horse on the day. I was quietly optimistic, but no more.

The great thing about 'Tyke', unlike Pontevecchio Notte, was that he could lie handy throughout the race. I told Fergal what I wanted him to do and we all took the lift to the top of the grandstand. My son Thomas – the lucky talisman – was there, while Alison was also in the party. We had decided that 1996 was her lucky year because she had won the Placepot at Cheltenham! It was the last race of the day, so television was no longer a distraction.

Fergal Lynch did everything in the race exactly as he was asked to do. Tykeyvor was always travelling well, and when they turned into the straight Fergal gave him a smack and set sail for home. 'Tyke' quickly went three lengths clear and never looked like getting caught. I found it difficult to keep my raceglasses steady and I delayed giving him a shout, ever mindful of the Fainne Lea syndrome. But he was home and hosed! The dream had come true. I stood with tears welling up in my eyes.

I shall never forget what Anne Herries and her assistant, Maxine

Cowdrey, accomplished for us that day. It was a wonderful achievement with an old horse who had come to them 18 months earlier as a jaded five-year-old and now had a spring in his step and a gleam in his eye – and had won at Royal Ascot! When he comes back to us at Burrough Green at the end of the season he is missed greatly at Angmering Park; and when he returns to Angmering the following February he leaves a great gaping chasm at home.

But 1996 had not started well. I was rusty after four months away from broadcasting and my first day of presentation was on the Thursday of the Grand National meeting.

Rough Quest, owned by Andrew Wates, had finished second in the Cheltenham Gold Cup. He was always a quirky horse, who needed to hit the front about 25 yards from the finish. I felt that he was an unsuitable horse for Aintree, especially so soon after the Gold Cup and I telephoned Andrew to tell him so. But Andrew and his trainer, Terry Casey, were determined to run and so, at 7.15 am on the Tuesday of Grand National week, we travelled down to Andrew's stables at Beare Green, near Dorking, to film Rough Quest.

We were driven in a four-wheel-drive vehicle up the side of a muddy hill, near Dorking. Our cameraman was climbing further uphill to find a suitable spot from which to film the gallop, when 'Whoosh', Rough Quest had flown by and we had missed the shot. We had missed out on the Grand National favourite's final gallop. This had never happened to me in 30 years of filming horses and I was apoplectic with rage. To make it worse, I could not be excluded from responsibility. To rub salt in my wound, Rough Quest proved me conclusively wrong by winning the National without being extended. I was delighted for Andrew and Terry, two exceptionally nice people, but my professional pride had taken a dent.

Furthermore, on the Friday of Aintree, I described the great American champion 'dirt' horse Cigar as a gelding – a real howler when he was a potential stallion of colossal value. There was an irony in that, when Cigar finally did go to stud in 1997, he was unable to get any of his mares in foal!

Brian Barwick had been appointed head of sport at BBC-TV and he suggested that we have lunch on 23 April. We talked about producers, commentators and the target audience of our racing programmes. Brian is a populist and he was determined to broaden our audience base. I suggested that we hold a seminar of all our racing commentators, contributors and senior producers, to discuss the way forward. It was arranged and took place at the end of August.

I had opened a Pandora's box. There were all manner of snakes slithering around and spitting their venom. None of them bit me, but there was menace in their body language. The innocent eye might have seen them as glow-worms, but there was ambition and a private agenda in those fangs. One or two of the more passive members of our team left that meeting in a state of shock.

The meeting was a microcosm of racing itself, in that everyone was pulling in different directions, and I was in danger of losing control. The following spring that was exactly what happened.

It was four weeks after this meeting that we were involved in a quite extraordinary and history-making broadcast. It is here that I must pay tribute to David Gordon. We were due to cover live the first four races of the Festival of Racing at Ascot, but I asked David about the technicalities of recording the last three races. Normally, after the end of our transmission, the BT sound lines are relinquished to save money. 'Oh, I think I'll keep the lines up,' said David. 'You never know, Frankie might have ridden a few winners.' I laughed. 'I can't see him riding more than two,' I stated.

It is now a part of racing legend that Frankie Dettori rode all seven winners on that extraordinary day. We transmitted the fifth and sixth races live, but to cover the seventh live would have disrupted BBC-1's evening schedules, so 'Presentation' vetoed it. A shame. But the 'Magnificent Seven' was the lead story on the 9 o'clock news.

Frankie was fantastic and helped to make it an unforgettable occasion for the 20,000 plus crowd there on that famous day, thousands of whom stayed on after the last to induce him to sign their racecards. Sue Barker and I must have talked to Frankie five times collectively during the afternoon. The most memorable interview was on my balcony after the last race, with over a thousand racegoers cheering beneath. It was a magical moment, a unique broadcasting occasion and a quite astonishing achievement by Frankie.

When Alison and I flew to South Africa in December 1996, I had already decided, irrevocably, that I should be writing 'Broadcaster' on my entry visa for the last time. We stayed for six weeks and enjoyed a visit from my ex-wife Carolyn, and her parents David and Denise, who were staying at the Mount Nelson Hotel. We also enjoyed some pleasant afternoons with Lester Piggott, his friend Anna Ludlow and their son Jamie, who were staying nearby. Jamie is a chip off the old block and brave as a lion. A football smacked him bang in the face, but he was determined not to cry!

When we returned home on 12 February, I learned that Malcolm Kemp, a producer from New Zealand who up until now had specialized in rugby league, was to be appointed senior horseracing producer. This meant that he would be responsible for the coverage of the Grand National, Royal Ascot and Glorious Goodwood. He had also received a firm brief from Brian Barwick. The coverage was to be less 'élitist,' more pacey, and more directed at a young audience. Above all, there was to be less 'jargon'. In other words, we were to pursue the current BBC trend of 'dumbing down'.

Malcolm and I had several discussions in the spring. He made it clear that he wanted to enhance the status of Clare Balding, who had auditioned for us in March 1994. Her broadcasting contract was with BBC Radio, for whom she had done some excellent work in general sports coverage. She was presenting regular sports bulletins on radio's 'Five Live' and had even survived the jungle radio of Chris Evans on Radio One! I have known Clare all of her life, and have a clear recollection of reading her a bedtime story whilst I was staying with the family in the 1970s!

Up until now we had used Clare as a pundit and general reporter. Now Malcolm proposed to promote her to co-presenter, on an equal footing with myself. I had mixed feelings. I have never felt comfortable with the idea of a 'Richard and Judy' show in horseracing. But

Malcolm had made up his mind – he was determined to change the format to achieve a heightened female involvement and to make the programme more 'presenter-led'. That meant more contributors being seen on the screen, especially at the start of the programme. It entailed the use of more cameras, involved considerable technical complications, and demanded far longer rehearsals than we had ever had previously. Not everyone was happy, but we made it work and the feedback on the new formula was reasonably positive.

It was Royal Ascot that brought the tensions to the surface. Malcolm was determined to pursue the ideology of populism and to extend our crowd focus into the Silver Ring and the centre of the course. This was dangerous and logistically difficult. Furthermore, he was determined to dispense with our regular team of fashion commentators. The excellent Eve Pollard and two or three others were vetoed, while my friend Angela-Belle McSweeney was discarded on the insistence of a third party.

Various names were discussed quite seriously, some of which are too laughable to commit to print. The least absurd included Dani Behr, a former presenter of the excruciatingly awful 'The Word', Stella McCartney, a burgeoning young designer and 'cool', but with no broadcasting experience, and Boy George. In the end we reached a compromise. I was allowed to have the experienced and highly professional Linda Berry for day one, and newcomers would be used on Wednesday and Thursday. All I would say is that the weather did not help the newcomers, and by the end of the week the message was – literally – 'Bring back Linda Berry!'

It was a long and tiring week and on the Thursday and Friday we were on the air from 1.45 to 5.45 pm non-stop. The persistent rain washed out the cricket at Lord's, so we covered all six races at Ascot. I was soaked to the skin at the uncovered 'windy corner', chilled to the bone and my shoes and socks were sodden. Clare Balding worked flat out, presenting a mid-morning programme and the evening highlights. It was tough for the presenters and tough for the production team. As usual, Gerry Morrison achieved amazing feats in videotape control, and at the end of the week

Malcolm, to his credit, threw a champagne party in the production office.

It was one of those weeks that put you in mind of going to the dentist – it's nice when it's over. My overwhelming thought was: 'Thank God I don't have to go through this again.'

We moved on uneasily to Goodwood. This was a less happy outside broadcast. Several interviews were either curtailed or aborted because of technical problems, the race coverage was criticized, and the paddock coverage was either minimal or non-existent. We were snapping at each other. The final straw came when Malcolm shouted: 'What's going on? I haven't seen Clare on the screen for 15 minutes!'

Even Clare was starting to get on my nerves, so some friends and I hatched a plot. One of the successful features of our prolonged Royal Ascot programmes had been the invitation to viewers to send in faxes, with comments on the coverage and questions for the presenters. It was a programme idea that I had seen exploited very successfully by Jack Bannister on the South African Broadcasting Corporation's cricket coverage. It involves the audience and inevitably raises some interesting issues. We decided to run it again at Goodwood.

On the Thursday, Jonathan Powell interviewed Enn Reitel and my friend Rory Bremner. Rory ended the interview by stating that he must slip away for some paddock inspection. However, 'paddock inspection' had become the code-name for a specific sexual activity while we were in South Africa the previous winter. The following day at Goodwood, a fax arrived which read as follows:

> *Please could you tell me what 'paddock inspection' means and which of the BBC team is best at it? – Signed: Rebecca (Miss R. Soles)*

I slipped the fax into the pile of messages that Clare was to read out. Eventually she reached it and read it out – without the signatory. I leant over and asked: 'Who's that one from? Miss R. Soles?'

'Rebecca!', replied Clare brightly. 'Ah yes, Rebecca,' I said, 'I think she's got 'form'. I think you'll find that she wrote to Test Match Special last week.'

It did not *quite* work as I had hoped, but it was still extremely funny to those of the Brian Johnston school of humour. Poor Clare had no idea of what had happened, until a racing newspaper picked it up the following week and accused the BBC of having been 'duped'! 'Rebecca', by the way, is alive and well and living in Petworth.

Throughout the autumn I was awaiting the right moment to tell Brian Barwick that I would not be renewing my contract. Peter O'Sullevan had announced his retirement for 29 November and I felt that several months of having two broadcasters covering their 'last Ascot' and 'last Goodwood' was counterproductive. So I was determined to delay my announcement for as long as was reasonable.

In early October our coverage of the Prix de l'Arc de Triomphe was, I thought, outstanding. It was, however, heart-breaking to achieve an audience figure of just 1.2 million viewers – a loud statement about audience potential on a fine day in the summer and autumn. It was a pleasure, as always, working with the 'Sunday Grandstand' presenter Sue Barker, who is not only an exceptionally nice person, but a terrific professional.

I finally broke the news of my departure on 21 October. It was a quiet day for racing news and I received a widespread and generous coverage. There was one newspaper that spoke of my 'demise' and suggested that I had been 'driven out' by Clare and Sue Barker. Both girls were surprised and embarrassed to read it. Clare felt, quite wrongly, that she was not ready to take over as senior presenter, while Sue is quite happy with her work-load and has no ambitions whatever to become a regular racing presenter.

I decided that my final broadcast would be at Chepstow on Coral Welsh National Day, Saturday 27 December. It was a terrific finale. Rodger Farrant, the excellent and enterprising clerk of the course, named a race after me, whilst the big race was won by Earth Summit, whose principal owner, training team and jockey are all friends, and who went on to win the Martell Grand National. It was a perfect way to finish – highlighted, for me, by a brilliant and painstaking 'This Is Your BBC Life' sequence compiled by Gerry Morrison.

Alison and I flew off to Cape Town the following day for the end of the beginning, with a feeling of relief that I had stopped playing while I was still winning.

# *Postscript*

The sky was a violent blue, with a smudgy fingerprint of cloud. The green of the trees created the perfect contrast. I awoke from my slumber to see the sun high in the South African sky.

How long will this ephemeral haven of pleasure remain? At present, it is Alison's and my idea of Heaven. Our holidays have a character of their own because Alison and I are best friends, as well as companions for life.

The business of horseracing will always be the centrepoint of my life. What has changed is that now I can no longer be emotionally waylaid by the irritations of political correctness at the BBC; incompetence in the commercial departments; the bad manners and offensiveness of 'alternative' programmes; the lost concept of public service broadcasting; and the continual frustration of financial constraints.

Like so many, I have been offended by the BBC's increasing hostility towards the Royal Family. It came to a head when BBC Radio news took, out of context, some perfectly balanced comments by the Duke of Edinburgh on the Dunblane tragedy and tried to depict them as insensitive and offensive. Every Rent-A-Royal -basher was wheeled in to criticize the Duke. However, three separate telephone polls indicated that the majority of listeners supported his views. The Duke's private secretary advised me that his office had received a staggering number of telephone calls and letters, 'probably in the order of about ten in favour to one against'. I was ashamed for the BBC.

Nor shall I any longer be irritated by internal documents outlining a target employment quota of 12½ per cent from ethnic minorities, 7½ per cent homosexuals and 50 per cent women in management roles by the year 2000. Whatever happened to *talent*? Whatever happened to *qualifications*?

The BBC is not the same organization that I joined 32 years ago. Then it fulfilled its obligation to instruct and entertain. Now, it is a *slave* to political correctness and equal opportunities, and to organizations like Quality and Equality, whose high-priestess Dr Mee-Yan Cheung-Judge has been well paid to instruct top BBC management on 'the way forward'. *What happened to concentrating the BBC's resources into making programmes?*

There are so many people – young people – bursting with talent and energy, whose creative ambitions are being held in restraint by lack of resources. Those people are the future of the BBC and those are the people I shall miss. I have been very lucky to work with them.

But my whole life has been lucky. What makes me doubly blessed is that I shall always be involved in a sport that I love, and always have the opportunity to make a living from it.

# Index